The

THE UNIVERSITY OF
WINCHESTER

Martial Rose Library
Tel: 01962 827306

To be returned on or before the day marked above, subject to recall.

Musical lives

The books in this series each provide an account
of the life of a major composer, considering
both the private and the public figure. The main
thread is biographical and discussion of the
music is integral to the narrative. Each book
thus presents an organic view of the composer,
the music and the circumstances in which the
music was written.

Published titles
The life of Bach PETER WILLIAMS
The life of Beethoven DAVID WYN JONES
The life of Bellini JOHN ROSSELLI
The life of Berlioz PETER BLOOM
The life of Debussy ROGER NICHOLS
The life of Elgar MICHAEL KENNEDY
The life of Charles Ives STUART FEDER
The life of Mahler PETER FRANKLIN
The life of Mendelssohn PETER MERCER-TAYLOR
The life of Messiaen CHRISTOPHER DINGLE
The life of Mozart JOHN ROSSELLI
The life of Musorgsky CARYL EMERSON
The life of Schubert CHRISTOPHER H. GIBBS
The life of Richard Strauss BRYAN GILLIAM
The life of Verdi JOHN ROSSELLI
The life of Webern KATHRYN BAILEY

The life of Messiaen

CHRISTOPHER DINGLE

CAMBRIDGE
UNIVERSITY PRESS

CAMBRIDGE UNIVERSITY PRESS
Cambridge, New York, Melbourne, Madrid, Cape Town, Singapore, São Paulo, Delhi

Cambridge University Press
The Edinburgh Building, Cambridge CB2 8RU, UK

Published in the United States of America by Cambridge University Press, New York

www.cambridge.org
Information on this title: www.cambridge.org/9780521635479

First published 2007
Reprinted 2009

Printed in the United Kingdom at the University Press, Cambridge

A catalogue record for this publication is available from the British Library

ISBN 978-0-521-63220-1 hardback
ISBN 978-0-521-63547-9 paperback

For Liz

CONTENTS

ILLUSTRATIONS

Photographs are from the private collection of Nigel Simeone unless stated otherwise.

ACKNOWLEDGEMENTS

I have been blessed throughout the decidedly lengthy gestation of this book with help and support from numerous friends and colleagues. Thanks should go first of all to Penny Souster, Vicki Cooper, Rebecca Jones, Michael Black, Jackie Warren and Clive Unger-Hamilton at Cambridge University Press for their guidance and, above all, patience. My colleagues at Birmingham Conservatoire and, before that, the Department of Music at Sheffield University have provided much encouragement, while the British Academy generously funded much of the research that has fed into the book. I am indebted to Erin O'Neill at the BBC Written Archive Centre, Bridget P. Carr, archivist at the Boston Symphony Orchestra, Barbara Haws and Richard Wandel, archivists at the New York Philharmonic, and Wilhelm Schlüter for information about the Darmstadt Summer School. My thanks also go to everyone at United Music Publishers.

Ian Gorman, John Garner and David Kettle nurtured my enthusiasm for Messiaen at an early stage, and thus made a substantial contribution without realizing it at the time. Malcolm Ball, who it so happens was my percussion teacher, has very generously supplied me with various materials, as well as making life significantly easier for Messiaen enthusiasts by setting-up the marvellous website www. messiaen.org.uk. I am extremely grateful to George Benjamin, Paul Crossley and Alexander Goehr for helpful and illuminating interviews. Stephen Broad, Robert Fallon and Nicholas Armfelt each provided useful materials and prompted fruitful lines of thought, while Eric Clarke gave me sage advice at several key moments.

Peter Hill would deserve mention for his inspirational performances of Messiaen's piano music alone. However, I am also fortunate to have benefited from his wisdom, numerous conversations and his insightful comments on my writing. Similarly, it would be hard to overstate the enormous contribution that Nigel Simeone has made to our understanding of Messiaen. In addition to his unstinting support and enthusiasm, he commented upon drafts of every chapter and gave me extensive access to his personal collection of photographs and documents, while our expansive conversations are not merely helpful, but also great fun. Particular thanks should also go to Phil Rostant for his comments on each chapter, and my mother, Marie Dingle, whose questions improved the comprehensibility in several places. Needless to say, any remaining deficiencies are entirely my own.

Finally, greatest thanks go to Liz for much more than I can express in words, and to Wilfred and Nathaniel, for giving me more joy than they can possibly realize.

NOTE ON THE TEXT

Hill and Simeone

References to Peter Hill and Nigel Simeone's seminal work, called simply *Messiaen*, are given as 'PHNS', followed by page number.

Messiaen's Conversations with Claude Samuel

Messiaen's conversations with Claude Samuel were originally published in French in 1967 and translated into English in 1976 by Felix Aprahamian. The original interviews were extensively revised and extended in 1986 and republished; this edition was then translated by E. Thomas Glasow in 1994. Finally, in 1999, Claude Samuel republished (as author) the 1986 French edition with additional commentaries. As the most widely available version, page references are to Glasow's 1994 translation except for where the earlier version of the conversations contains different material. Messiaen did not wish to appear as author of the conversations and, as a consequence, the author is given as Samuel.

TECHNIQUE DE MON LANGAGE MUSICAL

Originally published in two volumes, text and musical examples respectively, Leduc has recently published single-volume French (1999) and English (2001) editions of *Technique*. As a consequence, references are given for both the two-volume and single-volume English versions respectively.

1 The burgeoning artist 1908–31

Since childhood I've been irresistibly and powerfully drawn to a musical vocation.[1]

A boy sits reading on a stone bench in the town park of Grenoble. Far to the north, the battles on the western front of the First World War are at their most attritional, but the only hint here of the cruelty that humanity can inflict upon itself is the brooding presence of the town's 'bastille'. The sight of the old battlements glowering down from their high rocky vantage point on the other side of the River Isère is itself dwarfed by the mountains that dominate the surrounding skyline. To the east is the Romanche valley, with its dramatic gorges eventually leading to the dazzling glaciers of the Meije, on some of the highest peaks of the Rhône Alps. To the south the Route Napoléon rises resolutely for more than a thousand metres before reaching the sedate plateau of the Serre, marked by a series of four lakes and flanked by mountains that are distinctly genteel in comparison to the spectacular scenes along the Romanche river. This countryside of the Isère region, along the Romanche and around the lakes of the Serre, will provide a strong source of inspiration for the seven-and-a-half-year-old boy, who will become one of the creative giants of the twentieth century and one of the greatest religious artists of any era. Until this point he might have seemed destined, despite a remarkable facility at the piano, for a literary career. His beloved mother, Cécile Sauvage, is a poet, whilst his father is a teacher of English, and the boy has already developed a passion not just for fairy stories but also for poetry and Shakespeare. Now, though, he is not reading *A Midsummer Night's Dream* or *Hamlet*, but the vocal score of an opera whose message of love overcoming death, and conviction in the power of music, will later find resonances in his own scores: Gluck's *Orphée*. As Olivier Messiaen later recalled: 'I noticed an extraordinary thing. I was reading, sitting there and I could hear what I was reading in my head. So, I *was* a musician.'[2]

From the outset, Messiaen's life was dominated by the creative influence of women. Where Berlioz, his fellow Dauphinois, starts his memoirs by commenting wryly on his mother's lack of premonitions of the artistic greatness of her unborn child, Messiaen's arrival into this world was greeted by *L'Âme en bourgeon*, a garland of twenty poems by Cécile Sauvage.[3] Lest there be any doubt, he was absolutely unequivocal about the importance of this collection, going so far as to say that 'There has been only one influence in my life, and it happened before I was born ... thus before my birth there was [in *L'Âme en bourgeon*] this exchange between mother and child, and I believe it was *that* which influenced my entire destiny.'[4] In later life Messiaen drew attention to lines such as 'I suffer from an unknown, distant music', 'All the Orient is singing here within me, with its blue birds, with its butterflies' and 'The anguish of art's mysteries will be dispersed', as evidence of his mother's visionary abilities, foretelling not only that he would be a composer, but also that he would be interested in birdsong, have a love for Japan and be a great teacher. Messiaen might have taken all sorts of different career paths and still found prophetic intimations in his mother's poetry. Nonetheless, leafing through *L'Âme en bourgeon* aged eight and being told by Cécile that 'it is for you',[5] he could scarcely remain indifferent to the poetic chaplet that greeted him into the world: 'I didn't understand it, I did not realise it was about a mother expecting a child, I knew nothing. All the same, it certainly influenced me, not only my destiny, but also my way of thinking. It gave me a sense of wonder.'[6]

1. Pierre, Cécile and Olivier, Avignon, September 1910.

Olivier was born in the Provençal town of Avignon at midnight on
Thursday 10 December 1908, prompting the overjoyed new Grandpère
Sauvage to start singing the old French carol 'Il est né le divin enfant'.[7]
On Christmas Day the baby was duly baptized Olivier Eugène Prosper
Charles Messiaen. Pierre and Cécile had married the previous year, on
10 September 1907,[8] much to the chagrin of Pierre's parents, Charles

and Marie, who disapproved of their son choosing a bride who never went to church. He had grown up on the Bois-Franc farm, close to the Belgian border on the outskirts of Le Blaton, a hamlet between the villages of Linselles and Wervicq. He had been working in Saint-Étienne on the editorial staff of the literary journal *Revue Forézienne*[9] when, one morning in May, the manuscript of *Les Trois Muses* by Cécile Sauvage arrived. The daughter of a history teacher at the lycée in Digne, she was born on 20 July 1883 in La-Roche-sur-Yon in the Vendée, and, aside from a few trips to Avignon and Marseilles, she had spent her formative years in the small Provençal town. About a month after their marriage in the little church of Sieyes in Digne, the Sauvage family moved to Avignon and Pierre entered the barracks of the 58th Infantry Regiment, 3rd Battalion, 9th Company to fulfil his National Service.

In February 1909, Pierre was appointed to a secondary school teaching post at Ambert in the Puy-de-Dôme region of the Auvergne, though Cécile and Olivier did not join him until the Easter holidays. It was in Ambert, the birthplace of Chabrier, that Olivier first began to experience 'the revelation of nature',[10] and it was here also that he started learning to read, soon developing a voracious appetite for the stories of Perrault and Madame d'Aulnoy. At the same time, Pierre was studying for the highest teaching diploma, *agrégation*, not helped by the disturbed nights that followed the arrival of a second son, Alain, on 30 August 1912. Following his new qualification, Pierre was appointed to the lycée in Nantes, and Olivier began school where he was 'the best pupil in his class'.[11] The family's first stay in this western Loire city was either forgotten or overlooked in later life by Messiaen. It was only brief, for in the summer of 1914 France mobilized in response to the threat of German invasion.

With the onset of war in 1914, Cécile took her two sons to Grenoble to live with their grandmother, Marie Sauvage, at 2 cours Berriat, the house of her brother André, who, like Pierre, had been sent to the front. Any influence that his Flemish roots, his Provençal beginnings or the years spent in Ambert and Nantes might have had on Olivier was firmly supplanted by a lifelong attachment to the Dauphiné region,

2. Cécile, Olivier and Alain in 1913.

nurtured during these formative years in Grenoble. As he put it in a
self-authored biographical entry published in the *Dictionnaire de musique*
of 1970, 'The mountains of the Dauphiné ... are his true home'.[12] The
family had already spent an idyllic summer at André's house during
1911, going on trips by car to Grande-Chartreuse and Lake Bourget to
the north, and Bourg d'Oisans to the East. At other times they went and

sat in the public gardens: 'Cécile and her sister [Germaine] took needlework, Olivier made heaps of sand where he planted sticks, I read the novels of Dostoyevsky to grandfather Sauvage, who pretended not to like them'.[13] The happy family life evoked by this brief vignette was not to last. Cécile's physical health was rarely strong, and, pessimistic by nature, she also suffered from what both Pierre and Olivier Messiaen describe as a profound melancholy and which today would probably be diagnosed as depression. In Ambert she worked each morning between nine o'clock and half-past eleven in the bedroom on the first floor.[14] She told Pierre 'It is necessary to collect pollen to make honey' and would feel that the day had been wasted if she had not spent time alone, in quiet solitude, to work on her poetry,[15] a work ethic that Olivier would inherit. Nevertheless, there was more to her isolation than a desire for peace and quiet to work. According to Pierre, Cécile went into town barely ten times during the years in Ambert.[16] The war acted as a catalyst for a decline in her spirits and she rarely wanted to go out with the children, often locking herself in her bedroom so that she could not hear their games or hear them running about the house. This is certainly not to suggest that Cécile did not love her children. She noted their progress and foibles with delight, thinking of herself with pride as mother hen as she walked with them to school in Grenoble, and recalling that the other children had at first thought that Olivier was English or Russian on account of his blonde hair.[17] At the age of eight, Messiaen was already the same height as his mother and he had appointed himself her 'chevalier rose'. *L'Âme en bourgeon* sent him into raptures of adoration, telling Cécile that she was 'as poetic as Shakespeare'.[18]

Messiaen was, by his own admission, a solitary child with few friends apart from Jean Licou, 'who I liked very much, but he died when he was seven, so I was alone'.[19] Olivier devoted his time instead to his books and his new love, music. There being no musicians in the family, he taught himself to play the broken-down old piano that had been gathering dust in his uncle's house. Cécile and Marie Sauvage cannot have taken long to realize that they had a precocious talent on their hands. Rather than toys or books, Father Christmas began to receive requests for operatic vocal scores. Olivier's treble voice could subsequently be heard singing complete performances of each work. Within little more than three years, his repertoire included Mozart's *Don Giovanni* and *The Magic Flute*, Berlioz's *The Damnation of Faust*, Wagner's *Die Walküre* and *Siegfried*, and Gluck's *Alceste* had joined the score that first made Olivier aware of his musical vocation, *Orphée*. He made frequent trips to Deshairs, the big music shop in Grenoble, to look at the scores, and friends and family also fed his appetite for music with gifts of piano works. Recent pieces, such as Debussy's *Estampes* and Ravel's *Gaspard de la nuit*, figure prominently in Messiaen's recollections, but he also devoured the works of Bach and Beethoven, even if they left fewer obvious imprints on his own music. An important discovery at Deshairs was Grieg's *Peer Gynt* with its 'beautiful Norwegian melodic lines with the taste of folk song . . . They gave me a love of melody'.[20]

Olivier had begun to compose almost as soon as he started to play the piano, creating simple two-part canons. Only one piece of his juvenilia survives, a piano piece inspired by Tennyson's poem *The Lady of Shalott*. Never published, *La Dame de Shalott* is nonetheless instructive, as is clear from Messiaen's note to the sole recording made of the work, for his belief in the ability of music to portray, for the notes to convey meaning:

> In this *Lady of Shalott* a child's imagination runs unleashed. Nothing is missing: the castles, the inflection of the spoken word, the song of Lady Shalott (weaving!), Sir Lancelot on horseback, the broken mirror, the tapestry which flies out the window, the falling willow leaves, and the death of the lady who lies in a boat drifting down the river (barcarole!). Despite its extraordinary naivety, this work is nonetheless my op. 1.[21]

Furthermore, the way the music jumps from one passage to the next in following the narrative in *La Dame de Shalott* is prophetic of the sectional formats of Messiaen's mature works, not least the quasi-dramatic unfolding of events in some pieces of *Catalogue d'oiseaux*.

Although music was now his métier, Messiaen's love of literature was also flourishing, inspiring him to construct a toy theatre. Taking the cellophane from sweet boxes and patisserie bags and painting it with Indian ink or watercolours, Messiaen placed it in front of a windowpane. The simple coloured lighting effects produced by the sun shining through the cellophane foreshadowed his subsequent enduring interest in colour and, specifically, stained-glass windows. Thus equipped with his own personal equivalent of the Globe Theatre, in function if not design, Olivier performed the plays of Shakespeare using cardboard figures, and with Alain acting as assistant or audience as appropriate. On at least one occasion he also tried his hand as a dramatist, for the manuscript still exists of *Anymoné*, a play written in a school exercise-book at about the age of ten. Fifty-eight lines of text are squeezed on to the solitary surviving page of this short drama based on a passage in the Greek legend of the *Danaïdes*.

Messiaen claimed to have performed all the plays of Shakespeare in his theatre, but *Macbeth*, *A Midsummer Night's Dream* and *The Tempest* were given significantly longer runs. He later recalled that it was the magical and the mysterious aspects of Shakespeare that attracted him, though he put it more colourfully at the time, declaring to Cécile that 'I prefer everything that frightens.'[22] It was the phantasmagorical that enthralled the young Messiaen rather than 'certain disillusioned comments on love and death, such as can be found in *Hamlet*, comments that a child of eight obviously couldn't understand',[23] and the same can be inferred from his choice of operatic repertoire, preferring *Don Giovanni* and *The Magic Flute* to *Così fan tutte* or *Die Walküre*, and *Siegfried* to *Tristan und Isolde*. This affection for legends and the miraculous never left Messiaen. Rather, when he was old enough to understand love and death, they were also interpreted as falling within the dominion of the supernatural.

Given his predilection for the theatrical arts, Messiaen might have seemed destined for a career as an opera composer. In fact, he had reached an age by which most people would have retired before finally embarking, in 1975, upon his sole work of music theatre. The reasons for his reluctance are complex, but it is worth remembering that his formative dramatic experiences were essentially private, even internal, affairs, with their greatest resource being his imagination.

Following the Armistice in November 1918, Pierre was soon reunited with his wife and children. He had spent the War with the British forces as an interpreter, a posting that, if it did not keep him out of the frontline trenches, contributed to his survival. His two brothers were not so lucky. The eldest, Paul, fought with the 237th infantry regiment at Lorraine, Argonne and Artois, before being hit in the head by shrapnel in the attack on Craonne. He died in hospital in Troyes. Léon, who was eighteen months younger than Pierre, was a sculptor, who had spent time in the workshops of Gréber, Rodin and Bourdelle before entering the École des Beaux-Arts. Assigned to the 279th infantry regiment, he was injured three times, at Lorraine, Souchez and Verdun, before being killed outright by a shell on 15 September 1918, less than two months before the Armistice.[24] It is difficult to comprehend the devastating effect that the First World War had on an entire generation. Reading the early chapters of Pierre Messiaen's book of autobiographical reflections, *Images*, it is disquieting how the vast majority of his portraits of friends and acquaintances of a similar age end with recording that they died during one or other battle of the war.

The family now returned to Nantes and it was here, far from his beloved mountains, that Messiaen's formal musical education began in earnest. He later recalled several local teachers, such as Gontran Arcouët and the Véron sisters,[25] who gave him free piano lessons on account of his exceptional talent. The most momentous contribution, however, came from Jean de Gibon, who gave Messiaen his first harmony lessons. Gibon, who despite being poor, also declined to charge for his services, dutifully made Messiaen work from the standard textbook of the day, Reber and Dubois's *Traité d'harmonie*. However, Gibon also gave his ten-year-old protégé a score of Debussy's *Pelléas et Mélisande*, itself less than twenty years old. In a composer with as rich a language and as broad a range of influences as Messiaen, it would be misleading to name one work as decisive, but, by his own admission, the gift of *Pelléas et Mélisande* was a defining moment: 'Debussy's music is like water – water is still, unmoving, but immediately you throw a pebble in there is a shock wave around the pebble and the water is set in motion. Debussy's music is like that – there are stops and all of a sudden it moves. It was those stops that seized my imagination.'[26] The ten-year-old Messiaen immediately fell in love with the understated colours and dappled light of Debussy's setting of Maeterlinck's symbolist drama, spending many hours repeatedly playing and singing through the score until he knew the entire opera from memory; 'a provincial teacher had placed a veritable bomb in the hands of a mere child'.[27]

Messiaen spent just six months in Nantes before he had to bid farewell to his 'provincial teacher' (although they stayed in contact until Gibon's death in 1952). In 1919, Pierre took up a new job in Paris at the Lycée Charlemagne and, after a brief stay on the quai de Bourbon on the Île Saint-Louis, the family moved to 65 rue Rambuteau. It is not known whether he specifically requested this post so that his son could receive the training that his remarkable talents deserved, but Olivier now entered the Paris Conservatoire aged just ten. The Messiaen apartment was above a café on the corner of rue Quincampoix, in the Marais district, right in the heart of the city. Freezing cold in winter and baking in summer, there was always noise from lorries, trams and cars. Encountering the teeming cultural riches of Paris must have been as thrilling in the 1920s as it had been for Berlioz a century earlier.

Olivier was taken by his parents on educational trips to the city's cultural jewels, such as the Louvre, the Opéra and the Comédie Française. The 'shining revelation' of being dazzled by the coloured light of the extraordinary stained-glass windows at the Sainte-Chapelle remained with Messiaen throughout his life, inspiring a particularly succinct exegesis of his music:

> Stained glass is one of the most wonderful creations of man. You are overwhelmed. And I think this is the beginning of Paradise, because

in Paradise we are overwhelmed. We won't understand God, but we will begin to see Him a little . . . Real music, beautiful music – you can listen to it without understanding it: you don't need to have studied harmony or orchestration. You must *feel* it. And here, also, one is overwhelmed – by the shock of the sound.[28]

The première in 1921 of Milhaud's *Prothée* provided a salutary lesson on the reception periodically meted out to new works, for the audience at the Concerts Colonne booed so loudly that nothing of the work could be heard. Upon completing the performance, the conductor, Gabriel Pierné, stoically turned to the audience and said 'The piece was listed on the programme; it was performed. And it shall be a second time.' Fervid booing immediately started up again.[29] Such experiences provided the background to the development of Messiaen's own passionately held views. His antipathy to neoclassicism remained emphatic throughout his life, and he denounced it with venom for its superficiality: 'The principle is totally reprehensible; I'll even say it's a complete absurdity'.[30] The vehemence of such remarks is redolent of Berlioz's attacks on the dilettanti in his day. Cocteau's *Le Coq et l'arlequin*,[31] with its flippant remarks decrying nature, condemning Wagner and deriding *Pelléas et Mélisande*, could have been written specifically to taunt Messiaen. Nevertheless, Messiaen's anger is the product of more than simple aversion to the music associated with Cocteau's pamphlet, for there must have been numerous other works and styles that he disliked but did not feel provoked into lambasting. Rather, it seems that there is an added sense of great artists wasting their creative resources. Whilst the aesthetics associated with *Le Coq et l'arlequin* were anathema to him, Messiaen nevertheless held Cocteau's poetry and films in high regard, and bemoaned in later life the neglect of Honegger's *King David* (1921), *Judith* (1925) and *Antigone* (1927) as well as Milhaud's *L'Homme et son désir* (1918) and *La Création du monde* (1923). Similarly, hearing *The Rite of Spring*, *Les Noces* and *Pulcinella* in one evening left a deep impression, with the latter presumably avoiding the opprobrium of Messiaen (and Boulez several decades later) on account of it being not so much a new composition as an arrangement of Pergolesi. Having fallen in love with the ballets of his Russian period, Messiaen viewed Stravinsky's emergence as the apparent high priest of neoclassicism as an incomprehensible betrayal.

All the while, he was developing an ardent, passionate faith. Messiaen claimed to have been born a believer, but his faith nonetheless needed guidance and nurturing, a task that, given Cécile's atheism, fell upon Pierre. It seems that, at first, the earnest young *croyant's* knowledge of the vibrant Parisian tradition of sacred music would have been limited. He worshipped at the relatively modest church of St-Leu and St-Gilles on the Boulevard Sébastopol, just a few yards walk, dodging prostitutes, from the rue Rambuteau. There can be little doubt that, once he began learning the instrument himself in 1927, Messiaen would have followed the well-trodden organists' pilgrimage around the city's big churches. On a single Sabbath, an organ connoisseur could hear Louis Vierne at Notre Dame, Charles Tournemire at Sainte Clotilde (previously Franck's church), and Charles-Marie Widor at Saint-Sulpice with Marcel Dupré often deputizing. These were not just highly talented musicians, but also men of faith, whose belief in the scriptural and liturgical texts that provided the extra-musical inspiration for their improvisations was a world away from the cabaret tunes, pastiche and postwar cynicism prevalent in the concert halls. The musical genes of Tournemire's *L'Orgue mystique*, an enormous liturgical cycle of organ meditations based on plainchant and collectively lasting about as long as J. S. Bach's output for the instrument, permeate Messiaen's own organ works. Tournemire also composed sacred orchestral pieces, such as *La Symphonie du triomphe de la mort*, thus paving the way for the younger composer to write religious works for the concert hall. The influence of the organist-composers on Messiaen was immense, not so much in terms of technique, but in the more fundamental realm of the purpose of composition. For his part, Messiaen would make the single most important contribution to ensuring that the organ repertoire retained its relevance throughout the twentieth century.

Astonishingly, Messiaen first played an organ just eight days before entering Marcel Dupré's fearsome class at the Conservatoire as an *auditeur* after the Easter holiday in 1927.[32] It was Jean Gallon, his harmony teacher, who, impressed by his improvisational ability more than any consideration for his strong Catholic faith, sent Messiaen to Dupré. Progress on his new instrument, which rapidly superseded the piano in his affections, was swift, for just two years later Messiaen was awarded a *premier prix* in organ and improvisation. As well as introducing Messiaen to Dupré, it was under Jean Gallon that Messiaen first received a prize, *deuxième prix* in harmony at the age of fifteen. Almost as revolutionary as his pupil was to be two decades later, Gallon introduced the music of Debussy and Ravel into the harmony syllabus. As he recalled seventy years later, Messiaen's first encounter with Gallon, upon entering the Conservatoire fresh-faced from the provinces, was a rude awakening: 'In Nantes, I was taken for a little child prodigy, Paris brought me down to earth. I found myself before Jean Gallon who told me "You are nothing at all, you know nothing".'[33] Messiaen's tutor at the Conservatoire was Gallon's brother, Noël, who, in addition to being his official counterpoint teacher, gave him wide-ranging private lessons in music theory for about ten years: 'I really think that at the start he took me for a complete idiot. I don't blame him.'[34]

Messiaen had entered the Conservatoire as a pianist, studying with Georges Falkenberg, but he had little desire to be a true virtuoso concert performer, not least because the sheer quantity of practice required would allow little time for composition. Despite Falkenberg initially encouraging him to work towards a career as a concert pianist, Messiaen chose, after just a few years, to study the instrument under his own volition. The only prize the instrument brought Messiaen, therefore, was a *premier prix* in accompaniment under the tutelage of César Abel Estyle, reflecting his empathy for the subtleties of the instrument.

Messiaen's experience with the piano was typical. Each of his teachers, including Dupré, encouraged him to specialize in their

3. The harmony class of Jean Gallon at the Paris Conservatoire in 1924. Messiaen is at the far right.

particular field, but he simply wanted to learn the craft of a composer. Ironically, the certitude with which he pursued his vocation is responsible for the surprising lack of compositional productivity during his early years at the Conservatoire. Messiaen had decided that he should first serve his apprenticeship, learning the various components of his craft, before devoting himself to his chosen profession. As a consequence, the only work listed by him as being written during his first five years at the Conservatoire is an unpublished setting from 1921 of two poems by Villon for voice and piano; and works only begin to appear with any regularity once he entered Widor's composition class, followed in 1927, by that of Paul Dukas. Inspired, when gazing out of the window, by the anaemic clouds covering Paris on a particularly sullen day in 1925, Messiaen added *La Tristesse d'un grand ciel blanc* (The sadness of a large white sky) to his modest portfolio. He recalled that this short piano piece was rather Stravinskian in character,[35] but, like the two Villon songs, *La Tristesse d'un grand ciel blanc* now exists only as a frustratingly enticing title.

Of all the lost works from Messiaen's compositional apprenticeship, the most tantalizing is *Esquisse modale* (Modal sketch), an organ work from 1927, the title of which suggests a possible early foray into the melodic and harmonic world of the modes of limited transposition. Like Satie and Debussy before him, not to mention Tournemire, Messiaen was fascinated by creative potential in scales outside the major and minor confines of the tonal system prevalent in Western European music for the previous three centuries. In addition, the modes of plainchant melodies were a natural source of interest for a young Catholic composer. However, Messiaen did not simply resurrect the modes of antiquity, but discovered new, unmistakably modern-sounding modes with their own distinctive qualities. Due to the symmetrical nature of their construction, the number of possible versions that can be created of each of these modes is limited. The constrictions created by the structural symmetries within the modes paradoxically provided the catalyst for Messiaen's freedom of expression, not least by partly enabling the release of melody and harmony from the conventional approach to the temporal domain. Messiaen not only gave his discoveries their rather cumbersome collective name, modes of limited transposition, but was also to analyse their qualities at great length in his writings. These often extensive elucidations of his music can be misleading, suggesting a dry approach to composition. In this respect, the recollections of Langlais are instructive:

> Messiaen was a great composer even when he wrote the first [published] work, *Le Banquet céleste*. And he knows – he knew at this time – that he was a very gifted composer, but he did not know his system. He told me later on: he discovered his system by analysing his works. He discovered the scales and everything. So he did not decide before – he discovered afterwards.[36]

In other words, Messiaen's analyses often represent the composer trying to explain the works to himself as much as to his audience. In the case of his modes, Messiaen first discovered sounds that pleased him when improvising. Emmanuel and Dupré had alerted Messiaen to the possibility of unorthodox modes and the latter also encouraged his student to be methodical in working at improvisation, sparking a lifelong penchant for lists. Whilst his fingers will have instinctively picked out sounds used by, among others, Musorgsky and Stravinsky, Dupré's systematic approach will have revealed to Messiaen the hidden framework existing behind his intuition and enabled him to extend it. This exploration of modes was also nurtured by his history teacher, Maurice Emmanuel, who also awakened Messiaen to the possibility of using the metres of Greek poetry to musical ends. As such, Emmanuel joins Dupré and Dukas to form a trinity of affectionately remembered teachers whose influence permeates Messiaen's entire output.

Very little is known as to what his classes at the Conservatoire were like, and Messiaen also spoke rarely about his fellow students, usually only noting that someone had been in the same class as him. One thing that can be said with certainty is that he was not as solitary a figure at the Conservatoire as he had been during his time at Grenoble. The seeds of several long-term friendships were sown during this long apprenticeship. For instance, Daniel-Lesur, who would later join Messiaen as a member of La Jeune France, was a classmate from the age of thirteen. Several years later, Dukas's composition class cultivated a spirit of camaraderie and mutual support. Elsa Barraine, who won the Prix de Rome in 1929 for her sacred trilogy *La Vierge guerrière*, Jean Cartan and Claude Arrieu were among the friends that he made here. Barraine later recalled that Messiaen was 'extremely reserved, extremely timid and inward-looking' noting that he 'never spoke, just brought his music and played it on the piano. We could tell what power and technique he already had, what passion and originality of language was making itself felt.'[37] Five years his senior, though a couple of years later in gaining her *premier prix*, Arrieu's relationship with Messiaen throughout the 1930s is like that of a sister, acting as confidante and each doing everything to help the other to progress and sustain their compositional careers.

It is thanks to the memories of another fellow pupil and a lifelong close friend of Messiaen, that we have some illuminating glimpses of life in one of the Conservatoire classes. Jean Langlais became an *auditeur* in Marcel Dupré's class on the same day as Messiaen.[38] Several months after Messiaen and Langlais, a new batch of *auditeurs* joined the class, including Gaston Litaize and Henri Cabié. These four officially entered the class following an exam on 17 December 1927, joining three existing students, Joseph Gilles, René Malherbe and Noëlie Pierront.[39] The class met three times a week, from 1:30pm to 3:30pm, studying fugal improvisation on Mondays, improvisation on a free theme on Wednesdays and working on repertoire on Fridays. Dupré was a strict disciplinarian, welcoming newcomers by saying 'Those who arrive at 1:31 will find the door closed, and can consider themselves excluded from the class'.[40] He also expected his students to work hard, very hard: 'At your age I worked for twelve hours a day. You would be well advised to do the same.'[41] For the repertoire classes, the students had to learn to play a new work from memory every single week. Early on, Langlais brought the Bach B minor fugue for a second week, provoking Dupré to comment tersely 'If you want to spend the

4. The composition class of Paul Dukas at the Paris Conservatoire, 1929–30. Messiaen and Claude Arrieu are seated at the right. Maurice Duruflé is standing next to Messiaen.

whole year on the same piece, I don't think that it will get you very far'.[42] Nevertheless, there was more to Dupré's class than the regimentation. Rachel Brunschwig, who entered the class a year after Messiaen and Langlais, recalled that in the free improvisation classes he was very attentive to the individual character of each pupil: 'Messiaen, who was already tremendously interested in modes (he had in his pocket some small bits of numbered paper on which he noted harmonic formulas, modal turns, sequences, and certain Debussyan collections), had to improvise on Greek rhythms'.[43] In 1929, the *concours* (competition) for the organ and improvisation class was held on Friday 31 May, with the *premier prix* being awarded to Messiaen at his first attempt and Joseph Gilles at his second. Langlais was awarded *deuxième prix*, as was Henriette Roget. Also a friend of Messiaen, Roget later gave the first performance of his *Préludes*, thus attracting the dedication of one of his earliest works to have been published. Both Langlais and Roget were awarded *premier prix* the following year.

The summer following Messiaen's admission to Dupré's class as an *auditeur*, he suffered the first tragedy of his life. On 26 August 1927 his beloved mother, Cécile Sauvage, died. During the first few years in Paris her spirits and her health had improved, but, from about 1925, what Messiaen described as his mother's 'hidden despair'[44] increasingly affected family life. It was Pierre who would take the boys out, not just for walks and to friends' houses, but also to churches, for 'they showed signs of a true passion for religious ceremonies and music'.[45] 'She is a little tired' was his response to enquiries about his wife's health, not wishing to say that Cécile 'refused all recreation'.[46] The increasingly anxious Pierre wondered why she did not wish to spend the holiday with his family in the Dauphiné, scene of some enjoyable summers with the children. Cécile also asked him increasingly often to take the children out in the evenings to a restaurant so that she could have some calm. In July 1927, Cécile implored Pierre to go to Chartres, taking with him Alain, the son who hummed and whistled all day, irritating with his constant running about looking for tools for making his theatre sets. She assured him that, in September, they would all go to stay with Pierre's mother in the Dauphiné. Pierre acceded to this request. A few days after father and youngest son arrived in Chartres they received a long letter from Cécile, who seemed to be in better spirits, mentioning having had an excellent meal with Olivier at the Reine Blanche restaurant, and that they were both enjoying a new lease of good health: 'The enthusiasm for work is returning to me. Next autumn, I will return to Primevère [Primrose]. I've got to find again this poetry bordering on the supernatural, which is my reason for being, something bright blue and bright red like the stained glass at Chartres.'[47] It was not to be. Shortly after this upbeat and uncharacteristically optimistic letter from Cécile, Pierre received a telegram from the family doctor to say that she was dying. After taking her body to be buried in Grenoble, the family went to Fuligny to grieve.

Pierre's mother had sold the farm in Champagne after the Armistice, and moved with two of her daughters, Marthe and Agnès, to Fuligny, near Rheims, to the east of Paris in the Aube region. Here they bought a much smaller farm complete with an orchard, a kitchen garden, three cows and some hens. More unusually, it was ornamented with sculptures by Pierre's younger brother, Léon. This farm had already provided a welcome retreat from the city before Cécile's death, boosting the delicate health of both Olivier and his mother. Messiaen's aunts ensured that he ate properly, feeding him plenty of 'milk, eggs and good food'.[48] In order to build his strength, Olivier was also put in charge of the cows. Unfortunately the hapless young composer soon became the scourge of the village. His herd (if three cows can constitute a 'herd') managed to escape into a field of beets, ravaging them over a period of some hours and leaving a scene of minor devastation.[49]

In addition to being a kind of alfresco sanatorium, the farm became a peaceful compositional retreat from the city and Messiaen spent time in Fuligny each summer until after his marriage in 1932. Appreciating his gifts, Messiaen's aunts set aside a large room in which he could work, complete with an old Érard piano, and his most important and characteristic early works were composed there. It is from this time that he got into the habit of being a summer composer, making it a sacrosanct period away from the multitudinous distractions of the city. It was in Fuligny, too, that Pierre worked on his translation of the works of Shakespeare. With its many trees and meadows, the plain of the Aube countryside cultivated Olivier's profound appreciation of nature.[50] Apart from his rather disastrous experience as a cowhand, Messiaen witnessed vivid sunrises and sunsets and, more importantly, he really began to take notice of the many birds that are indigenous to the region, occasionally attempting to jot down their songs.

By 1928, Messiaen's self-imposed restriction on composing had most definitely been lifted with five works being composed during the course of the year. Although just one of these, *Le Banquet céleste*, has been published, the titles betray a distinct disparity between Conservatoire necessities and the first serious attempts to express more personal themes. Two works were written in Paris, Fugue in D minor for orchestra and, rather inconceivably, a set of *Variations écossaises* (Scottish variations) for organ. It seems likely that these two uncharacteristic pieces, to judge by their titles, were written to fulfil requirements of the Conservatoire composition course.

By contrast, away from the Conservatoire and the bustle of Paris, the tranquillity of Fuligny produced three contemplative, and entirely idiosyncratic, religious works – the orchestral *Le Banquet eucharistique* (The Eucharistic banquet) and two organ works, *Le Banquet céleste* (The celestial banquet) and *L'Hôte aimable des âmes* (The kind host of souls). Nothing is known of the latter beyond its title. *Le Banquet eucharistique* was performed at the Conservatoire by the student orchestra under Henri Rabaud on 22 January 1930, providing Messiaen with his first opportunity of hearing whether he possessed his teacher's mastery at orchestration. He did not regard it as a success: 'It was a very long work, neither very well scored, nor very well constructed. But I never hesitated about the title. It always seemed obvious to me.'[51] *Le Banquet eucharistique* was not performed again, but it was not entirely wasted for, as the titles suggest, *Le Banquet céleste* is related to it, drawing on material from the orchestral work.

It is quite natural that Messiaen's first religious works should be meditations on the Eucharist since it forms a central pillar of his Catholic faith. According to Church doctrine, Christ's sacrifice is not just *commemorated* during the celebration of Mass but that unique event is made present through the transubstantiation of bread and wine into His body and blood. One of the manifold consequences of this abstruse theological concept is that it provides Catholics with an instance of the timeless aspect of God. Namely that Christ's Passion, an event that is fixed at one moment in the human perception of time, is also present in the realm of eternity, where the concept of time does not exist. The representation of the eternal coexisting with the temporal is a basic objective, and achievement, of much of Messiaen's art. As his earliest work to have been published, *Le Banquet céleste* announces that intention with astonishing assurance. The piece seems almost to have ground to a halt on its very first chord and then moves at such a slow pace that even the shortest chords become aural entities in themselves. All this happens within the rather weightless soundworld of Messiaen's newly discovered modes. And yet it is not simply static. There is logical movement, but it happens almost in the realm of the unconscious. Messiaen creates not stasis but something much more profound. It is the simultaneous experience of movement and stillness, and thus a representation of one of the greatest theological mysteries – the ability of God to exist outside time yet to act within it. With the performance of pre-Renaissance music now commonplace, the experience of mini-malism, and a (non-liturgical) resurgence in the popularity of plain-chant, it may be difficult for current ears to appreciate the significance of this deceptively modest work. However, in 1928, little music earlier than that of Bach and Rameau was being performed. Rather than the evolution and progression conventionally expected of a musical work, *Le Banquet céleste* just *is*. At the age of nineteen, Messiaen was challenging the established perception of the function of music and hence the entire Western musical tradition since the Renaissance.

Messiaen's visits to Fuligny bore fruit again the following year in the form of eight *Préludes* for piano which 'don't form a suite in the usual sense of the word, but are essentially a collection of successive states of the soul and of personal feelings'.[52] The fingerprints of Messiaen's favoured composers can often be detected upon these delectable pieces, notably Debussy and Ravel, but also figures as diverse as Mozart, Liszt and Musorgsky. For instance parts of 'Le Nombre léger', the third Prélude, are redolent of 'The Limoges Market' from *Pictures at an Exhibition*. With titles such as 'Un Reflet dans le vent' and 'Les Sons impalpables du rêve', and the collective appellation of *Préludes*, these often introverted pieces might seem to owe a burdensome debt to Debussy. Nevertheless, the music ultimately reveals otherwise, for, if the influences are strong, Messiaen's voice is stronger.

The first piece, 'La Colombe' (The dove), is also Messiaen's first musical bird portrait. Despite having already made tentative attempts to notate the chirpings of the many birds around Fuligny, there is no link between the music and the title beyond the poetical. The mood is one of introverted simplicity and sets the tone for the collection as a whole. When Messiaen attempts to be extrovert, the effect is curiously forced, particularly in the last Prélude, 'Un Reflet dans le vent'. Having worked so hard to create music to represent eternity, the composer seems to have had trouble manipulating the same resources to produce genuinely fast music. Given the formative influence that Cécile provided during her son's artistic awakening, it may be that it was still too soon after his mother's death for Messiaen to feel creatively gregarious. The *Préludes* are permeated by a profound sense of melancholy, a remarkable trait coming from a composer who subsequently became renowned for his ecstatic outpourings of joy. Nowhere is this lugubrious spirit more potently felt than in the sixth piece, 'Cloches d'angoisses et larmes d'adieu' (Bells of anguish and tears of farewell).

In marked contrast to the three Fuligny works of the previous year, the *Préludes* have no overt theological pretensions. 'Cloches d'angoisses et larmes d'adieu' nevertheless provides the first example of a musical struggle between life and death or, more accurately, death and life. This concept of mortal conflict dominates Messiaen's early music and reappears in varying guises periodically throughout his career, the basic idea being the same every time. On each occasion, the movement in question divides quite clearly into large sections alternating moods of intensity and serenity. The vehement attacks by death, which usually climax with pounding dissonance in a torrent of ferocious violence, dissipate into the assuaging calm and tender, soaring melodies of eternal life. The two parts of 'Cloches d'angoisses et larmes d'adieu' correspond exactly to the division in its title. This, the most clearly defined of the *Préludes*, hints at the apocalyptic evocations that were to come, and ranks as one of the most powerful of Messiaen's early works. It is no coincidence that, though unstated, the religious overtones are clear: dissonant bells chime for Cécile, followed by Olivier's memories of his mother whilst his eyes, olive green like hers, shed tears.

It was with the *Préludes* that Messiaen first attracted the attention of a publisher. On being shown them, Dukas contacted Durand & Cie, publishers of his music and the great works of, among others, Debussy, Ravel and Saint-Saëns, suggesting that they take the set. Dukas was both influential and respected, but Durand were understandably nervous about undertaking the cost of engraving over half an hour of rather eccentric and, as yet, unperformed music by a twenty-year-old student. Having decided that they would hedge their bets and issue a selection of the *Préludes*, Durand found themselves being constantly chivvied by a far from satisfied Dukas. A private performance was given by Messiaen at Durand's offices on 28 January 1930, and Henriette Roget gave the official first performance at the Salle Érard just over a month later on 1 March. The entire set of eight *Préludes* appeared in the shops in June 1930 just a year after its composition.[53] Durand also agreed to take Messiaen's *Trois Mélodies* and an organ work, *Diptyque*, and it was the latter which has the distinction of being the first of Messiaen's works to appear in print, in May 1930. It is a rare example of a Messiaen work that contains all the materials but that somehow adds up to less than the sum of its two parts. This is particularly bemusing as when, in the *Quartet for the end of Time* (1940–41), Messiaen transcribed the rapt but cloying second half for violin and piano, he somehow transformed it into one of his most devastatingly beautiful paeans of yearning devotion.

Armed with the confidence of having works published, Messiaen's last two years at the Conservatoire saw a surge of creativity. In addition to the *Préludes*, *Diptyque* and *Trois Mélodies*, the two orchestral works and a mini-cantata (again to his own text) flowed from his pen. Of the pieces published, the orchestral *Simple chant d'une âme* being the sole rejection, three are variants of the life-versus-death concept. *Les Offrandes oubliées* (The forgotten offerings) is an astonishingly assured orchestral debut (if the unpublished works are discounted). Like *Le Banquet céleste* it is a meditation on the Eucharist, though at this point it is worth noting that, for Messiaen, a religious meditation was not *ipso facto* a calm experience. Indeed, the most striking aspect of *Les Offrandes oubliées* in the context of Messiaen's preceding works is the fearsome brutality of its breathless central lurch into sin. His score of Stravinsky's *The Rite of Spring* seems to be close at hand, as does that of Dukas's *The Sorcerer's Apprentice* (notwithstanding the latter's darker side having since been neutered by Mickey Mouse in the Walt Disney film *Fantasia*). Iniquitous tumult evaporates into a timeless Elysian ecstasy recalling the world of *Le Banquet céleste*. A slow pseudo-plainchant melody representing Christ on the Cross precedes the mortal struggle, to create a musical sandwich of dying life/death/life. So that there should be no mistake about the serious religious messages of the *Les Offrandes oubliées*, Messiaen furnished it with a poetic preface, its three verses reflecting the titles Messiaen gives to the three sections: 'La Croix' (The Cross), 'Le Péché' (Sin), 'L'Eucharistie' (The Eucharist):

> Arms extended, sad unto death
> on the tree of the Cross you shed your blood.
> You love us, sweet Jesus: that we had forgotten.

> Driven by folly or the serpent's tongue,
> on a panting, frantic, ceaseless course,
> we went down into sin as into a tomb.

> Here is the spotless table, the fount of charity,
> the banquet of the poor, here the Pity to be adored,

offering the bread of Life and of Love.
You love us, sweet Jesus: that we had forgotten.

No such verbalization was necessary for the mini-cantata *La Mort du nombre* (The death of the multitude) since Messiaen sets his own, poetically lucid, text. Scored for soprano, tenor, violin and piano, it consists of a dialogue between two souls. In this, the most intriguing death/life representation, the boundary between the two types of music is fragmented but still distinct. The radiant soprano is already close to heaven, while the increasingly fraught tenor is stuck in purgatory and seems to be being dragged deeper and deeper by the piano on each appearance. The soprano offers words of comfort to each of the tenor's outbursts before the transcendent violin first joins, and then consumes, her soaring melody. This innately dramatic work owes its final gestures to the 'Liebestod' of Wagner's *Tristan und Isolde*, which Messiaen had, by now, studied at some length.

The titanic struggles of *Diptyque*, *Les Offrandes oubliées* and *La Mort du nombre* are absent from the set of *Trois Mélodies* composed in the first part of the year. These sublime songs containing hints of late Fauré still inhabit the nebulous world of the *Préludes* and, although it is not stated, the set must surely be a remembrance of Messiaen's mother. The first song 'Pourquoi?' (Why?) puzzles at the diminished allure now proffered by nature. In a unique instance of Messiaen setting words by another poet, Cécile's 'Le Sourire' (The Smile) is the foundation of the second song's hushed intimation of the gossamer-like delicacy of love. Taking its cue from the *Song of Solomon*, the final song rejoices in the memory of the loved one by extolling the delectations of (divine) nature, before concluding with a beseeching prayer for benevolence on her soul, made all the more poignant by Sauvage's atheism.

Messiaen gained his *premier prix* in composition in 1930 and, treading in the footsteps of many predecessors, he entered for the prestigious Prix de Rome. For this he was required to compose a fugue on a theme by Georges Hüe and to write a setting for chorus of 'Sainte Bohème', from Banville's *Odes funambulesques*. Despite the latter beginning with the phrase 'We are brothers of the birds' and containing lines such as 'lilies of diamond, colours of gold and honey',[54] neither work impressed the judges and Messiaen did not progress to the final round. Messiaen entered again in 1931, this time managing to reach the final round, in which he was required to compose a cantata entitled *L'Ensorceleuse*.[55] If, as seems likely, Messiaen knew Berlioz's writings, with their observation that Prix de Rome cantata texts always begin with a sunrise or sunset, he may have chuckled to see that Paul Arosa's text for *L'Ensorceleuse* begins 'At dawn . . .'. The competition for the Prix de Rome had seemed arcane to Berlioz, and little had changed in a hundred years. The process still involved locking the candidates away from the world in rooms at Fontainebleau, from eighteen hours for the fugue to a fortnight for writing the cantata in the final. For the fugue, the competitors could bring a case with food, and they were checked upon regularly, but this was not a happy process for Messiaen:

> He was on time: that was probably the only time in his life he was on time – at 6 o'clock. And they gave him the studio and the theme. The man came at 8 o'clock and said 'is everything all right?', he said 'yes'. At 10 o'clock he said 'is everything alright?', he said 'no'. At noon he said 'any better now?' – 'No'. And every two hours like that. At four o'clock the man said 'but what's the matter with you?'. Messiaen said 'I need to eat', and [the man] said 'well you have to eat!' He said 'yes, I would like to very much.' 'So why don't you eat?', [Messiaen] replied 'Because I cannot open my suitcase.'[56]

When the six cantatas called *L'Ensorceleuse* were played through to the judges on 4 July 1931, First Prize was awarded to Jacques Dupont, with Yvonne Desportes receiving Second Prize and Henriette Roget also being given a prize. Not surprisingly, none of the works written for the Prix de Rome are mentioned in any of Messiaen's official listings and, unlike Ravel and Berlioz, he would not keep trying year after year.

The young composer had now completed his apprenticeship at the Conservatoire. The great attraction of the Prix de Rome was not so much the prestige involved as the financial security brought by winning. Messiaen would later state on several occasions that he never had any doubts about his own faith. However, such certitude neither made him immune from ill fortune or severe tests of his character, nor averted the sometimes difficult consequences of his heartfelt belief in Christian, specifically Roman Catholic, teaching. If he possessed his mother's reputed premonitory gifts, he would know that, believer or not, the years to come would often be extremely tough. In 1931, though, the immediate priority was to earn his daily bread.

Notes

1. Samuel, Claude, *Olivier Messiaen: Music and Color – Conversations with Claude Samuel*, trans. E. Thomas Glasow (Portland, Oregon: Amadeus, 1994), p. 19. Originally published in 1986 as *Olivier Messiaen: Musique et couleur – nouveaux entretiens avec Claude Samuel*, Paris: Pierre Belfond.
2. Alan Benson (producer/director), *The South Bank Show: Olivier Messiaen – The Music of Faith*, London Weekend Television film broadcast on Good Friday, 5 April 1985.
3. Published as part of *Tandis que la terre tourne*.
4. Dennis Marks (executive producer), 'Messiaen at 80', programme broadcast by BBC2 on 10 December 1988.
5. Cécile Sauvage, *Oeuvres complètes* (Paris: La Table Ronde, 2002), p. 244.
6. Benson, *South Bank Show: Messiaen*.
7. Pierre Messiaen, *Images* (Paris: Desclée de Brouwer, 1944), p. 191.
8. It may have been two days earlier with *Images* stating on page 117 that the wedding was on 10 September 1907 and on page 134 that it was 8 September. This may be explained by the fact that French weddings happen in two parts.
9. In November it moved to Lyons and became the *Revue de Lyon*. Pierre Messiaen, *Images*, p. 124.
10. Samuel, *Music and Color*, p. 33.
11. Pierre Messiaen, *Images*, pp. 171–2.
12. Messiaen, Olivier (1970), 'Olivier Messiaen', in Marc Honegger (ed.), *Dictionnaire de musique*, 2 vols, Paris: Bordas ii, p. 713.
13. Pierre Messiaen, *Images*, p. 147.
14. ibid, p. 136.
15. ibid, pp. 141–2.

16. ibid, p. 136.
17. Sauvage, *Oeuvres complètes*, pp. 242–3.
18. ibid, p. 244.
19. Benson, *South Bank Show: Messiaen*.
20. ibid.
21. Olivier Messiaen, notes to Erato LP set OME1.
22. Sauvage, *Oeuvres complètes*, p. 244.
23. Samuel, *Music and Color*, p. 26.
24. Pierre Messiaen, *Images*, p. 46.
25. Literally, *Les mesdemoiselles Véron*.
26. Benson, *South Bank Show: Messiaen*.
27. Samuel, *Music & Color*, p. 110.
28. *Everyman: Stained Glass*, BBC Television, 1988.
29. Samuel, *Music & Color*, p. 113.
30. ibid, p. 195.
31. Jean Cocteau, *Le Coq et l'arlequin: notes autour de la musique* (Paris, 1918); reproduced in *Oeuvres complètes IX* (Genève: Editions Marguerat, 1950).
32. Nigel Simeone, private communication.
33. Brigitte Massin, *Olivier Messiaen: une poétique du merveilleux* (Aix-en-Provence: Éditions Alinéa, 1989), p. 39.
34. Massin, *Une Poétique du merveilleux*, pp. 39–40.
35. Messiaen, Olivier, *Entretien avec Claude Samuel*, rec. Paris, October 1988, Erato disc ECD75505.
36. Jean Langlais, 'Interview at the Österreichisches Orgelforum, Vienna, 19 June 1982', CD Edition Lade EL CD 002.
37. PHNS p. 24.
38. The most extensive source of his recollections is Marie-Louise Jacquet-Langlais, *Ombre et Lumière – Jean Langlais 1907–1991*, (Paris: Edition Combre, 1995).
39. Jacquet-Langlais, *Ombre et Lumière*, p. 45.
40. ibid, p. 46.
41. ibid, p. 47.
42. ibid, p. 46.
43. ibid, p. 51.
44. Samuel, *Music & Color*, p. 16.
45. Pierre Messiaen, *Images*, p. 153.

46. ibid, p. 153.

47. ibid, p. 155.

48. Peter Hill, 'Interview with Yvonne Loriod' in Peter Hill (ed.), *The Messiaen Companion* (London: Faber and Faber, 1995), p. 294.

49. Samuel, *Music & Color*, p. 33.

50. ibid, p. 33.

51. Massin, *Une Poétique du merveilleux*, p. 45.

52. José Bruyr, 'Olivier Messiaen' in *L'Écran des musiciens, seconde série* (Paris: José Corti, 1933), pp. 124–31, cited PHNS, p. 38.

53. Nigel Simeone, *Olivier Messiaen: A Bibliographical Catalogue* (Tutzing: Verlegt bei Hans Schneider, 1998), p. 7.

54. 'Nous sommes frères des oiseaux' and 'Des lys de diamant, des couleurs d'or et de miel', cited Pierette Mari, *Olivier Messiaen: l'homme et son œuvre* (Paris: Éditions Seghers, 1965), pp. 17–18.

55. See Mari, *Olivier Messiaen*, pp. 17–18 and Simeone, *Catalogue*, pp. 189–91.

56. Langlais, 'Interview'.

2 Le jeune français 1931–9

> Now I turn to the matter of musical language. No – it isn't crazy!
> For many years I have studied harmony, fugue and composition
> so that I can lay claim to knowing my craft.[1]

For a composer who was criticized for his verbosity, it is striking how little Messiaen spoke about his life before the Second World War. The only substantive comments that can be gleaned from the many interviews that he later gave are a number of well-rehearsed anecdotes about his childhood, some choice phrases about his parents, especially his mother, and an acknowledgement of the debt owed to various teachers. In short, Messiaen studiously avoided discussing the earlier part of his life. Instead it has taken the invaluable and voluminous research of Nigel Simeone to shed light on Messiaen's early career. Substantial gaps in our knowledge and understanding still remain, but one thing is certain: the earnest, bespectacled young man who emerged from the Paris Conservatoire in 1931 was a very different figure from the serene, established composer who years later deftly skirted around questions regarding his first adult years. Forthright in his opinions, self-assured yet patently still finding his way, filled with a burning passion when discussing music, many of the differences between the young and the old Messiaen are not, on reflection, especially surprising. Nevertheless, a feeling of anger can sometimes be perceived behind his remarks, suggesting that the spiritual calm that permeates the music, and ultimately the man, was not attained easily. Which is not to suggest a truculence of the kind with which Pierre Boulez burst onto the scene a decade and a half later. Rather, at this stage Messiaen has a tendency to define himself as much by what he is not as by what he is, or wishes to be, as a composer. That, in contrast to the studious tact of later years, he is refreshingly feisty, reflects in part the difficulty of being heard in any context, whether as musician or polemicist.

Messiaen may have been unworldly throughout his life, and he was certainly shy and decidedly awkward in his early years, but he was not so naïve as a young man as to think that a career as a composer was simply about writing great music. Many of his remarks suggest a close acquaintance with the memoirs of Berlioz, one of his favoured composers and a natural model for a serious-minded young French musician. Messiaen's struggles were not as extreme as those of Berlioz, but he spent much of the 1930s fighting for, and defending, his own music and that of his friends. Through sheer determination, hard work and a punctiliousness that frequently resulted in comically pernickety missives to those involved in performances of his music, Messiaen was quickly identified as a significant talent, and his star rose steadily. That he had the self-belief required to survive the inevitable slings and arrows confronted in embarking upon an artistic career is evident from comments on learning of a setback that he made in a letter postmarked 21 June 1933 to his friend Claude Arrieu:

> It would mean nothing to be played alongside mediocrity and to compose pot-boilers ['demi-œuvres']. Since we are four genuine talents,[2] let's keep looking, collect our thoughts and write our masterpieces. Then it will be the sheer beauty of our ideas which gets us noticed; and if it doesn't, at least we'll have had the satisfaction of doing something important.[3]

The Romantic side of Messiaen's personality manifests itself in this determination to follow a true artistic path; a trait that runs like a leitmotif through many of the public and private statements of his early career. Indeed, it helps to explain the fiery, proselytizing zeal that underpins so many of his activities. Not that finding the right path was always easy, for he had already tried his hand at what can only be described as an attempted pot-boiler with the short piano piece *Fantaisie burlesque*. At best it can be described as an intriguing experiment, with Messiaen forcing his already distinctive harmony into a jazzy world redolent of Poulenc in clowning mood. Aside from any spiritual or aesthetic objections that he may have had, Messiaen was simply not very good at writing light music.

As an older man Messiaen generally avoided talking about music for which he did not care, but such diplomacy was acquired. In 1931 he had few qualms about evincing forthright views on the state of French music or attacking leading figures of French musical life, including composers whom he generally admired:

> It is possible to be a humorist and a great musician at the same time. Ravel is like that. I think it's inconceivable that Ravel could really have taken the Largo of his new concerto seriously, this Largo which turns a phrase reminiscent of Fauré on a bad day into Massenet. [. . .] Then again, there's the question of current fashion. Ravel himself is now a prisoner of this fashion, if not of the dreadful publicity which claims him as the Debussy of recent years, then of himself.[4]

Ravel was not the only one of Messiaen's boyhood heroes whose recent music was an aberration from the right course, for the composer of the *Rite of Spring* had also strayed: 'All French music today seems to me to be polarized by Albert Roussel . . . and by early Stravinsky. I say early because I still hear nothing in his later music [. . .].'[5] Messiaen's solution was 'not to destroy tonality but to enrich it', not least through the use of Gregorian chant, 'a source which is still living'.[6]

The fault line that he identified running through the nation's musical life merely reflects the fragmentation in French society as a whole during the 1930s. There is, of course, never an easy time to begin earning a living as a musician, especially a composer, even for someone as gifted as Messiaen. Nevertheless, even in the context of France's

often turbulent history, 1931 was an especially inauspicious moment to be embarking on any kind of career. The backward-looking nature of large parts of the country's economy initially insulated France from the impact of the Wall Street crash in 1929. When the inevitable downturn came, the largely agrarian economy suffered all the more harshly. Far from experiencing a *belle époque*, France was in turmoil between the wars. As political opinion drifted towards the extremes, the already embattled Third Republic lurched from one crisis to the next, with governments rarely lasting more than a few months and some managing just a few days or even a matter of hours. Messiaen did not come from a poor background, but the uncertainty, the instability and periodic outbursts of political violence left their mark on every level of society. Hunger, or at least the fear of hunger, affected the bourgeoisie as well as the working class. Messiaen's achievements as a young man may have been remarkable, but, even towards the end of the 1930s, he was far from secure financially.

In this respect the harsh regime in Dupré's organ class at the Paris Conservatoire had been an excellent preparation for Messiaen's chosen career, for the habit it instilled of unceasing hard work provided the only chance of success. It was a lesson that Messiaen learnt well, being tremendously busy not just as a young man but, as is becoming apparent from his pocket diaries, retaining this work ethic throughout his life. At the beginning of his career this meant composing as much as possible in order to give himself the best chance of getting his music heard. The result was a flurry of relatively short works, of which the orchestral pieces are the first to catch the eye. Just as the regular summer visit to Fuligny in 1930 had borne the fruit of *Les Offrandes oubliées*, Messiaen's stay on the farm with his aunts in 1931 produced another musical harvest with the symphonic poem *Le Tombeau resplendissant*. A year later, he produced a further religious orchestral meditation *Hymne au Saint Sacrement* and began work on yet another piece, the four-movement cycle *L'Ascension*. A lot of time and effort is involved in composing a piece for large orchestra, and the fact that these works were not written to fulfil commissions underlines the scope of Messiaen's ambitions. He evidently felt that they were essential to being taken seriously as a composer, and they stand as an early marker of his intention to operate primarily on the big stage of orchestral repertoire.

If there is a small incongruity in a shy young man wishing to occupy the most conspicuous forum for his art, there can only be astonished bemusement at the way in which Messiaen so publicly bares his soul in *Le Tombeau resplendissant*, or, to be precise, in the desperately vivid imagery of the text that prefaces the score:

> My youth is dead: I am its executioner. Anger bounding, anger overflowing! Anger like a spurt of blood, anger like a hammer blow! A circle at the throat, hands full of rage, a face of cold hate! Despair and weeping!
>
> My youth was lived in a music of flowers. I had in view an enchanted stairway. On it shone the plumage of the bluebird of illusions. The melody of the atmosphere rose up, joyously sad.
>
> My youth is dead: I am its executioner. Where, fury, are you leading me? Why, trees, do you gleam through the night? Advance, retreat, hold out your arms! A sea swells at my ears! and it cracks, spins, dances, shouts, yells: the void enters into me!
>
> What is this resplendent tomb? It is the tomb of my youth, it is my heart. Lit by the flame forever surging, lit by the blinding clarity of an inner voice:
>
> "Come unto me, all you who labour and are heavy laden, and I will give you rest. Blessed are the meek, for they shall inherit the earth. Blessed are they that mourn, for they shall be comforted. Blessed are the pure in heart, for they shall see God."

Speaking to José Bruyr at what can only have been a matter of weeks after completing the work, Messiaen explained that 'I wanted to write a kind of Beatitude for those who discover in their faith something more than illusions of a distant youth'.[7] Even taking into account the assuaging quotation from the Sermon on the Mount at the end of this outburst, this hardly explains the extreme picture of anger and despair portrayed by the first and third parts of the text. It is not the graphically violent language that shocks those accustomed to Messiaen's other prefaces, for there is plenty of evidence throughout his life of his penchant as a child for 'everything that frightens'.[8] Rather, it is the sense of a frank autobiographical confession that disconcerts. Quite what prompted these painful outpourings is unclear, although it is tempting to speculate that, remembering his stay at Fuligny three summers earlier, Messiaen is attempting to lay to rest some aspects of the grief that he felt at the death of his mother. That Cécile is still the great influence on his life is not in doubt though, for, as he explains to Bruyr, 'it often seems to me now that it is my mother, after her death, who guides my hand or my spirit'.[9] Nevertheless, his comments to Bruyr about 'illusions of a distant youth' suggest that in his early twenties Messiaen was clarifying the distinction between the fairy-tales or Shakespearean fantasies with which he was besotted as a child, and the 'marvellous' aspects of his faith in which 'it was no longer a matter of theatrical fiction but of something true'.[10]

Messiaen also had to come to terms with the fact that, for his father, life would move on after the death of Cécile. Pierre and his two sons had spent time in Fuligny grieving, and his sisters spent some time in Paris helping him with the household (it appears that Olivier may have inherited his blind spot for the practicalities of life from his father). The valiant assistance of Messiaen's aunts could not disguise the fact that, as women of the country, they were not suited temperamentally to life in the very heart of Paris. Marguérite, a friend and former fellow-student of Pierre's also helped. Before long (he is determinedly vague in *Images* about the timing), Pierre asked Marguérite that she 'devote herself to us; without hesitating a second, without the least objection or condition, she accepted', and they were married.[11] According to Pierre, Olivier and Alain were happy about their stepmother, writing to their grandmother shortly after the wedding to say that 'Marguérite is for us a second mother'.[12] In the eyes of Pierre, she also brought a breath of fresh air to the apartment at rue Rambuteau. This may have been wishful thinking, for, however much they liked her, it seems beyond the bounds of credibility that Olivier and Alain would not have had mixed feelings about Marguérite. Nevertheless, this can only be speculation as Messiaen barely spoke of Pierre in interview, beyond his being an English teacher and translator of Shakespeare, and did not mention Marguérite at all. This silence, which is in marked contrast to the effusive praise of Cécile, can be explained by a desire on Messiaen's part only to discuss publicly the people, or aspects of them, that impinged upon his music. After all, Alain only tends to get a passing mention from his older brother. It does not really explain, though, the cursory mentions of the father who had such a profound knowledge of Messiaen's beloved Shakespeare and Keats, a man who would have been a ready source of literary insight, and the parent who shared rather than rejected his faith. Not that Olivier fares much better at the hands of his father, being conspicuous by his absence from vast tranches of *Images*, Pierre's autobiographical set of essays written during the Occupation. When he does appear, Messiaen is rarely the focus of his father's attention and there are few insights into his character considering the lengthy discussion of Cécile. Though not hostile, the father and son who barely saw each other during the First World War, did not have the closest of relationships. As Messiaen put it to Brigitte Massin, 'You know well that it wasn't my father who counted for me so much as my mother'.[13] Despite this, they saw each other most weeks when Olivier was in Paris until Pierre's sudden death on 26 June 1957.

Pierre does observe in *Images* that 'my children do not like to discuss the Great War and the following years'.[14] Messiaen remained discreetly silent not only about this period, but about the various problems and tragedies with which his personal life was blighted, making the very public agonies of *Le Tombeau resplendissant* even harder to fathom. While the twenty-two-year-old Messiaen may have had few qualms about parading his growing pains so publicly, it would appear that doubts did not take too long to emerge. *Le Tombeau resplendissant* was given its first performance by the Orchestre Symphonique de Paris under Pierre Monteux at the Salle Pleyel in Paris on Sunday 12 February 1933.

Following this, although Messiaen did not actually withdraw the score, performances during his lifetime were rare in the extreme. He made little effort to have it published (Durand held the material but a printed score did not appear until 1997), and no recording was made until several years after his death.

By contrast, Messiaen appears to have had no second thoughts about the *Hymne au Saint Sacrement*, which was first performed by the Orchestre Straram under Walther Straram at the Théâtre des Champs-Elysées on 23 March 1933, just forty days after *Le Tombeau resplendissant*. However, it owes its continued existence to Messiaen's extraordinary memory. In Autumn 1942, the publisher, Durand, sent all of the material for the *Hymne* from occupied Paris to Lyon, which was in the 'Free Zone' and it was never seen again. When Leopold Stokowski enquired in 1946 about performing the work in New York on 13 March 1947, Messiaen, no doubt at pains not to disappoint the conductor made a household name by Disney's *Fantasia*, decided to reconstruct the score. If this seems to be a remarkable feat, it is worth noting that Messiaen was able to play the entirety of *Pelléas et Mélisande* from memory. Furthermore, two movements of the *Quartet for the End of Time* are transcriptions from memory of works that Messiaen wrote years earlier. Publication of the reconstruction of the *Hymne* was entrusted not to Durand but, uniquely in Messiaen's output, to an American firm, Broude Brothers of New York. However, the absence of the *Hymne* from the catalogues of Messiaen's main French publishers has contributed to performances attaining a rarity value amongst the composer's works matched only by the limbo in which *Le Tombeau resplendissant* languished for six decades. This is a minor tragedy. Taken together with *Les Offrandes oubliées*, *Le Tombeau resplendissant* and the *Hymne* form a striking triptych of early orchestral meditations creating a succession and progression of subjects, ideas and musical invention that is truly remarkable for a composer who was not yet twenty-five years old. From the plainchant-inspired slow string melodies that frame *Les Offrandes oubliées*, via the dramatic free-falls and dizzying turbulence of *Le Tombeau resplendissant*, to the bubbling sunny climax of the *Hymne*, Messiaen is clearly at home in an orchestral medium. Admittedly aspects of language and instrumentation, notably the inclusion of timpani, place them closer to Dukas and early Stravinsky than the composer of *Turangalîla-Symphonie* or *Des canyons aux étoiles* . . .. Nevertheless, if these three symphonic poems seem to be further removed from the works of Messiaen's maturity than the early organ works, it is, perhaps, because there have been far fewer opportunities to hear his first orchestral outings.

Messiaen's next foray into the medium, *L'Ascension*, was begun when the ink was barely dry on the *Hymne*, underlining the extent to which he regarded himself as being primarily a composer of orchestral works. A cycle of four meditations, its forward-looking bold structure and gestures have stolen the limelight from its three predecessors. With a majestic opening chorale for winds, and a luminescent slow final movement for strings, which are both dedicated to aspects of the figure of Christ, *L'Ascension* is an early example of the musical structure supporting the theological symbolism. Christ is the Alpha and the Omega, the beginning and the end, encompassing everything in the orchestra from winds to strings. As important as the symbolism itself is the audacity with which it is conveyed. Leaving entire sections of the orchestra silent for whole movements is a considerable risk, but it is clear from the outer movements of *L'Ascension* that Messiaen already has a steady nerve and the force of personality to make it work. Nevertheless, in addition to the undoubted advances, it has to be admitted that aspects of *L'Ascension* are relatively weak, representing a retrogressive step from the earlier pieces. Messiaen effectively acknowledged this a decade later when he rated the compositions in his catalogue of works in his first treatise, *Technique of my Musical Language*. Like a Michelin rating, Messiaen awarded one star to works that he regarded as 'characteristic' of his musical language, and two stars to 'very characteristic' works. The double star rating tends to be given to more recent works, such as *Les Corps glorieux* and *Visions de l'Amen*, but most of the more substantial early works, including both *Les Offrandes oubliées* and the *Hymne au Saint Sacrement* are awarded one star. It is no shock that the Cinderella of Messiaen's œuvre, *Le Tombeau resplendissant*, receives no stars. What is astonishing is that *L'Ascension* is also bereft of stars. Messiaen places his most substantial orchestral work to date on a par with the distinctly uncharacteristic *Fantaisie burlesque*.[15] The chief culprit for undermining the overall effectiveness of *L'Ascension* is the third movement, 'Alléluia sur la trompette, Alléluia sur la cymbale'. Messiaen lacks the necessary tools to whip up a genuine head of steam towards the end of the movement, instead creating pseudo-Stravinsky with added fugue but without the impetus. When he came to transcribe *L'Ascension* for organ, a task that he found uncommonly arduous, he struggled interminably with this movement, only to end up replacing it with what rapidly became one of his most celebrated toccatas, 'Transports de joie'. Organists may not like the idea, but, with the exception of the new movement, the transcription of *L'Ascension* was just that: a transcription. Messiaen did not regard the organ version as a work in its own right. For him, *L'Ascension* was an orchestral work, and the organ transcription simply enabled a wider audience to acquaint themselves with it, in much the same manner as the piano version of *Les Offrandes oubliées*. The difficulty that he encountered when transcribing *L'Ascension* seems to have clarified for Messiaen that he could not follow Milhaud's example and increase his productivity (and fees) by producing several versions of each work for different genres. They might explore similar subjects, but Messiaen never again allowed his orchestral and his organ music to overlap in terms of substance.

As it happens, the organ was the first area of music-making to produce a regular income for Messiaen. He had deputized since 1929 for Charles Quef, the organist at the Trinité, a large church about a quarter of a mile north of the Opéra Garnier. Following the death of Quef in July 1931, Messiaen was not slow to appreciate the opportunity that now presented itself. The Trinité may not have been the most prestigious of the great Parisian churches, but it possessed a magnificent Cavaillé-Coll organ. Furthermore, even though each church needs at least two organists, years may pass between vacancies appearing

5. The Trinité.

in the city for the post of titular organist. In 1931, Messiaen's own widely acclaimed teacher, Marcel Dupré, was still two years away from becoming titular organist at Saint-Sulpice, having been Widor's assistant there since 1906 and having substituted for Vierne at Notre-Dame for five years. Messiaen was Quef's substitute, and he was prodigiously talented, but he was still very young and only had two years' experience as a regular church musician. He would be far from an automatic choice for the vacant post. He realized that he may have ruffled a few feathers already with his playing at the Trinité, for he felt it necessary to write an assuaging letter to the curate on 8 August, making reassuring noises that his music would be appropriate:

In music one always has to seek what is new, but reserve that for chamber and orchestral works in which fantasy is admissible. As far as the organ is concerned, and in particular the church organ, the liturgy is the primary factor. The pattern of this, and the instrument itself, are not suitable for modern music, and one must not disturb the piety of the faithful with wildly anarchic chords. Furthermore, do not imagine that I am incapable of writing anything but dissonances. If they are not suitable for religious music, neither are they suitable for Conservatoire competitions, and if I have gained prizes it is because, thanks to my teachers, I possess a solid grounding in harmony, and in the technique of composition and organ playing ... I can, therefore, safely explore new avenues, but I can also be sensible and classical ...[16]

Tournemire, who Messiaen regarded as a kind of mentor, and Dupré were also pressed into action, exerting influence on his behalf. André Marchal, organist at Saint-Germain-des-Prés, went so far as to tell his other pupils not to apply for the post, saying that it should go to Messiaen.[17] Just twenty-two years old, Messiaen was duly appointed, making him by far the youngest titular organist in Paris. Whether or not he felt obliged to visit the confessional after sending his letter to the curate, it is hard to think of a phrase more apposite than 'wildly anarchic chords' to describe the extraordinary sounds emanating from the Trinité organ twenty years later.

We tend to think of Messiaen in the 1930s very much as an organist composer, and yet the first four years following his appointment to the Trinité are not marked by many works for his instrument. He produced just one relatively short organ piece, *L'Apparition de l'église éternelle*, a powerful exercise in crescendo and diminuendo redolent of Debussy's sunken cathedral, and the transcription of *L'Ascension*. Why this paucity of music for the organ from the composer who would make one of the greatest contributions to the instrument? To start with, Messiaen was still learning how to reconcile the conflicting demands of his artistic instincts with liturgical necessity and the sensibilities of members of the congregation. He later recalled that he was 'the object of hatred and protest from the parishioners, espe-cially the old ladies who heard the devil in the organ pipes'.[18] It is also worth remembering that, despite his love for the instrument and devotion to his duties, Messiaen did not want to make his name as an organist but as a composer. Rather, having secured the modest income together with the much more sizeable prestige that came with his post at the Trinité, and no doubt fulfilling his duties with utter diligence, Messiaen wisely channelled his compositional energies in other directions. In any case, he needed more income than the Trinité provided and that was not going to come from writing organ music. Far from sitting in an ivory tower, or even a draughty organ loft, waiting for the world to recognize his gifts, he concentrated on writing music for the concert hall, securing additional income and giving concerts.

In the early years of his career, much of Messiaen's musical activity relied upon the mutually supportive network of friends that he had built up through the classes of Dukas and Dupré at the Paris Conservatoire. To start with, they did their best to help each other in getting their music published and in gaining positions where their voices would be more influential. Having had no fewer than six of his works published by Durand, Messiaen acted as an advocate with the firm for Claude Arrieu, arranging a meeting for her with the managing director, René Dommange in November 1931. A year later Messiaen needed Arrieu's help, writing to her on 10 October to ask if she could 'please be at the general assembly of the Société Nationale this year. I am standing for membership of the committee.'[19] Messiaen's sup-porters turned out for him and he was elected, giving him a say regarding which new works would receive support for performances. He was soon able to repay Arrieu for her support, writing that 'Your work has been taken up straightaway by the Nationale. Bravo!'[20]; and again, in 1934, he could report that 'Your piano pieces are accepted at the Nationale'.[21] Messiaen's early successes meant that even as early as 1932 his inclusion was regarded as an asset for a project, as is apparent from the approach by Jacques Porte, a fellow musician who was planning to set up a new society: Les Jeunes Musiciens Français.

Messiaen accepted the position of vice-president but, as is the way with many such proposals, little else was heard of it.[22] In addition to Arrieu, the cohort of Dukas pupils included Jean Cartan, who died in 1932 aged just twenty-five, and Elsa Barraine. Messiaen was instrumental in trying to get their music performed, making plans for a concert on 1 April 1933 at the Concert Servais, and in June of the same year he went to see the conductor and well-known supporter of new music Roger Désormière on behalf of 'les quatre'. The meeting was a disappointment, for Désormière was prohibitively expensive, asking a fee of 50,000 francs, prompting Messiaen to observe in a letter to Arrieu postmarked 21 June that 'it would be vanity and folly to spend so much money on a kind of glory which would be dubious and transitory'.[23] The episode also provoked an outburst of frustration of the kind all too common in young artists attempting to make their name: 'Well-known amateurs have money thrown at them and Les Six have profited from society connections which we've never had, and from special circumstances which no longer exist: Cubist painting, Picasso, Chirico, Dadaism etc'.[24]

Whatever support he gave his friends, and vice versa, it is clear that Messiaen undertook his positions of responsibility with the utmost propriety. He was not interested in promoting a coterie of friends merely for the sake of advancement, but in supporting those he saw as kindred artistic spirits and genuine musical talents. Nowhere is this demonstrated better than in his duties as a member of the selection committee for the Société Nationale, in which position his abilities were given a tough test, for he 'had to sight-read something like one to two hundred manuscripts!'[25] Among the many scores to pass under his studious gaze in this generally thankless task, the String Quartet sent by André Jolivet in the autumn of 1934 stood out, prompting a rapturous response from Messiaen: 'Monsieur, you write the music I would like to write. Can we meet?'[26] On a cold November evening, the Jolivets went round to Messiaen's apartment, and a close friendship was immediately formed. Hilda Jolivet recalled that the two men spent much of the evening in conversation that 'went on, and on . . . At last, they reappeared with smiling faces, confirming the next meeting.'[27] It was through Jolivet, who was three years his senior, that Messiaen developed his familiarity with progressive composers from elsewhere in Europe, including works by the Second Viennese School (Schoenberg, Berg and Webern) and Bartók.

In addition to his fellow Dukas pupils, and new friends and acquaintances such as Jolivet, Messiaen also kept in close contact with Jean Langlais, who was himself now in Dukas's composition class. Langlais's blindness threatened to pose problems in the class on account of the lack of scores in Braille. Messiaen's response to this demonstrates the devotion he had to his friends. Every Wednesday evening he would spend from five o'clock until nine o'clock reading through scores for Langlais 'from the piccolo to the double bass'.[28]

This generosity of spirit also characterized Messiaen's approach to the only area of his life aside from the Trinité to provide a regular income: teaching. By 1933 at the latest, Messiaen was teaching at the École Normale de Musique, a post he would hold until the outbreak of war in 1939. Not much is known of his duties there, as the École Normale no longer has records of his employment, although it is clear that Messiaen's first steps as a pedagogue were relatively modest.[29] Over and above Messiaen's own recollection that he 'taught a piano sight-reading course'[30] it can be deduced from short pieces that he wrote as exercises or for exams that he also taught *solfège*,[31] and aspects of harmony. Messiaen also benefited from the sweeping reorganization of the Schola Cantorum in December 1934, being appointed to a post by its forward-looking new director Nestor Lejeune.

As he approached his twenty-fifth birthday, Messiaen's National Service could not be delayed any further. During his holiday in August 1933, Messiaen was anxious about how busy he would be when he returned to Paris in September, telling Arrieu in a letter postmarked 8 August that he had to 'do everything at the Trinité (the choir organist is on holiday) and must spend some Sundays doing military service'.[32] Even for an army used to dealing with all manner of conscripts, it cannot have been easy to assign appropriate duties to Messiaen. His superiors surely did not take long to reach the conclusion that this young man, who was so inept that he could not successfully negotiate the lock on his own suitcase during the fugue exam for the Prix de Rome, should be kept as far as possible from any munitions. At any rate, Messiaen was able to report to Claude Arrieu early in January 1934 that he was now 'doing a gentler kind of military service. I am giving harmony lessons to the officers and soldiers and write on average two assignments for them every day. (It's just as well that I work fast, half an hour for a melody or a bass!).'[33] It is unclear how unusual a posting this would have been, but it certainly capitalized upon Messiaen's talents, whilst avoiding the potential dangers of his weaknesses.

Throughout his national service, Messiaen still tried to maintain his playing and teaching, explaining in a letter to Arrieu on 23 July 1934 that 'I am frantically busy with the preparation of sight-reading tests for the Ecole Normale and some army exercises at Maisons-Laffitte'.[34] He also continued to give Langlais advice by post. By half-way through his national service, the strain of Messiaen's conflicting obligations was beginning to show. In March 1934, he stepped in at the last minute to play for the annual Mass at the Trinité organized by Nadia Boulanger as a memorial for her sister Lili, who had died at the age of twenty-four in 1918. It is clear by the defensive tone of the letter sent to Nadia Boulanger shortly after the service on 15 March that she had expressed her displeasure to Messiaen about his performance:

Chère Mademoiselle,
   I am completely distraught that things did not happen according to your wishes. You asked me if I could perhaps play at the beginning of the service – in this instance – the first of Bach's Advent chorales. I did that. I was given no other instructions whatsoever. Seeing that Monsieur Bonnet had not arrived and not knowing the keys of the pieces with the small organ or the time that you had set aside for me between these pieces, I thought that the wisest course was to improvise from start to finish. There you are! And I am not to blame!
   I remain distraught about your disappointment and completely understand that any programme – even an ultra-magnificent one – would always seem to you unworthy of your sister's memory.[35]

As a member of the committee of the Société Musicale Indépendante (SMI), Boulanger had been acquainted with Messiaen's music (and his fretful letters) at least since early 1931, when *La Mort du nombre* received its première at an SMI concert. Within a few years Messiaen was a fellow teacher at the École Normale de Musique, whilst the Trinité was Boulanger's local parish church, so there was plenty of opportunity for making close acquaintance with the precociously talented titular organist's improvisational style. It may well have been a desire on the part of Boulanger not to have him at the keyboard that provided the original impetus for inviting Joseph Bonnet to play at Lili's memorial service. The previous year Messiaen was 'absolutely delighted to cede the organ to my maître',[36] for Marcel Dupré had been pressed into service. It is scarcely surprising that Messiaen was uptight at the prospect of having upset Boulanger. As the grande-dame of the neo-classical camp, her aesthetic was poles apart from that of the young composer, but she was a formidable and highly influential woman capable of opening, and closing, many doors.

Despite the more genteel duties, Messiaen's National Service was capable of imposing restrictions of a more direct, physical nature. In a letter dated 23 July, Messiaen complained to Arrieu that 'things go from bad to worse at the barracks!'.[37] Things evidently came to a head a couple of weeks later with Messiaen writing on 21 August to explain that 'I've recently had a lot of bother at the barracks and a ridiculous incident has prevented me from going out for the last 15 days (Sundays excepted!). I'm calmer about it now and should be free in 45 days.'[38] Whilst this tantalizing letter is ambiguous about whether Messiaen was confined to barracks for two weeks or for two months, it is evident from this sorry episode that he was temperamentally as well as practically unsuited to military life.

After the abundance of riches over the previous few years, 1934 bore a fallow harvest for Messiaen, the completion of the organ transcription of *L'Ascension* being the sole addition to his catalogue. The effect that National Service had on Messiaen's domestic life must have been at least as frustrating as the impact upon his career, for, like his father a quarter of a century earlier, Messiaen was not a bachelor when he entered the barracks. He had already met and married the woman who, after his mother, stands as the second great female inspiration of Messiaen's life: Claire Delbos.

Born on 2 November 1906[39] and the daughter of Victor Delbos, a teacher at the Sorbonne, Claire had studied at the Schola Cantorum, being a violinist and an accomplished composer in her own right. Claire and Messiaen were married on 22 June 1932. Claude Arrieu was Claire's Maid of Honour, giving them a crystal decanter, and a few months later Messiaen produced a musical wedding present of his own in the form of a *Thème et variations* for violin and piano. During the summer, Claire and Olivier moved into 77 rue des Plantes in the 14th arrondissement on the Left Bank, a task that prevented him from finding much time to devote to his music: 'I am taking only three weeks holiday in the countryside and have had to endure the stifling heat of Paris. I have not had time to compose and that distresses me.'[40] Situated in a block on the corner of place de la Porte de Châtillon in the south of the city, 77 rue des Plantes would be the couple's home for the next six years. Although hardly set in docile suburbia, the new apartment was markedly more peaceful than the bustling rue Rambuteau. Apart from external noise, quiet moments at rue Rambuteau were rare thanks to the playful havoc wreaked by a toddler, in the form of Messiaen's half-brother, Charles-Marie. Born in 1930, it is not known what Messiaen thought of his half-brother for, as with Marguérite, he never mentioned him outside family circles. Not being in the very centre of the city did mean that Messiaen now had a much longer trek to the Trinité, and there must have been days when he rued their choice of location after his appointment to the École Normale in the north-west of the city. Nevertheless, like any newly-wed's first home, 77 rue des Plantes was also full of beginnings. It was here, for instance, that Olivier and Mi, Messiaen's pet name for Claire, first met the Jolivets, and it was also the venue for the lengthy discussions of music amongst friends that would eventually evolve into the famed private analysis class. In addition to the Paris apartment, marriage to

Claire brought the benefit of a new refuge about 300 miles to the south to which they could escape during the summer months: 'I am staying in an old feudal château which is very conducive to composition and I am getting a lot of work done.'[41] Owned by the Delbos family, the Château St Benoît, at Neussargues in the Cantal area of the Auvergne, was where much of *L'Ascension* was composed as well as providing the picturesque location for several of Claire and Olivier's early holidays together.

On Saint Cecilia's day, exactly five months after they got married, the young couple gave the first public performance of *Thème et variations* as part of a concert given at the Salle Debussy by the Cercle Musical de Paris. Like Berlioz a century earlier, Messiaen worked hard at rounding up support in advance of a première, writing, for instance, to Langlais a couple of days before the concert asking him to come and 'make lots of noise'.[42] A review in *Le Ménestrel* duly noted lively applause from the sympathetic audience. As an abstract work with no poetic title or inscription, the *Thème et variations* is unusual in Messiaen's output, but it seems that the success of this little party-piece prompted the composition of another work for Mi, *Fantaisie*, the following year. However, Messiaen must have had second thoughts, for it was never published and it is unclear whether it was even performed in public. The work still exists, though, for Yvonne Loriod has recently rediscovered the manuscript. A similar fate befell a setting of the Mass, written at Neussargues during the summer of 1933 on the same holiday that he completed *L'Ascension*, which Messiaen never permitted to see the light of day. This sudden bout of self-censorship, having had several years' worth of compositions of all types published, suggests that during 1933 Messiaen began to perceive more strongly which compositional path he should follow and which he should avoid. In particular, the Mass setting appears to have clarified that although his music would be inspired by his faith, it would not, with the notable exception of his organ works, be written for use within the liturgy. He summarized his outlook towards the end of his life, reflecting that he had 'written works which meditated on the Mystery of Christ, which is little or badly known. These works, it seems to me, were more interesting than endlessly repeating "Have mercy on us, have mercy on us", because everyone knows that we are unfortunate and that we need someone to have mercy on us.'[43] Similarly, Messiaen's love for Claire would not manifest itself in abstract trifles vaunting their respective talents on violin and piano, but necessitated a much deeper mode of expression. When in 1936 he finally wrote another piece for Claire, three years after the aborted *Fantaisie*, it was not a short violin showpiece but a chaplet of nine songs celebrating the sacramental bliss of marriage: *Poèmes pour Mi*. The dedication of the title is far from being the only way in which the cycle is inspired by Messiaen's relationship with his wife. His human love for Claire is placed within the context of the divine love of God. This results in some juxtapositions that can be uncomfortable for unbeliever and believer alike, with the language of heartfelt religious devotion, such as long, melismatic *Alléluias* nestling alongside personal revelations about life with Claire, such as the intimate picture conjured by the eighth song, 'Le Collier' (The necklace):

> Printemps enchaîné, arc-en-ciel léger du matin,
> Ah ! mon collier ! Ah ! mon collier !
> Petit soutien vivant de mes oreilles lasses,
> Collier de renouveau, de sourire et de grace,
> Collier d'Orient, collier choisi multicolore
> Aux perles dures et cocasses !
> Paysage courbe, épousant l'air frais du matin,
> Ah ! mon collier ! Ah ! mon collier !
> Tes deux bras autour de mon cou, ce matin.

> [Spring enchained, light rainbow of morning,
> Ah! my necklace! Ah! my necklace!
> Little living support for my weary ears,
> Necklace of renewal, of smiling and grace,
> Necklace of the Orient, chosen, multicoloured,
> With hard, whimsical pearls!
> Curving landscape, fitted to the cool morning air,
> Ah! my necklace! Ah! my necklace!
> Your two arms around my neck, this morning.]

For Messiaen, the boundary between sacred and secular subject matter simply did not exist. In a vigorous defence of his next song cycle, the equally autobiographical *Chants de terre et de ciel*, he explained:

> If there is such a thing as religious art, then it is equally essentially diverse. Why? Because it expresses ideas about a single being, who is God, but a being who is ever-present and who can be found in everything, above everything, and below everything. Every subject can be a religious one on condition that it is viewed through the eye of one who believes.[44]

The logical conclusion of this approach, and one that Messiaen himself implied on numerous occasions, is that all of his music is 'religious', regardless of whether or not this is made explicit. This assertion helps to explain how a phrase depicting the changing colours of a lake during sunset in the piano work *La Fauvette des jardins* can reappear as a chorale espousing the glory of carrying the cross in *Saint François d'Assise*. Nevertheless, while all of Messiaen's works may be 'religious', some are undoubtedly more religious than others. He need not make a distinction between the *Alléluias* and the image of Claire's arms as a necklace around his neck in *Poèmes pour Mi*, for the latter is not a secular act but a facet of the sacramental relationship that he has with his wife. For Messiaen, the question is not why are these two sentiments contained within the same work, but why would one be included without the other?

It is possible that Claire may have provided a further spur, for she had composed a song cycle, *Primevère* (Primrose), the previous year to five poems by Cécile Sauvage. Not that the influence would have extended much beyond the idea of a song cycle, for the sumptuous music of *Poèmes pour Mi* with its rich vein of melodic invention and elongated melismas is worlds apart from the more astringent approach of Delbos. *Poèmes pour Mi* was first performed complete under the auspices of La Spirale on 28 April 1937. In the Wagnerian soprano Marcelle Bunlet, Messiaen had an understanding advocate for his music. Appropriately the cycle shared the programme with *L'Âme en bourgeon*, Delbos's new setting of nine poems from the collection that Messiaen's mother had written whilst expecting him. This was doubly apposite for Delbos was by now pregnant herself, giving birth on Wednesday 14 July, Bastille Day, to a son, Pascal. Paris was in an even greater state of fervour on Bastille Day 1937 than usual, for the spectacles of the Exposition Internationale were approaching their zenith. Messiaen was one of eighteen composers commissioned to write works for the series of 'Fêtes de la lumière', in which the music played an integral part in displays of water, light, fireworks and sound along the banks of the Seine.[45] Messiaen's contribution to these spectacular events was *Fêtes des belles eaux*. Knowing that the music would need to be recorded and then broadcast from loudspeakers in trees and on barges in the river, he opted not for conventional instruments or voices, but for a sextet of ondes Martenot, the electronic instrument which, although included in works by composers such as Milhaud, Jolivet, Koechlin, Schmitt, Ibert, Honegger and Varèse, would become almost synonymous with Messiaen's music. *Fêtes des belles eaux* was first experienced on 25 July 1937, just eleven days after the birth of Pascal, and a further two times during the Exposition, on 12 September and 3 October. Lasting about half an hour, some parts of *Fêtes des belles eaux* now sound like futuristic Muzak, the effect of these strange new sounds coinciding with the light and water effects for those walking alongside the Seine during the three Sunday evening performances must have been extraordinary. There are also some profound passages, for even in an occasional work for a public show Messiaen found expression of his religious sentiments: 'in the most worthwhile moments of *Fêtes des belles eaux* when, on two occasions, the jets of water shoot up to a great height, a long, slow phrase is heard – almost a prayer – which makes the water a symbol of Grace and Eternity'.[46] Not surprisingly, Messiaen did not manage to compose anything new in the summer after Pascal was born, contenting himself with orchestrating *Poèmes pour Mi*, but the next year he was getting enough sleep to be able to produce *Chants de terre et de ciel*, inspired this time by the joys of family life with 'baby Pilule'. By this time the

Messiaens had moved into 13 villa du Danube, on the eastern side of Paris in the 19th arrondissement. This town house is tucked away about as far from a road as it is possible for any but the richest to be in Paris; it is about half-way along villa du Danube, a walkway linking rue David d'Angers and rue de l'Égalité. This was not a fashionable part of Paris, but Claire and Olivier had found an ideal house for two composers, and, with a nice park just around the corner, it was a fine home in which to bring up a child.

The arrival of Pascal was a particular blessing for the Messiaens as Claire had suffered several miscarriages during the early years of their marriage. It was probably on account of Claire being pregnant or convalescing after a miscarriage that Messiaen asked Arrieu if a meeting to discuss concert arrangements could be at her house as 'I'm afraid of tiring my wife if we meet at mine'.[47] The first time that the Messiaens and the Jolivets spent an evening together, in November 1934 at the apartment in rue des Plantes, Claire was unexpectedly frank on the subject with Hilda Jolivet: 'We had heard about the white wedding of these two ethereal beings, so I was astonished when my hostess started to confide in me about her difficulties with pregnancy, and her regret at not having children'.[48] The distress caused by these miscarriages was thrown into relief by events back at rue Rambuteau. Four years after the birth of Charles-Marie, Marguérite and Pierre had another son, Jacques, but this time tragedy struck. On Saturday 21 July 1934, after twelve fraught days, Olivier's second half-brother died. It may be that a desire to support Pierre and Marguérite at this time was the cause of Messiaen's problems at the barracks, for it was just two days after the death of Jacques that he mentions things going 'from bad to worse' in a letter to Arrieu.

With so much of his domestic life preoccupied with pregnancies and thoughts of bringing a new life into the world, it is natural that Messiaen's musical thoughts in the mid-1930s should turn to the birth of Christ with *La Nativité du Seigneur*. The work that marks a watershed in Messiaen's early career, *La Nativité* forms his first true organ cycle, with nine meditations lasting the best part of an hour. The impetus for

6. Messiaen's summer house at Petichet in 2002.

writing the cycle came in part from a major rebuilding of the organ at the Trinité that began towards the end of 1934. At least as significant, though, must be that it was written during the summer of 1935. On 12 September, he wrote to Arrieu that 'I have been able to compose a little and I think I have made progress from a rhythmic point of view (though perhaps I am fooling myself!). I've seen the most stunning mountain landscape here. The Dauphiné is really one of the greatest things in France!'[49] Messiaen had rediscovered the scenery that would act as his muse for the remainder of his life.

It is in La Nativité that Messiaen begins to formulate a rhythmic approach in his music that is equivalent to, and as distinctive as, the rich harmonies and melodies derived from his modes of limited transposition. Two developments in particular find coherent expression in La Nativité. Firstly, he incorporates ancient Hindu rhythms as categorized by Çarngadeva and reproduced in Lavignac's Encyclopédie. Divorced from their original context, these Indian rhythms provided the impetus for the second advance, the addition of small values to otherwise straightforward rhythms. The technical upshot of these innovations is that Messiaen's rhythms build upwards from the smallest value, rather than dividing downwards from a larger value, such as a bar. Of more significance is their impact on the sound of the music, which has a far greater fluidity than anything emanating from other organ lofts around Paris at the time: 'With the use of Hindu rhythms in *La Nativité* I produced the proof, at least I believe I did, that it was possible to write music for organ other than in a post-Franckist aesthetic'.[50] This is apparent even from the simple little harmonized melody that opens the cycle in 'La Vierge et l'Enfant' (The Virgin and the Child). As it unfolds, periodically decorated with little arabesques, it sounds as if it is following a beat, and yet what that beat might be remains elusive, bending one way then the other. The effect is both supple and subtle, whether in the slow music that dominates the first half of the cycle or in the thunderous power of the seventh piece, 'Jésus accepte la souffrance' (Jesus accepts suffering) or the dazzling closing toccata of 'Dieu parmi nous' (God among us). As a consequence, the advances made in *La Nativité* not only marked out Messiaen as being a great organ composer, but also moved organ music from the fringes to the centre of progressive musical thought.

Messiaen performed individual movements of *La Nativité* at the Trinité during late 1935, but, according to Daniel-Lesur, he felt at that time that it was too difficult for one player. The official première was thus shared between three friends, Daniel-Lesur, Langlais, and Jean-Jacques Grunenwald at a concert put on by Les Amis de l'Orgue on 27 February 1936, with Messiaen reassuring them that the music 'wasn't as difficult as all that'.[51] Nevertheless, his decision not to take any part in the première emphasized his role as composer rather than organist, a point underlined by the little manifesto distributed at early performances of the work:

> The emotion, the sincerity of the musical work.
> Which will be at the service of the dogmas of Catholic theology.
>   Which will be expressed by melodic and harmonic means: the progressive growth of intervals, the chord on the dominant, pedal notes, embellishments and extended appoggiaturas.

Still more by rhythmic means: rhythms immediately preceded or followed by their augmentation and sometimes increased by a short value (adding half the value).

And above all by modes of limited transposition: chromatic modes, used harmonically, the strange colour of which derives from the limited number of their possible transpositions (2, 3, 4 and 6 according to the mode).

The theological subject? The best, since it contains all subjects. And this abundance of technical means allows the heart to overflow freely.[52]

If La Nativité marks the point at which Messiaen's music begins fully to sound like Messiaen, then the curious combination of effusive religious sentiment with the dry assurances of technical rigour espoused by this manifesto is equally typical of the composer's explanations of his own music. As Paul Griffiths has observed, the choice of the word 'theological' rather than 'mystical' is important, for Messiaen is not unveiling a personal vision, but conveying the truths espoused by the doctrines of the Catholic Church. Like the Church, Messiaen makes full use of simple symbols as a springboard to a deeper understanding of the subject. Some of these, such as the use of numerology, help the composer to define the parameters of the work. For instance, the number of movements, nine, is associated both with the Virgin, by virtue of the nine months of her pregnancy, and with the Trinity, being three times three. Other symbols emerge through the music. On the one hand, Messiaen draws upon the musical heritage of his faith by quoting the Christmas plainchant Puer natus est. On the other hand, there are examples of direct musical representation, such as the cavernous descents of 'Le Verbe' (The Word) and 'Dieu parmi nous', representing the extraordinary notion of God descending to live in the world, the enormous power of which is juxtaposed with the fragile vehicle for this existence in the form of the baby Jesus.

While La Nativité is seminal in terms of style and approach, it can also be regarded as the work with which Messiaen's international career began in earnest, being the reason for his trip across the

Channel to London for the ISCM[53] festival in 1938. This was certainly not the first time that his music had been heard abroad. *Le Banquet céleste* had been performed in London in October 1936 and *L'Apparition de l'église éternelle* a month later by Noëlie Pierront and André Marchal respectively, whilst Serge Koussevitzky had been responsible for bringing Messiaen's music to American audiences with the US première of *Les Offrandes oubliées* given by the Boston Symphony Orchestra on 16 October 1936. In December of the following year, four movements from *La Nativité* itself were heard in a London recital by André Fleury, drawing an insightful response from Edwin Evans, music critic for *The Times* who noted that *La Nativité* is 'harmonically daring, and composed in a very free rhythm, without time-signature. This, incidentally, is not very modern, since it is the common usage of the plainsong. The effect, however, is anything but orthodox, and the music would flutter some organ lofts, but one feels its sincerity.'[54]

So, by 1938 there had been some limited outings overseas for Messiaen's music. Nevertheless, the ISCM festival that summer marks his first experience of the nerve-racking task of himself performing in front of a foreign audience and without understanding a word of the language. The irony of the language in question being English, from which his father made his living, was surely not lost on Olivier or Pierre. To this was added the responsibility of representing not just himself, but his country, a point underlined by the fact that he stayed at the Eaton Square home of the First Secretary of the French Embassy, Roland de Margerie.[55] Given that *La Nativité* had not been submitted to the French jury for consideration as part of the festival, it must have come as a surprise to all concerned that it was included at all. The unexpected advocate was none other than Poulenc, a composer whose music Messiaen seems barely to have been able to bring himself to discuss. Nonetheless, Poulenc had been overwhelmed by *La Nativité* and made a personal representation to the international jury so that some of the work could be heard in London.[56] The subsequent performance of two movements, Les Mages and Le Verbe, was far from ideal, for the organ in the dry acoustic of Broadcasting House was not remotely up to the task. Thanks to the efforts of Felix Aprahamian, an opportunity was found to hear the entirety of *La Nativité* in a much more appropriate setting, the Anglo-Catholic church of St Alban the Martyr, Holborn, which had both a fine instrument by Willis and a more resonant acoustic.[57] The conditions may have been more favourable, and the event a greater success, but this did not prevent Archibald Farmer in the *Musical Times* dismissing Messiaen's music: '... the work, indeed, is the very negation of phrasing; hence these endless ramblings, meaningless and inchoate, without form and void.'[58] Such sentiments set the tone for the regular onslaughts of critical invective with which Messiaen would be increasingly showered over the next twenty years or so, not only in Britain and America, but also in his native France. He always possessed a distinctive musical voice, but it is no coincidence that these critical attacks grew steadily more vitriolic as his music matured, moving out of the shadow of his teachers and forebears to become unmistakeably, idiosyncratically Messiaen.

Later in life he saw little point in engaging with his critics, but as a young man Messiaen was not averse to giving a spirited defence of his music. With the publication of his second song cycle, *Chants de terre et de ciel*, just a few months after Farmer's attack in the *Musical Times*, Messiaen made a pre-emptive strike: 'As this is a very individual work (more than just the title!) which has been, is, and will be vigorously discussed and attacked, I want to provide some commentary on it'.[59] Even though he had found his feet as a composer in his own right, he was keen to justify his musical language by demonstrating his musical lineage: 'My models were: first, Debussy, then plainchant and the work of the great Hindu rhythmician Çarngadeva. Certain pages of Schoenberg and Jolivet, certain French and Russian traditional melodies have not left me indifferent. Add to that the fact that I love Massenet because his music is tonal and well harmonized, and you have some idea of my style.'[60] For the most part this list is not so different from similar declarations made later in life, although less prominence is given to Schoenberg and Jolivet. It is the final sentence that leaps off the page, though, for within a few years Messiaen's effusive citation of kinship with Massenet had been discreetly swept under the carpet. Messiaen completed his apologia of *Chants de terre et de ciel* with a forthright dismissal of his less progressive detractors: 'As for those who moan about my so-called dissonances, I say to them quite simply that I am not dissonant: that they should wash their ears out!'[61]

Whilst his music was making its first excursions overseas, on the domestic front Messiaen and various close friends were adopting a policy of strength in numbers. The mid-1930s saw Messiaen take a prominent role in two overlapping groups dedicated to the cause of new music.[62] Along with several other recent appointees made to the Schola Cantorum after Nestor Lejeune wielded his new broom, Messiaen joined the committee of La Spirale upon its foundation in 1935. Very much a circle of friends, other members around the table included Claire, Jolivet and Messiaen's old classmate Daniel-Lesur. Primarily a forum for promoting the performance of contemporary chamber works, the manifesto of La Spirale stated that it 'wishes to serve music and in order to do so, it will give fewer world premières; instead, it will give repeat performances of significant works'.[63] The inaugural concert at the Schola consisted exclusively of works by the committee members, while subsequent events looked much further afield, with concerts dedicated to American composers, contemporary Hungarian music, women composers and the works of Alban Berg. For his part Messiaen made regular contributions as a performer, whether it be accompanying songs by Ives, John Alden Carpenter, Claire and his former teacher, Maurice Emmanuel, playing organ music by Jules le Febvre, or piano pieces by Barraine, Ravel or Milhaud. As with so many ventures of this kind, La Spirale was a short-lived one, its activities spanning just eighteen months. By the time that La Spirale's last concert was given on 4 May 1937, Messiaen was involved more prominently in another group with remarkably similar aims: La Jeune France.

It was the self-taught Yves Baudrier who, having been bowled over by a performance of *Les Offrandes oubliées*, approached Messiaen with the intention of capitalizing upon the spiritual goals that he perceived were spurring several young French artists. Messiaen suggested three further members to Baudrier; Jehan Alain, Daniel-Lesur and Jolivet. Of these, Alain declined, but the others were enthusiastic and, for the second time, Messiaen was one of 'les quatre'. These four soon became a close-knit group and 'plotted various ideas and schemes, mainly at Yves Baudrier's house ... [which was] cluttered with books, scores and records, all muddled up with his pots and pans in an indescribable mess'.[64] The staple fare of La Jeune France was to be orchestral rather than chamber music and, to this end, Baudrier financed many of the activities of the group, so that for the inaugural concert it was possible not only to engage Désormière and the Orchestre Symphonique de Paris, but also a celebrity soloist in the shape of the pianist Ricardo Viñes.

Messiaen had signed up to the stated aims of La Spirale and he had outlined his personal approach with the slip of paper distributed at performances of *La Nativité*. In this most political of decades, he now put his name to the manifesto of La Jeune France, the opening sentence of which was an effective rebuke to the previous generation: 'As the conditions of life become more and more hard, mechanical and impersonal, music must bring ceaselessly to those who love it its spiritual violence and its courageous reactions'.[65] The foundation of La Jeune France placed Messiaen more clearly than ever centre stage, not only in the promotion of new orchestral works by French composers, but also as a polemicist reacting against the aesthetics of Satie and of Cocteau's *Le Coq et l'arlequin*, not least the flippancy and the calls for a decidedly urban modernity and populism. By 1939, Messiaen was leading an all-out attack in a front-page article for La Page Musicale entitled 'Contre la paresse' (Against laziness) that is extraordinary for the force of its rhetoric:

> This feverish century, this crazy century is nothing but a century of laziness.
> Lazy: those composers who produce nothing any more. Lazy: those composers who produce too much without ever taking the time to think, to let their hurried work ripen.

Lazy: those artisans of sub-Fauré and sub-Ravel. Lazy: the fake Couperin maniacs, writers of rigadoons and pavans. Lazy: the odious contrapuntalists of the 'return to Bach' who offer us, without remorse, dry and doleful lines poisoned by a semblance of atonality.

Lazy: the vile flatterers of habit and *laissez-faire* who scorn all rhythmic undulation, all variety, all respiration, all alternation in the subtle art of musical metre, giving us instead on the illusory platter of perpetual motion, vague 3-in-a-bars and vaguer 4-in-a-bars, native to the most vulgar of public dances and the most limping of military marches.

[. . .]

What thunder, what treasure-troves of furious hailstones or of sweet snow will be brought to bear on this kind of laziness by the genius we await, the great anticipated liberator of the music of the future?[66]

One of the strengths of La Jeune France from the outset was that, aside from a common dislike of neoclassicism, the four composers explicitly did not aspire to create a school or to espouse one particular manner of composition. On the contrary, they celebrated their stylistic diversity in their manifesto, stating that 'their only unqualified agreement is in the common desire to be satisfied with nothing less than sincerity, generosity and artistic good faith'.[67] It was a point that did not go unnoticed, an anonymous critic from *Revue Musicale* observing that 'Nothing – or almost nothing – seems to unite these composers [. . .]', before going on to repeat a favoured analogy of Messiaen's, that 'Daniel-Lesur and Baudrier occupy the right [i.e. traditionalist] wing of the group in which Jolivet represents the extreme left [i.e. progressive], while Messiaen is equidistant from the two poles [. . .]'.[68] Other composers, notably Jehan Alain, Claude Arrieu, Alan Bush, Georges Migot and Alan Rawsthorne, also benefited from the stated aim of La Jeune France to support performances of 'one or several works characteristic of some interesting trend within the bounds of their aspirations'.[69]

From the current perspective, Messiaen stands head and shoulders above the other three members of La Jeune France, both as a creative musician and for his pedagogic influence upon the post-war avant-garde.

Jolivet might be described as a fine, though not a 'great', composer, whilst the more conventionally tonal Daniel-Lesur tends to be admired more as an administrator than a composer, and Baudrier is really only remembered as being the 'fourth' member of the group, if at all. By contrast, although it was clear in 1936 that Messiaen was prodigiously talented, it was Jolivet who was regarded as the more progressive composer, shocking the musical establishment and acting as *de facto* mentor to his younger colleagues. As deputy to his teacher Tournemire at Sainte-Clotilde since 1927, Daniel-Lesur was already establishing a reputation as a fine organist-composer. Critics and audiences may not have enthused about Baudrier's music as they did about Messiaen's, but neither did they disparage it, and he was recognized as being 'the driving force' behind the group.[70] Although Messiaen is the main reason that La Jeune France is remembered today, it was, along with La Spirale, invaluable to the development of his career. These groups also gave Messiaen some sense of status, of belonging to an establishment, if not the Establishment, providing him with a platform for his works and views that he would have struggled to find on his own.

7. Claire, Pascal and Olivier Messiaen, in 1939.

As the 1930s came to a close, Messiaen could look back with some satisfaction. His domestic life was happy with Claire and Pascal, and he was secure as titular organist at the Trinité. He had forged a career as a composer, developing a musical style that was recognizably his own with a body of works of increasing confidence and sophistication. *La Nativité* is rightly viewed as a defining moment, but with each of the succeeding large-scale works, Messiaen manages to raise his sights even higher. Now, following the two domestically inspired song cycles, *Poèmes pour Mi* and *Chants de terre et de ciel*, he produced another organ cycle, *Les Corps glorieux*. These 'seven brief visions of the life of the resurrected' delve much deeper into the heart of Messiaen's faith than the quasi-narrative Christmas meditations of *La Nativité*. However picturesque the shepherds and Magi might be, it is the theological territory explored by *Les Corps glorieux*, not least the 'mystery of the Holy Trinity' in the final movement, that is typical of the composer's music as a whole. As such, the cycle reflects Messiaen's greater confidence in both his compositional craft and the understanding of his faith. The concluding meditation on the Holy Trinity is a case in point, being a ninefold Kyrie eleison, with three simultaneous musical lines creating not counterpoint but heterophony, in that three seemingly independent strands occur at once, each apparently operating in its own time-frame whilst the whole remains comprehensible to the ear. That Messiaen manages to work in references from earlier in the cycle would be the icing on the cake, except that this is no grand hurrah in the manner of 'Dieu parmi nous', being quiet and 'distant' throughout in a transcendent cultivation of the mysterious. It is clear in every page of *Les Corps glorieux* just how far Messiaen had travelled since leaving the Paris Conservatoire. It is apposite, then, that for the movement that forms the centrepiece of the cycle, Messiaen returned to the same bipartite 'darkness vanquished by light' formula as can be found in several works of his student days, notably the *Diptyque* for organ and 'Cloches d'angoisse et larmes d'adieu' from the piano *Préludes*. Written as it was becoming clear that no amount of diplomacy was going to prevent war, it is hard to regard the unusually stark directness of

Messiaen's title for the movement as coincidental, for it could stand as an epithet for the catastrophe that was about to engulf the world: 'Combat of death and life'.

Notes

1. Olivier Messiaen, 'Autour d'une parution' in *Le Monde musical* (April 1939), p. 126, cited PHNS, p. 81.
2. Messiaen, Arrieu, Elsa Barraine and Jean Cartan.
3. Simeone, 'Offrandes oubliées', *Musical Times* (Vol. 141, Winter 2000), 35.
4. Bruyr, 'Olivier Messiaen' cited Nigel Simeone, 'Offrandes oubliées 2', *Musical Times* (Vol. 142, Spring 2001), 21.
5. ibid.
6. ibid.
7. Bruyr, 'Olivier Messiaen' cited Simeone, 'Offrandes oubliées 2', 21–2.
8. Sauvage, *Oeuvres complètes*, p. 244.
9. Bruyr, 'Olivier Messiaen' cited PHNS, p. 38.
10. Samuel, *Music and Color*, p. 26.
11. Pierre Messiaen, *Images*, p. 238.
12. ibid, p. 238.
13. Massin, *Une poétique du merveilleux*, p. 125.
14. Pierre Messiaen, *Images*, p. 153.
15. When a new edition of *Technique* appeared in 1999, several years after Messiaen's death, *L'Ascension* had magically acquired two stars. It is presumably a mere coincidence that Alphonse Leduc publishes both the *Technique* and *L'Ascension*.
16. Catherine Massip (ed.), *Portraits d'Olivier Messiaen* (Paris, 1996), p. 11.
17. PHNS, p. 35.
18. Samuel, *Music and Color*, p. 118.
19. Simeone, 'Offrandes oubliées', 33.
20. Undated letter to Claude Arrieu, cited Simeone, 'Offrandes oubliées', 34.
21. Letter to Claude Arrieu, before 4 January 1934, cited Simeone, 'Offrandes oubliées', 35.
22. Simeone, Nigel, 'Group Identities: La Spirale and La Jeune France', *Musical Times* (Vol. 143, Autumn 2002), 10.
23. Letter to Arrieu, postmarked 21 June 1933, cited PHNS, p. 47.

24. ibid.

25. Undated letter to Arrieu cited Simeone, 'Offrandes oubliées', 34.

26. Hilda Jolivet, *Avec André Jolivet* (Paris, 1978), p. 83.

27. Jolivet, *Avec André Jolivet*, p. 84.

28. Jaquet-Langlais, *Ombre et lumière*, pp. 83–4.

29. Jean Boivin, *La Classe de Messiaen* (Paris: Christian Bourgois, 1995), p. 28, footnote 1.

30. Samuel, *Music and Color*, p. 176.

31. The French system of aural training.

32. Simeone, 'Offrandes oubliées', 35.

33. PHNS, p. 49.

34. Simeone, 'Offrandes oubliées', 35–6.

35. Simeone, 'Offrandes oubliées 2', 22.

36. ibid, 22.

37. Simeone, 'Offrandes oubliées', 35–6.

38. ibid, 36.

39. Not 1910 as she later claimed.

40. Letter to Claude Arrieu, 5 September 1932, from Lévigny, Aube, cited PHNS, p. 41.

41. Letter to Arrieu, postmarked 8 August 1933, cited Simeone, 'Offrandes oubliées', 35.

42. Letter to Langlais, 20 November 1932, cited Jacquet-Langlais, *Ombre et lumière*, 71.

43. Messiaen, 'Entretien avec Claude Samuel', ECD 75505.

44. Messiaen, 'Autour d'une parution', *Le Monde musical* (April 1939), cited PHNS, p. 80.

45. For an excellent account of the musical activity engendered by the Exposition, see Nigel Simeone, 'The Science of enchantment: Music at the 1937 Paris Exposition', *Musical Times* (Vol. 143, Spring 2002), 9–18.

46. Olivier Messiaen, disc notes for REM 311306.

47. Letter to Arrieu, late 1932 or early 1933, cited Simeone, 'Offrandes oubliées', 34.

48. Hilda Jolivet, *Avec André Jolivet*, p. 84.

49. PHNS, p. 56.

50. Massin, *Une poétique du merveilleux*, p. 172.

51. *Olivier Messiaen, homme de foi: Regard sur son œuvre d'orgue* (Paris: Trinité Media Communication, 1995), p. 89.

52. Reproduced in Simeone, *Catalogue*, p. 46.

53. International Society for Contemporary Music.

54. E. E. (Edwin Evans), 'A Mystic Composer' *The Times*, 11 December 1937.

55. Felix Aprahamian, disc notes, *Composers in Person: Olivier Messiaen*, EMI CDC 5 55222 2 (1994), p. 6.

56. ibid.

57. The original church was destroyed by German firebombs on 16 April 1941.

58. A. F. (Archibald Farmer), 'Organ Recital Notes', *Musical Times* (December 1938, 925–6).

59. Messiaen, 'Autour d'une parution', cited PHNS, p. 80.

60. Messiaen, 'Autour d'une parution', cited PHNS, p. 82.

61. ibid.

62. For an excellent detailed study of the activities of *La Spirale* and *La Jeune France*, see Simeone, 'Group identities', 10–36.

63. Manifesto of *La Spirale*, cited Simeone, 'Group identities', 11.

64. J. J. Brothier, *La Jeune France: Yves Baudrier, André Jolivet, Daniel-Lesur, Olivier Messiaen* ([Paris] Les Amis de la Jeune France, [1954]), pp. 5–6.

65. Manifesto of *La Jeune France*.

66. Olivier Messiaen, 'Contre la Paresse', *La Page musicale* (17 March 1939), 1, cited Stephen Broad, 'Messiaen and Cocteau' in Dingle and Simeone (eds), *Olivier Messiaen: Music, Art and Literature* (Aldershot: Ashgate, forthcoming).

67. Manifesto of *La Jeune France*.

68. Cited Simeone, 'Group identities', 19.

69. Manifesto of *La Jeune France*.

70. Andre Coeuroy, 'Manifeste et Concert des Jeune France' *Beaux-Arts* (5 June 1936), cited Simeone, 'Group identities', 16.

3 Occupying time 1939–45

There he was, playing the piano with such beautiful sound in spite
of the deformity of his hands.
> Yvonne Loriod[1]

When France mobilized in September 1939, Messiaen, like his father
twenty-five years earlier, had to leave his family and become a soldier.
His poor eyesight precluded a combat role, although he was still close to
the front line. In the tense winter months of the phoney war, his first
posting was with the Engineers [Pionniers] at Sarreguemines, on the very
edge of the German border. The religious composer who had spent the
First World War in a rarefied literary world of poetry and fairy-tales was
far from happy as a conscripted workman. On 2 November 1939, 'Soldat
Messiaen Olivier, 620^e R. I. Pionniers – 2^e Bataillon, 5^e Compagnie –
secteur postal 42' wrote in frustration to Jean Langlais:

> My grazed and blackened hands, using a pickaxe, the flies, [and]
> carrying unbelievably heavy weights [. . .] prevent me from keeping on
> intimate terms with music [. . .] Everyday, or nearly, I receive a letter
> from my wife, which is an indescribable consolation for me. But I am
> not helping with the progress of my little boy! . . . a tremendous regret!
> Pray for peace and for your old pal.[2]

Things had not improved by the time he wrote to Claude Arrieu on
30 January 1940, with Messiaen revealing concern that he would fade
from the Parisian musical scene:

Thank you for your kind letter which has really touched me. I was completely unaware of the performance of *Les Offrandes oubliées* which you told me about. So they haven't forgotten me – that's nice! No, I am not able to tell you where I am: I only know that it is in the first zone and in a regiment which specialises in manual labour. Here I am obliged to carry heavy weights, cut down trees and dig holes, to be a removal man and to push wagons by hand. It is useless my telling you how unhappy I am, or that these labours are beyond my strength. Having asked for a change of regiment in order to work in a hospital, I am awaiting the result of my request: I will surely be a passable nurse, which is better than being a useless labourer![3]

In the same letter, he beseeches Arrieu to ask Tony Aubin (artistic director of the French radio station Paris Mondial) whether a post can be found at a radio station so that he can be recalled from his miserable life at the front. It is not known whether or not Arrieu spoke to Aubin, but Messiaen did not get his longed-for return to civilian life. His request for a transfer out of the pioneers was successful, though, and he soon moved about ten miles south to Sarralbe, where he donned the white coat of a medical orderly.[4]

By the time of the surprise German invasion in the searingly hot May of 1940, Messiaen was at Verdun, where his commanding officer also happened to be a professional cellist, Étienne Pasquier, and where a fellow soldier, Henri Akoka, was a clarinettist from the Orchestre National. In the face of the German advance, Messiaen, Pasquier and two companions, tried to get from Verdun to Epinal further south. Messiaen was pushing a bike astride which were two cases with manuscripts and music. On 20 June a small force of German soldiers surrounded them:

> . . . we were taken prisoner in a forest, by means of choirs of speaking voices [*des chœurs parlés*] . . . The Germans posted themselves at the four points of the compass, in small numbers, and rhythmically scanned certain words. The different sources of the sounds of these words multiplied, giving the illusion of a large troop. The chorus closed in a small circle on the Frenchmen, who believed themselves outnumbered.[5]

After their capture, Messiaen, Pasquier and Akoka had to walk more than forty miles to a large field at Toul, near Nancy. Along with 30,000 other French soldiers, they were kept in the field for ten days, then transferred to another camp for a further ten days whilst the German army, unprepared for the sheer scale of their victory, made arrangements for their transit to prison camps. Akoka had been allowed to keep his clarinet, and, whilst they awaited their fate, he began to learn 'Abîme des oiseaux', a piece that Messiaen had been writing for him in Verdun.[6] With Pasquier acting as his music stand, Akoka combined practising with complaining about the technical difficulties of the work. Messiaen countered with a deadpan 'You'll manage'.[7]

It was in the makeshift transit camp that the seeds of another friendship were also made. Throughout his time in the army, his capture and subsequent internment as a prisoner of war, Messiaen somehow retained a haversack containing a small, eclectic library of miniature scores of works ranging from the *Brandenburg Concertos* to Berg's *Lyric Suite*. As he explained in his letter of 31 January 1940 to Arrieu:

> I read them in the dead of night. Thanks to that, perhaps I will be able to maintain my technique – I am really afraid (if this goes on for long) that I will forget everything I know about music.[8]

Whilst reading one of these treasured scores in the transit camp, Messiaen was approached by another prisoner. The man observed admiringly that the score was Stravinsky's *Les Noces*, and introduced himself as an Egyptologist and musician named Guy Bernard-Delapierre. The men immediately recognized each other as kindred spirits attempting to retain their humanity in the face of the desperate circumstances. Unfortunately, the composer was transferred to another camp that night. Not wishing to wake his new-found friend, Messiaen instead wrote his name and telephone number and left it on Bernard-Delapierre's coat.[9] Their chance meeting would bear fruit several years later, once both men had been repatriated to Paris.

In the meantime, Messiaen, Pasquier and Akoka were herded along with thousands of others into padlocked cattle trucks and transported half-way across Europe to Görlitz in Silesia, about fifty-five miles east of Dresden. As a result of this horrendous four day journey 'among the urine and the poo, nothing to drink, nothing to eat',[10] Messiaen contracted dysentery and spent a month being cared for by Polish nuns in a hospital in which each room had a portrait of Hitler hanging between a crucifix and a picture of the Virgin. Once he recovered, Messiaen was interned as prisoner no.35333 in barrack 19A of Stalag VIIIA.

He had not been in the camp long when he discovered a fourth professional musician there, the violinist Jean Le Boulaire, who, like Akoka, had been allowed to keep his instrument. Messiaen composed a short trio for his fellow musicians which, after a collection by the prisoners to buy Pasquier a cello, received a private première in the illustrious setting of the washrooms. Messiaen helped to set up the camp theatre and the musicians periodically gave concerts, notably the Beethoven Trio with Akoka and Pasquier in December 1940. These performances were enthusiastically received both by their fellow inmates and the German guards, all of whom were grateful for any diversion from the incessant tedium of life in a Stalag.

Lunch in the camp was a thin, anonymous stew made from just throwing potatoes, cabbage and turnips into boiling water. Pasquier had been assigned to kitchen duties and attempted to give Messiaen extra portions wherever possible, but this did little to keep hunger at bay and did not prevent the composer from fainting many times. The winter of 1940–1 was bitterly cold, even for Silesia, with its short days lasting just a few doleful hours. Lack of food combined with the cold induced Messiaen to have vivid coloured dreams, reminding him of the vibrant, often violent imagery of the Apocalypse, with its rainbow-encircled angels heralding the end of time. When vast curtains of purple and green tore across the sky before dawn one morning, Messiaen, watching from the desolation and fear of the prison camp, believed that the prophecies were coming true. A fellow prisoner explained that he had actually witnessed the spectacular phenomenon of the aurora borealis.[11] Inspired by these experiences, Messiaen took the little trio he had composed for Pasquier, Akoka and Le Boulaire, and added seven further movements. He worked in a corner of the priests' hut after completing his duties for the day, using manuscript paper and pencils provided by a German officer, recently identified as Captain Karl-Albert Brüll.[12] In addition to finishing 'Abîme des oiseaux', Messiaen wrote a fearsome depiction of the trumpets of the Apocalypse for the ensemble to play in unison, two movements dedicated to the Angel who announces that there will be no more Time, and a contemplative evocation of the eternal to open the work. To balance the latter, Messiaen transcribed passages from two earlier works. The slow section of the *Diptyque* became a soaring solo for violin, gently supported by piano, to form a suitably luminescent conclusion to the work. Similarly, he took a long slow passage from *Fêtes des belles eaux* and turned it into a sublime paean of praise to 'the eternity of Jesus' for cello and piano. If it is initially surprising that Messiaen should use music originally written as a *pièce d'occasion* for the *Fêtes de la lumière* extravaganzas in the 1937 Paris Exposition, the connection is clear from his commentary on *Fêtes des belles eaux*, in which he assigns words from Saint John's Gospel to this beautiful melody: 'Anyone who drinks the water that I shall give will never be thirsty again: the water that I shall give will turn into a spring inside him, welling up to eternal life.'[13] In any case, the music that had first been heard in the shadow of the imposing, and opposing, Russian and German pavilions at the 1937 Exposition, was now to be heard in the middle of what had been Poland, the country that had been vanquished by these two dictatorships. Messiaen claimed that the title of the resulting *Quartet for the End of Time* referred not to the circumstance of his captivity but to passages in Revelation, and also to a desire to overturn conventional notions of musical metre. Nevertheless, he would have understood that the eternal is not in any way analogous to a long period of time. The oppressive abundance of unoccupied hours that made up camp life must surely have been instrumental in turning his attention to the passage in Scripture where the entire notion of Time itself is abolished.

In addition to his work with the camp theatre, Messiaen gave a lot of his time to his fellow prisoners, talking with them and helping to comfort them. Pasquier recalled that 'In the camp there were intellectuals, musicians, painters [. . .] And they would come to arrange interviews with Messiaen. You should have seen it: we were dressed in rags. We had to wait outside in the dreadful cold, and yet people would stand in line to make an appointment with Messiaen.'[14] Understanding 'the importance of the presence of this young and already famous master',[15] the camp Commandant not only gave permission for the composer's new work to be performed within the camp, but also gave special dispensation to attend for prisoners in quarantine awaiting repatriation due to ill health.[16] The musicians rehearsed for months. At first there was no piano, but, in November, an old upright was eventually provided, though with keys that stuck. Rehearsals were held each evening from six o'clock until lights out at about ten, always watched, very respectfully, by at least one guard.[17] The first public performance of the *Quartet for the end of Time* took place inside Stalag VIIIA at 6.00pm on the evening of Wednesday 15 January 1941, preceded by a short lecture by Messiaen on its inspiration, the Book of Revelation.

This famous première stands as one of the most remarkable events in musical history. The following is an amalgam of Messiaen's recollections:

> The Stalag was shrouded in snow. We were 30,000 prisoners (mostly French, with a few Poles and Belgians). The four instrumentalists played on broken instruments: Étienne Pasquier's cello had only three strings, the keys of my piano would stick . . .[18]
>
> It was on this piano, with my three fellow musicians, dressed very strangely, myself clothed in the bottle-green uniform of a Czech soldier, badly torn, and wearing wooden clogs . . . that I was to play my *Quatuor pour la fin du Temps*, in front of an audience of five thousand, among which were gathered all the different classes of society: peasants, labourers, intellectuals, career soldiers, medics, priests . . .[19]

This story has passed into legend. However, as with all legends, it contains certain embellishments. In the years immediately before his death at the age of ninety-three, Étienne Pasquier gave a series of interviews to Hannelore Lauerwald[20] and Rebecca Rischin[21] providing new information about Messiaen's time in captivity, the genesis of the *Quartet* and its first performance. Whilst confirming the essence of Messiaen's account, and adding many new details, Pasquier's recollections diverge from those of the composer on two points. First, and simplest, is the notion that the cello had just three strings. Pasquier is unequivocal:

> Yes, he [Messiaen] repeatedly made this claim, but in point of fact I played on four strings. A piece as difficult as the one that Messiaen wrote can't be played on three strings. In telling this story he presumably wanted to illustrate the inadequacies surrounding this first performance.[22]

Although not directly contradicting Messiaen, Pasquier's version of events also raises important questions about another aspect of the composer's account:

> [the performance took place] in the hut that we used as the theatre. It consisted of an auditorium, a stage and a room where the props were stored . . . expectations amongst the prisoners ran high. Everyone wanted to come and hear us, including the camp commanders. They sat in the front row. All the seats were taken, around four hundred in all . . . the performance was a great success and we often repeated it.[23]

Even allowing for many prisoners sitting on the floor or standing, it is difficult to reconcile this with Messiaen's claim that the audience was a distinctly Biblical 5,000 in number. Although it can clearly be seen now as an exaggerated figure, nobody thought, in the fifty years between first performance and the researches of Lauerwald and Rischin, to question whether even the most tolerant of German commandants would have countenanced such a large gathering of prisoners. Nevertheless, Pasquier's account does not suggest that Messiaen's recollections are entirely false, even if 'it amused him' to claim that the cello only had three strings.[24] None of these inaccuracies detract from the fact that the première and subsequent performances were extraordinary events. It is easy, also, to envisage Messiaen telling of this experience on his repatriation, embroidering the details of the story slightly in order to convey succinctly the remarkable nature of performing the work inside the prison camp. It is hard to imagine what these concerts sounded like, with half-starved musicians trying to negotiate the demands of the music with frozen fingers on sub-standard instruments. As a beacon of hope in the face of the most desolate circumstances, the work transcended all such practical diffi-culties. In that first desperate winter of captivity, the *Quartet for the end of Time* provided a shared moment of escape from the cold and hunger. 'Never', Messiaen later recalled 'have I been listened to with such attention and understanding'.[25]

Messiaen wrote the *Quartet for the end of Time* 'to escape from the snow, from the war, from captivity and from myself . . . in the midst of 30,000 prisoners, I was probably the only man who was not one.'[26] A group of senior officers came to listen to the musicians rehearsing one evening: not in itself a particularly unusual occurrence. However, as they left, Pasquier recalls that Captain Brüll turned to Messiaen and said 'In a few weeks, there will be a return of prisoners to Paris. Don't miss the train'.[27] Messiaen asked in astonishment 'How is it that we're being allowed home?', only to be told 'You were musicians and so you had no guns.' Pasquier kept quiet about the rifle he was carrying when he was captured,[28] and he doctored his and Messiaen's documents, a move encouraged by Brüll who was keen to help the musicians get home.[29] The music that Messiaen had composed for spiritual release also hastened the end to his physical captivity.

Messiaen and Pasquier should have been joined by Akoka, who, as a genuine 'soldat-musicien', had the proper papers, but at the last moment he was prevented from boarding the train by a German officer who had spotted that he was a Jew and returned him to the camp.[30] Messiaen and Pasquier were transported to Constance in Switzerland, and then spent several frustrating weeks at Lyons in quarantine before being discharged.[31] By 10 March 1941, Messiaen was able to write to Arrieu with the jubilant message 'I am free!' and that he was back with his wife and 'little Pascal' at Neussargues, Cantal, in the neutral zone.[32] The same letter reveals, though, that Alain was still a prisoner, in Stalag VII B1. Messiaen spent just a few weeks recuperating from the effects of the prison camp, of which just one sign was a bout of bronchitis, before heading back to Paris in order to find work. He found time before returning to the capital, however, to write two *a cappella* choruses for Pierre Schaeffer and Pierre Barbier's extravaganza about Joan of Arc, *Portique pour une fille de France*. Messiaen later claimed that these were never performed, but in fact the production, which also included music by Baudrier and Léo Préger, was mounted in Lyons on 11 May 1941 with several hundred in the chorus, and thousands attending the event, though Messiaen was not among them.[33] Messiaen's reticence regarding his contribution to this production is not difficult to fathom: the Vichy government financed the production and, once France was liberated, even the loosest association with this regime was frowned upon. Having been interned for the first nine months after the fall of France, in need of some income and anxious to return to music-making as soon as possible, Messiaen accepted the Vichy-backed commission. Far from politically aware, he clearly did not realize its connotations until after returning to the occupied capital early in May. Once back in Paris, Messiaen resumed his duties at the Trinité and was given a post teaching harmony at the embattled Paris Conservatoire by its brilliant new director, Claude Delvincourt.

Like many institutions, the Paris Conservatoire struggled to remain a viable concern during the first year of the Occupation. Many of the staff and students left the capital on the morning that the Germans arrived, among them the previous director, Henri Rabaud, who took some of the archives to Bordeaux. Only seven members of staff and about twenty-five students remained.[34] Delvincourt, who had lost an eye and been decorated for bravery during the First World War, took over as director early in 1941 and immediately set about bolstering the institution in an attempt to preserve its integrity in the face of German edicts and cultural strictures. In a reflection of the broader population of occupied Paris, the majority of students at the Conservatoire during this period was female. One such student was Yvonne Loriod, a brilliant young pianist and composer. Her beloved teachers were Lazare Lévy for piano[35] and, for harmony, André Bloch. Both were Jewish and were soon forced out of their posts. Loriod was distraught and wanted to leave the Conservatoire, but she was persuaded to stay by Bloch and Lévy, the latter being replaced by Marcel Ciampi.[36] When, on 7 May, Delvincourt introduced a new harmony teacher, the students were struck by his poor condition. A painfully thin young man, he began with an examination of a work that is pointedly French, Debussy's *Prélude à l'après-midi d'un faune*. The students, including Loriod, were impressed that he played through the work from the miniature score rather than a piano reduction:

> At the first class the pupils were absolutely astonished, because here was a man who was quite young and whose fingers were swollen on account of the privations which he had suffered during his time in captivity in Silesia ... and there he was, playing the piano with such beautiful sound in spite of the deformity of his hands.[37]

Messiaen had made an indelible impression.

By the time that he became her harmony teacher, Messiaen's *Préludes* were already part of Loriod's rapidly expanding repertoire. They had been sent to Lazare Lévy who, being shortsighted, had asked his young protégée to play through them for him. A little later, on the suggestion of her Godmother, Mme Nelly Sivade, at whose salon she gave regular concerts, Loriod invited Messiaen and Jolivet to hear her perform the *Préludes* and *Mana*.[38] If Loriod had been won over by Messiaen in that first harmony class, the composer was clearly bowled over by the extraordinary talents of this young pianist. Since completing the *Préludes* in 1929, all of his substantial instrumental works had been for the organ. In the space of just two years, Messiaen now produced a seven-movement piece for two pianos, *Visions de l'Amen*; a work for choir and small orchestra with a significant part for solo piano, *Trois petites liturgies de la Présence Divine*; and *Vingt Regards sur l'Enfant-Jésus*, a twenty-movement cycle for piano lasting more than two hours. The first and last of these are dedicated to

8. Yvonne Loriod c. 1941.

Yvonne Loriod whilst the solo part of *Trois petites liturgies* was written for her. Like Clara and Robert Schumann, the incredible pianism of Loriod acted as a catalyst for Messiaen, and this trinity of religious works are only the first fruits of a creative partnership which would last right until the composer's final, unfinished work, *Concert à quatre*. In short, without Loriod, Messiaen's output would have been radically different.

In addition to providing Messiaen with his first opportunity to hear Loriod perform his own music, it was also at Nelly Sivade's salon that Messiaen began giving private analysis classes. Before the war, he had occasionally invited select friends to his house where, after they had been welcomed by Claire, he would lead musical analyses.[39] In the spring of 1941, soon after his repatriation, Messiaen mentioned to Jean-Louis Martinet his desire to have regular gatherings of musicians wishing to better their knowledge.[40] As Martinet later recalled, invitations were sent out to various colleagues and pupils of Messiaen for a series of meetings [*séances*] to be held on Monday evenings between 8pm and 10pm from 28 July at Mme Sivade's salon at 53 rue Blanche.[41]

However, Claire would not be able to greet the friends, for the authorities did not grant permission for her and Pascal to join Messiaen in Paris until late November 1941.

On that first Monday gathering, seated at Mme Sivade's Érard piano, Messiaen analysed Berg's Violin Concerto, a work far beyond anything studied at the Conservatoire and certainly not held in high esteem by the Nazis. Messiaen's approach was similar whether he was teaching analysis or harmony. Rather than take examples from textbooks, as was the custom of his colleagues, he worked directly with important scores by great composers. Furthermore, whereas other teachers at the Conservatoire stopped at the works of Fauré, the staple fare in Messiaen's classes was Debussy, Ravel, Stravinsky, Schoenberg, Berg and Bartók, together with passages from his own latest works. Inspired in part by the enthusiasm of his students, he spent the summer of 1942 in Neussargues writing a treatise on his own musical style, The Technique of my Musical Language. Several of Messiaen's works, notably La Nativité du Seigneur, had already appeared with lengthy prefaces amounting to mini-manifestos, but Technique, whilst specifically not a compositional treatise, gave a far more comprehensive elucidation of the aesthetic and technical concerns that underpinned his musical choices at this time:

> One point will attract our attention at the outset: the charm of impossibilities. It is a glistening music we seek, giving to the aural sense voluptuously refined pleasures. At the same time, this music should be able to express some noble sentiments (and especially the most noble of all, the religious sentiments exalted by the theology and the truths of our Catholic faith).[42]

Despite assuaging words about the sovereignty of melody, and building on existing harmony, The Technique of my Musical Language pointedly begins with six chapters devoted exclusively to rhythm. At the age of just thirty-three, Messiaen was making a firm statement of conviction regarding the future course of music.

The conversational style of The Technique of my Musical Language reflects Messiaen's intention to use it to support aspects of his teaching. During his Conservatoire class on Wednesday 2 December 1942, Messiaen gave a preview of his treatise with examples at the piano for his pupils and invited guests. The young composer and pedagogue was attracting a following amongst the brightest musicians of the new generation. The students attending the private analysis meetings even began calling themselves Messiaen's '*flèches*' [arrows] because, in the words of Yvonne Loriod:

> like all young people, we imagined that we were going to revolutionize the world and we were shooting these arrows in every sense; [. . .]the arrows represented the letter M, M for Messiaen, and that the O of Olivier Messiaen represented the circle of his disciples.[43]

In addition to Loriod and Martinet, the *flèches* included Yvette Grimaud, Serge Nigg, Ginette and Maurice Martenot, Françoise Aubut and, from November 1944, Pierre Boulez. By the autumn of 1943, there were more *flèches* than could be comfortably accommodated in Nelly Sivade's salon on rue Blanche. The classes moved to a larger apartment at 24 rue Visconti, behind the *École des beaux-arts*, which belonged to none other than Guy Bernard-Delapierre, the man Messiaen had met in the transit camp near Nancy. Bernard-Delapierre had kept Messiaen's telephone number safe throughout his captivity and, on repatriation, rang the composer. The clandestine classes continued at Bernard-Delapierre's apartment until 1947 and it was on his Bechstein grand piano that Messiaen first analysed Stravinsky's *The Rite of Spring* for his students. Whatever the repertoire, the music was examined thoroughly, for the sessions now began in the afternoon and often continued until late into the evening.

Whilst a small but fervent band of disciples formed around Messiaen during the war years as a result of the private analysis classes, he also began to cause a stir amongst the wider cultural community of occupied Paris. The *Quartet for the end of Time* was performed for the first time outside captivity at the Théâtre des Mathurins on Tuesday 24 June 1941. Le Boulaire was still in the camp, but did not play in performances after his repatriation early in

1942 either, being replaced by Étienne Pasquier's brother, Jean. Having spent seven years in military service, Le Boulaire felt that a career as a violinist was unobtainable and turned instead to acting.[44] Henri Akoka managed to escape captivity by jumping from a train whilst in transit and, having somehow kept hold of his clarinet, was in the process of making his way to Marseilles.[45]

Given the circumstances of its composition, the *Quartet for the End of Time* could hardly fail to make an impression in occupied Paris. An even greater boost to Messiaen's reputation, though, came from the championing of his music by Denise Tual, the organizer of the *Concerts de la Pléiade*. This remarkable concert series was conceived to circumvent Nazi controls on French music, specifically the ban on performances in concert halls of unpublished works by French composers, Jewish composers, exiled composers such as Stravinsky and composers living in the Free Zone such as Poulenc and Auric. Held in the Galerie Charpentier, and with admission strictly by invitation only, the first season of concerts in the spring of 1943 was a great success.[46] The driving force behind this 'clandestine revenge against the occupation',[47] Tual commissioned Messiaen to write a work for the *Concerts de la Pléiade* in the autumn of 1942 after hearing him playing at the Trinité one evening having stepped inside 'with the absurd idea of warming myself up'.[48] Bowled over by the remarkable music that she heard, Tual asked a verger the way up to the organ loft so that she could meet the organist, only to be told that this could be done only by making a written appointment. She wrote to Messiaen that evening, and he promptly replied, arranging to meet her a few days later 'at the Trinité, in front of the door leading up to the organ loft'.[49] Tual's account of this rendezvous paints a marvellous picture of Messiaen the shy titular organist taking her to the heart of his domain:

> I was expecting to meet a very young and rather trendy [«zazou»] man. I was still imagining the pre-war generation of musicians, the elegance of Désormière or the eccentricity of Varèse. I found myself in front of a man of the church, ageless, with a forehead balding and glasses, carrying a large, very heavy, briefcase that has never left him since. As it

was very cold that day, he wore a beret, a purple scarf and fingerless gloves. After a timid hello, quick and embarrassed, he took his bunch of keys and carefully opened the door of a spiral staircase leading to the organ. This staircase looks out onto the public gardens, in such a way that, the wind hitting all the openings at the same time, we were in a whirlwind that increased at each floor. Arriving at the fifth, Messiaen took a second key to let us into a kind of dark cubbyhole. He genuflected and prayed before a crucifix and, on getting up, he held a third key that permitted access to the organ. He asked me to sit beside him on the organ bench. Our conversation was in hushed tones and he seemed visibly frightened. His face lit up when I told him the purpose of my visit. A commission? He beamed.[50]

The result was *Visions de l'Amen*, a virtuoso showcase for two pianos to be performed by Yvonne Loriod and Messiaen. For the first time, the spiritual basis of a work, the idea of the 'Amen', comes not from Scripture but is inspired instead by theologian Ernest Hello, whose writings had been recommended to Messiaen by Alain about ten years earlier. There is also a very clear progression in the work from still, almost silent contemplation to an effulgent proclamation of joy. This is reflected in the progression of a cyclic theme, the 'Theme of God', which evolves from simply existing amidst the cosmic flotsam of the universe in the opening 'Amen de la Création' to being the driving force behind the ecstatic perorations of 'Amen de la Consommation'. This simple but effective method of unifying a work, which is analogous to the Wagnerian *Leitmotif* or the *idée fixe* of Berlioz, marks a breakthrough in Messiaen's ability to control large musical structures and is a crucial aspect in the success of *Visions de l'Amen*. To this can be added the inter-relationship of the two pianists, who are given distinct roles, the breathtaking pianism of the first piano (Loriod) taking wing from the principal unfolding of themes and harmonies in the second piano (Messiaen). The result is like a duel where the protagonists are inextricably bound together.

Originally intended for the third of the *Concerts de la Pléiade* on 3 May 1943 alongside works by Chabrier, Satie, Poulenc and Stravinsky,

9. Messiaen and Yvonne Loriod rehearsing at the Paris Conservatoire, mid-1940s.

Visions de l'Amen was rescheduled for a special concert a week later. The day before, Sunday 9 May, Messiaen and Loriod gave a private performance at Nelly Sivade's salon attended by, among others, Tual, Poulenc, Jolivet and Honegger. Tual later recalled:

> Messiaen announced in a mournful voice 'Les *Visions de l'Amen*'. Quickly the faces became serious, intense, lifting their gaze towards the pianists. Once the last chords had died away, there was a long silence. Messiaen thought we hated his work. Our reaction was eventually so enthusiastic that a broad smile lit up his face and that of his pupil Yvonne Loriod.[51]

Messiaen repaid his guests' enthusiasm for his fifty-minute religious cycle for two pianos by taking them 200 metres down rue Blanche to the Trinité for 5 o'clock Vespers, at which he played the organ.[52]

The concert the following day was a great success and led, in September 1943, to Tual offering Messiaen a second commission.

Her letter reached him towards the end of his annual holiday at Neussargues where he was enjoying time with his family:

> My wife is well, and Pascal is in particularly good form: he has grown, and his neck and arms are tanned from the fine air and the sunshine. He is interested in a thousand different things, and runs non-stop![53]

He could scarcely have known it at the time, but such periods of family happiness were rapidly to become a rarity. Despite his upbeat mention of Claire's health, the tragic illness that would blight the family was beginning to take hold.

Messiaen's initial response to the new commission was to write another work for two pianos. Less than a fortnight later, and fearing that he would just write a poorer version of *Visions de l'Amen*, he had changed his mind substantially. In a note left for Tual at her offices in the place de la Madeleine, Messiaen proposes a work of fifteen to twenty minutes requiring a male reciter, an ondes Martenot, three flutes, three trombones, a large grand piano, percussion (celesta, tam-tam, cymbals and tambourine) and ten strings.[54] He started work on 15 November and had completed *Trois petites Liturgies de la Présence Divine* by 15 March 1944. In the process, the work had grown to more than half an hour in duration and he had replaced the male reciter with a chorus of women's voices, added a vibraphone, enlarged the number of strings and omitted the flutes and trombones.

The première of the *Liturgies* was originally scheduled for May 1944. It was then delayed further until early June, only for the allied invasion of Normandy on D-Day, 6 June, to throw into disarray any pretence at normality in Paris. The occupied city was already experiencing shortages of food and paper, compounded by regular cuts to the supply of gas and electricity. As the Allies approached in August, fighting broke out in the streets, strikes were called and the Resistance erected barricades. It might seem odd that during all the fighting and chaos that led up to the liberation of Paris on 25 August, Messiaen spent the Spring and Summer months in the city composing. Nevertheless, with virtually no other daily activity possible, writing must have relieved the hardship and anxiety in much the same manner as in the prisoner-of-war camp.

Whatever the reasons, Messiaen was writing music at a ferocious speed, starting work on 23 March, just eight days after completing the *Liturgies*, on a set of piano pieces based around the Nativity. Having initially intended the text of the *Liturgies* to be recited rather than sung, it seems that Messiaen began with a similar idea for this new piano cycle, which would eventually become *Vingt Regards sur l'Enfant-Jésus*. Encouraged perhaps by the second performance of *Visions de l'Amen*, at the Salle Gaveau on 22 June 1943, which featured Guy Bernard-Delapierre reading the Biblical inscriptions for each movement, Messiaen himself would read the more expansive Scriptural and theological texts ascribed to all twenty movements at the première of the *Vingt Regards*. The practice of reciting these inscriptions may have been due in part to the severe paper shortages afflicting Paris, but Messiaen definitely had a spoken context in mind for his music. The new work was intended to fulfil a commission from Radio Paris to write fifteen minutes of music as an accompaniment for a broadcast of Maurice Toesca's *Les Douze Regards*, a dramatized account of the Nativity.[55] Taking his cue from the chapter on the Nativity in Dom Columba Marmion's *Le Christ dans ses Mystères*, Toesca uses the word "regard" to portray the contemplative gazes of various characters upon the newborn Jesus.[56] The exact chronology is unclear. The first mention of Toesca's *Douze Regards* in Messiaen's pocket diary for 1944 is on 31 March, a week *after* he began composing, and two months later comes a tantalizing reference suggesting that he was far from settled on a piano cycle at this stage in the work's genesis, noting that he must 'write music for Toesca: ready and orchestrated for 1 November at the latest'.[57] The entry in Toesca's diary for 20 July 1944 suggests, though, that the writer and the composer worked independently for some time:

> I arrive on the doorstep at the same time as Messiaen. We exchange greetings. Our smiles have the air of agreed complicity; we are thinking of the same things; we understand one another. I said to him, 'Here are

my words' and he replied, 'I will give you my sounds'. He has already composed eleven movements for our radio programme *Les Douze Regards*.[58]

It seems that the 'agreed air of complicity' was relatively short-lived, for Messiaen exceeded the terms of the original commission in every respect, composing twenty movements containing more than two hours of virtuosic piano writing. Messiaen was triumphant when he rang Toesca after completing *Vingt Regards* on 8 September 1944,[59] and, on hearing a private run-through of the music on 11 September, the writer felt that Messiaen's music was a 'magnificent illustration in sound' ('illustration sonore magnifique') for *Les Douze Regards*.[60] Toesca's enthusiasm led him to formulate ambitious plans for a de luxe edition of *Les Douze Regards*, his poems and Messiaen's music being placed alongside illustrations by Rouault and Picasso.[61] Ultimately, neither the publication nor the intended radio broadcast materialized, although as late as 31 October Messiaen was intending to 'cut the *Regards* so that they can be used in Toesca's piece and try out the cut version for him and Delapierre.'[62]

The precise reasons for the project falling through are unclear, but it cannot have been helped by the fact that, despite Messiaen's willingness to cut, the *Vingt Regards* exceeded Toesca's requirements not just numerically, but also conceptually. It is not known how much Toesca and Messiaen discussed the idea of the radio broadcast before they set to work, but they were evidently working under a misunderstanding from an early stage, for the text and the music have very different concepts as their foundations. *Les Douze Regards*, which was eventually published as *La Nativité* in 1952,[63] is a chronological narrative account bringing to life and elaborating upon the story of the Nativity. With its strong characterization of figures such as Joseph, it has a vivid simplicity suggesting that it was written with children in mind. Whilst this approach might have been appropriate for Messiaen a decade earlier, when he was happy to include several directly pictorial movements in *La Nativité du Seigneur*, it stands in marked contrast with the more conceptual spiritual contemplation which characterizes the works of the war years. Each movement of *Vingt Regards* is utilized as a springboard for theological reflection, finding a deeper symbolism. Messiaen uses the idea of the 'Regard' in much the same way as the concept of the 'Amen' in *Visions de l'Amen*. He explains in the preface to the score of *Vingt Regards* that, whereas Marmion and Toesca identify the four differing 'Regards' of the shepherds, the angels, the Virgin and the Father, Messiaen adds a further sixteen, such as the star, the Cross, Time and silence. In this way, *Vingt Regards* goes beyond simply being a work about the Nativity to become a contemplation of Jesus and the significance of his existence.[64] It seems that, inspired by Marmion, Messiaen had already started work on *Vingt Regards* before discovering that Toesca was working on what appeared to be a similar idea. However, after seeing Toesca's text, Messiaen must have realized just how little their respective ideas converged. Already finding himself constrained by just twelve movements, he abandoned any attempt to restrict the scope of his new work.

Like *Visions de l'Amen*, *Vingt Regards* starts with an extremely slow unfolding of its principal musical motif, the 'Theme of God', quietly, calmly, deep in the resonant low register of the piano so that the harmony is almost felt rather than heard. Like the earlier cycle, this opening is merely the first step on a journey to a jubilant final peroration in the vaults of heaven. However, the range and scope of expression in *Vingt Regards* is much, much wider. On the one hand, Messiaen introduces subsidiary themes, making the range of interrelationships between movements much more complex, both musically and symbolically. On the other hand, he is far more prepared to concentrate his attention fully for an entire movement upon a single compositional idea, pursuing it relentlessly to its conclusion, logical or otherwise. This pianistic Everest shares with *Visions de l'Amen* the same elated sense of joy, at times bottled up, certainly, but there all the same. If the turbulent backdrop to the composition of *Vingt Regards* can be felt at all, it is in the violently anarchic passages that immediately precede the most resplendently ecstatic pages of the work, notably in the sixth *regard*, 'Par Lui tout a été fait' (By Him was everything made), and the final movement, 'Regard de l'Église d'Amour' (Gaze of the Church of Love). In both cases, chaos seems to reign supreme until vanquished by the 'Theme of God' in the most resounding and unequivocal manner.

Vingt Regards marks the end of the burst of creativity for which Yvonne Loriod was the catalyst and the Occupation the backdrop. During the war Messiaen had attracted a significant following among the more radical minds of the younger generation, and the performances of *Quartet for the end of Time* and *Visions de l'Amen* won him many new admirers. However, he was still a controversial figure regarded by many with suspicion bordering on contempt, and by the time that *Vingt Regards* and *Trois petites Liturgies* finally received their respective premières in March and April 1945, the atmosphere had soured. Following the Liberation, Henry Barraud, the new director of music at French Radio organized a Stravinsky cycle in part as a kind of celebration of the restoration of artistic freedom. During a performance of a particularly recent work, the *Four Norwegian Moods* (1941–2), persistent and noisy whistling and shouting broke out from the gallery. A small, but extremely vocal group of students were publicly marking their disdain for the work. The *Danses concertantes* in the following concert drew the same reaction, provoking anger from other sections of the audience, notably Poulenc who shouted 'this is the real Stravinsky, it's *Apollon musagète*, it really is not *Le Sacre*'.[65] The perpetrators included several of Messiaen's *flèches*, who had gained a passion for Stravinsky's earlier works, notably *The Rite of Spring*, in the private analysis classes. It did not take long for the whistling protestors to be identified as '*messiaeniques*',[66] with the implication that their actions had been instigated by their *Maître*.[67]

If many of Messiaen's colleagues were happy to think the worst of him, they probably felt that they had good reason. Quite apart from the nature of his music, or the fact that he taught harmony in a most unorthodox fashion, his private analysis classes, regarded as composition classes in all but name, were blatantly disloyal to the established Conservatoire curriculum. All of this was underpinned by the

publication, in 1944, of *Technique of my Musical Language* with its pro-
vocative approach to the components of music. In the Spring of 1945,
Messiaen's critics began sharpening their knives. Bernard Gavoty,
writing as 'Clarendon' in *Le Figaro*, launched the opening barrage of
invective. In his review of the première of *Vingt Regards*, he compares
Messiaen to 'a lunatic curator of a vanished museum' and complains
that 'there's not a hint of tenderness [. . .] To evoke the eternity of the
stars, a great gaggle of chords, immobile to the point of nausea, which
then rear up in sudden convulsions. Is this heaven? No, it's purgatory!'[68]
Gavoty changed stances several times in what rapidly came to be
known, following the first performance of *Trois petites Liturgies* just a
month later, as *le cas Messiaen*. Similarly, Claude Rostand, who would
(after much longer and more considered reflection) become one of
Messiaen's most ardent defenders, picked the morning of the première of the *Liturgies*, Saturday 21 April, to launch his diatribe. Also
writing in *Le Figaro*, Rostand attacks Messiaen's explanatory prefaces
and inscriptions as being 'extravagant gobbledegook' with which the
composer 'wraps his music'. Despite ostensibly being a review of a
performance of *Les Corps glorieux* the previous Sunday, Rostand devotes
himself to lambasting Messiaen's descriptions of his music in 'the
recent *Visions* [sic] *de l'Enfant-Jésus*', concluding that 'either he [Messiaen]
takes me for an imbecile . . . or I fear for his reason.'

Rostand's scathing remarks had been provoked by phrases like
the one assigned to 'Par Lui tout a été fait', the fearsome sixth movement of the *Regards*: 'The abundance of space and time: galaxies,
photons, opposed spirals, inverted lightning; by "Him" (the Word)
were all things made'. What Rostand utterly fails to convey is how
Messiaen's inscriptions do not merely reflect the character of the
music, but are also intended to direct the contemplation of the listener.
In this case, Messiaen, inspired by his books on astronomy, is direct-
ing the listener to consider the earliest part of creation. Not the land
and the sea or the plants, flowers and animals, and certainly not Adam
and Eve, but that part of the creation story which equates with the
moments immediately after the big bang. Rostand's article set the tone

for the reception of the *Liturgies* amongst hostile critics, who, rather than attack the music directly, tended instead to concentrate upon vilifying the poem that Messiaen had written himself with, in the words of Auric 'a touching and unfortunate perseverance'.[69] Unlike others who were initially hostile, notably Gavoty, Rostand later had the decency to apologize to Messiaen in print for his hurtful remarks.

Debate about *le cas Messiaen* continued for several years within the Press and it was a time when 'no criticism was too low, too facile or too insultingly expressed'.[70] That Messiaen was hurt by the more vitriolic attacks against him is not in doubt for he was, in his own words, 'martyred by the critics'.[71] What surprised him was not the reaction to the music so much as the anger expressed questioning the propriety of the religious text. He later mused 'I imagine it was a kind of native distrust by right-thinking people, comfortably settled in their armchairs and worn slippers, opposed to anything out of the ordinary, especially in the spiritual domain . . . the poem is replete with quotations from Holy Scriptures . . . the people attacking me didn't know these texts . . . but, all the same, they were roused from their complacency!'[72] Although certain detractors 'carried on to their hearts' content, heaping abuse upon me for ten years after the première',[73] Messiaen was always clear, with good reason, that the *Trois petites Liturgies* was a great success with the public. As the first of the *Concerts de la Pléiade* following the liberation of Paris, the première was a grand celebration of renewed artistic vigour and freedom. In addition to the *Liturgies*, the programme included the first performances of Poulenc's *Un Soir de neige* and Milhaud's *Quatrains valaisans* and the concert was attended by many of the most distinguished musicians, artists and poets, including Honegger, Poulenc, Auric, Jolivet, Georges Braque and Paul Éluard. Messiaen's pupils were all present, having also been allowed to attend the rehearsals. The exotic instrumentation enthused them, boasting another orchestral novelty aside from ondes Martenot: the vibraphone. Its inclusion alongside the more traditional instruments prompted amazement amongst the *flèches*[74] and the work itself 'seemed to symbolize the spiritual renewal of the country'.[75] Nor was it just Messiaen's protégés who were vigorous in their support, for the overwhelming majority of the audience were enthusiastic.[76] There were some supportive voices amongst the critics, too, notably the Ravel disciple Roland-Manuel, whilst on 27 April, the Friday after the concert, Poulenc wrote to Paul Collaer describing *Trois petites Liturgies* simply as being a 'marvellous work'.[77]

During his time as a conscripted soldier in the early months of the war, Messiaen had been worried not only about losing his technique, but also fading from the musical scene in Paris. In fact, the war was a turning point in every respect for Messiaen, as a composer, as a teacher and especially in terms of his stature and profile. In addition to the premières of *Vingt Regards* and *Trois petites Liturgies*, the first few months of 1945 were notable for performances of *Les Corps glorieux*, the orchestral version of *L'Ascension*, the *Quartet for the End of Time* and *La Nativité du Seigneur*. As Poulenc wrote to Collaer on 25 June, 'Messiaen remains the event of the winter, which is entirely justified'.[78]

Notes

1. Hill, 'Interview with Loriod', p. 289.
2. Jacquet-Langlais, *Ombre et lumière*, p. 114.
3. Cited Simeone, 'Offrandes oubliées', 37.
4. Goléa, *Rencontres*, p. 59.
5. Antoine Goléa, *Rencontres avec Olivier Messiaen* (Paris: Julliard, 1960), pp. 59–60.
6. Rebecca Rischin, *For the End of Time – The Story of the Messiaen Quartet* (Ithaca, New York: Cornell University Press, 2003), p. 12.
7. Hannelore Lauerwald, 'Er musizierte mit Olivier Messiaen als Kriegsgefangener', *Das Orchester* (January 1999), 21.
8. Simeone, 'Offrandes oubliées', 37.
9. Goléa, *Rencontres*, p. 60.
10. Pierre Messiaen, *Images*, p. 340.
11. Marks, 'Messiaen at 80', programme broadcast by BBC2 on 10 December 1988.
12. Rischin, *For the End of Time*, p. 29.

13. John 4:14, cited by Messiaen in the disc notes for REM 311306.

14. Rischin, *For the End of Time*, p. 37.

15. ibid, p. 36.

16. ibid, pp. 61–2.

17. Étienne Pasquier, 'Hommage à Olivier Messiaen' in *Olivier Messiaen – homme de foi* (Paris: Trinité Média Communications, 1995), p. 92.

18. Notes to Erato disc ECD71597.

19. Goléa, *Rencontres*, p. 63.

20. In addition to the *Das Orchester* article, Hannelore Lauerwald is author of a book about Stalag VIIIA, *Im Fremdem Land. Kriegsgefangene in Deutschland am Beispiel des Stalag VIIIA Görlitz 1939–1945* (Görlitz: Viadukt Verlag, 1997).

21. Rischin, *For the End of Time*. Rischin also interviewed Le Boulaire and relatives of Akoka.

22. Lauerwald, 'Er musizierte mit Olivier Messiaen' 22.

23. ibid.

24. Rischin, *For the End of Time*, p. 66.

25. Goléa, *Rencontres*, p. 63.

26. ibid, p. 67.

27. Rischin, *For the End of Time*, p. 72.

28. Lauerwald, 'Er musizierte mit Olivier Messiaen' 23.

29. Rischin, *For the End of Time*, p. 73.

30. ibid, pp. 73–4.

31. Lauerwald, 'Er musizierte mit Olivier Messiaen' 23.

32. PHNS, p. 103.

33. Nigel Simeone, 'Messiaen: the dark years', paper given at Messiaen 2002 conference in Sheffield.

34. Marcel Dupré, *Marcel Dupré raconte* ... (Paris: Éditions Bornemann, 1972), pp. 132–3.

35. Who had earlier taught Langlais.

36. Both Bloch and Lévy survived the war, but one of Lévy's sons was deported and killed.

37. Hill, 'Interview with Loriod', p. 289.

38. ibid.

39. Boivin, *La Classe de Messiaen*, p. 44.

40. ibid.

41. Martinet's recollections, in Boivin, *La Classe de Messiaen*, pp. 44–5, place this first gathering in 1942. However, 28 July 1942 was a Tuesday,

while 28 July 1941 was a Monday. Given that the invitation explicitly indicates Monday evenings, either the date was 27 July or the year was 1941. Messiaen did not get permission to leave Paris to join Claire and Pascal for the summer in 1941 until the very end of July. In 1942, he met his deputy at the Trinité, Line Zilgien on Saturday 25 July 1942 to confirm the summer arrangements before beginning his holiday (see PHNS, pp. 114 and 119).

42. Olivier Messiaen, *The Technique of my musical language*, translated by John Satterfield (Paris: Alphonse Leduc, 1944, translation 1956), p. 13 (single vol. edn, p. 8).

43. Hill, 'Interview with Loriod', p. 291.

44. Rischin, *For the End of Time*, pp. 85–6.

45. A full account of Akoka's remarkable story is contained in Rischin, *For the End of Time*.

46. For a much more detailed account of the *Concerts de la Pléiade*, see Nigel Simeone, 'Messiaen and the Concerts de la Pléiade: "A kind of clandestine revenge against the Occupation"', *Music and Letters* (November, 2000), 551–84.

47. Messiaen, given in Nouritza Matossian, *Iannis Xenakis* (Paris: Fayard-SACEM, 1981), p. 52.

48. Denise Tual, *Le Temps Dévoré* (Paris: Fayard, 1980), p. 194.

49. Tual, *Le Temps Dévoré*, p. 195.

50. ibid.

51. Denise Tual, *Itinéraire des Concerts de la Pléiade*, unpublished typescript, cited Simeone, 'Messiaen and the Concerts de la Pléiade', 560.

52. PHNS, p. 126.

53. ibid, p. 129.

54. ibid, pp. 130–1.

55. Charles E. Seifert, 'Messiaen's *Vingt Regards sur l'Enfant-Jésus*: A Historical and Pedagogical Study', PhD thesis, University of Illinois (1989), pp. 4–5.

56. 'Regard' is one of those words that does not have an exact equivalent in English. It can be translated as 'look at', 'gaze' and 'contemplation', and incorporates elements of each.

57. Nigel Simeone, 'Olivier Messiaen: *Vingt Regards sur l'Enfant-Jésus*', booklet essay for Hyperion disc CDA67351/2, p. 5.

58. Maurice Toesca, *Cinq ans de Patience (1939–45)* (Paris: Emile-Paul, 1975), p. 298.

59. Toesca, *Cinq ans de Patience*, p. 348.
60. ibid, p. 349.
61. Simeone, 'Messiaen: *Vingt Regards*', p. 6.
62. ibid.
63. Maurice Toesca, *La Nativité* (Paris: M. Sautier, 1952).
64. A more detailed account of the relationship between *Les Douze Regards* and *Vingt Regards* can be found in Edward Forman 'L'Harmonie de l'Univers: mystical and literary influences on the *Vingt Regards sur l'Enfant-Jésus*' in Dingle and Simeone (eds), *Olivier Messiaen: Music, Art and Literature* (Ashgate: forthcoming).
65. Serge Nigg, cited in Boivin, *La classe de Messiaen*, p. 65.
66. Goléa, *Rencontres*, p. 10.
67. Jésus Aguila intimates that the whistling was actually incited by René Leibowitz: Jésus Aguila, *Le Domaine Musical* (Paris: Fayard, 1992), p. 178.
68. Cited Simeone, 'Messiaen: *Vingt Regards*', 12.
69. Cited Claude Samuel, *Permanences d'Olivier Messiaen: Dialogues et Commentaires* (Actes Sud, 1999), p. 256.
70. Pierre Boulez, *Orientations – Collected Writings*, trans. Martin Cooper (London: Faber and Faber, 1986), p. 505.
71. Håkon Austbø, 'Olivier Messiaen: le prêche aux oiseaux, *Diapaison-Harmonie*, no.344 (December, 1988), p. 77.
72. Samuel, *Music and Color*, p. 130 [1986, pp. 140–1].
73. ibid.
74. Boulez, *Orientations*, p. 160.
75. Serge Nigg, cited in Boivin, *La Classe de Messiaen*, p. 65.
76. ibid.
77. Paul Collaer, *Correspondance avec des amis musiciens*, ed. Robert Wangermée (Sprimont, 1996), p. 385, n. 8.
78. Collaer, *Correspondance*, p. 384.

4 Songs of love and death 1945–8

> Music is much better than the other arts at expressing what is
> inside us, the surreal, the hallucinatory, the world of dreams.[1]

In the years immediately following the end of the Second World War,
Messiaen appeared to the outside world to be riding the crest of a wave
of creativity and good fortune. Before the outbreak of war he had gained
a reputation in Paris as an important young talent. There had even been
his first taste of international recognition, with *Les Offrandes oubliées* being
performed in America, and his appearance at the ISCM festival in London
in 1938. However, Messiaen was just one of many young composers
vying for attention, and at that stage he was regarded as being neither
the most progressive nor the most successful of his generation.

By September 1945, just a few months after peace returned to Europe,
Messiaen had acquired the epithet 'Atomic bomb of contemporary
music'.[2] The composition and premières of three large works during
the latter years of the war made him the talking point amongst artistic
circles in Paris. Three further substantial works now appeared: a song
cycle *Harawi*, the *Turangalîla-Symphonie* for piano, ondes Martenot and
large orchestra, and an *a cappella* piece for twelve voices, *Cinq Rechants*.

An indication of this burgeoning reputation is given by the commission from the Director of Music at Radio France, Henry Barraud, of
Chant des déportés for a concert, in November 1945, in remembrance of
the victims of the concentration camps. For many years, few people

knew that this fascinating piece existed. After the single performance on 2 November 1945 conducted by Manuel Rosenthal with the twenty-one-year-old Pierre Boulez at the piano,[3] the score for *Chant des déportés* was deposited in the library at Radio France and forgotten. In 1991, Messiaen mentioned his sorrow at the apparent loss of the work to an interviewer, who decided to search for, and subsequently found the piece in the Radio France library, exactly where it had been tucked away since the performance forty-six years earlier.[4] *Chant des déportés* is in many respects an anomalous work in Messiaen's output. Despite swirling ostinatos and gamelan-inspired rhythmic machinations in the manner of *Trois petites Liturgies* and *Turangalîla*, *Chant des déportés* appears to have been a consciously populist work, a public chorale. The unison vocal lines have a strong tune, with the overall effect being curiously reminiscent of Berlioz's arrangement of *La Marseillaise*. As a direct comment on the distinctly terrestrial and horrific events of the war, it marks a stark contrast with the image of a composer whose head is resolutely stuck in the celestial clouds. Indeed, with a climax on the words 'Ma France', *Chant des déportés* demonstrates that Messiaen was far from impervious to the inevitable nationalistic fervour following the liberation. Even the title seems to be an allusion to Méhul's popular revolutionary song *Chant du départ*. Moreover, if *Chant des déportés* is significant for its style and its message, the fact that Messiaen was commissioned to write it underlines his seemingly omnipresent position in Parisian artistic life at this time.

Nor was it just his music that was creating a frisson of excitement around Messiaen. He was rapidly gaining a reputation as a kind of godfather to the radical voices of the younger generation. As a consequence, Messiaen was held responsible for their actions. Attacks on the establishment might have been expected, but the booing of Stravinsky, still regarded by most as the epitome of modernism, startled even progressively minded figures. It was against this backdrop that the most aggressively vocal of Messiaen's protégés, Pierre Boulez, mounted a petition in the Conservatoire for Messiaen to be given the position of composition teacher. Although supportive of Messiaen, Claude

Delvincourt, the Director of the Conservatoire, had little room for manoeuvre as such a move was far too radical to be countenanced by the conservative-minded *Institut.*[5] Delvincourt also had to contend with a powerful lobby pushing for Nadia Boulanger to be made composition tutor, following her appointment to the piano accompaniment post in November 1945. Having heard of Messiaen's unofficial, private lessons, Delvincourt eventually solved this politically tricky problem in 1947 by creating a class in aesthetics and analysis especially for him. Though still a controversial move among Messiaen's fellow teachers at the Conservatoire, who were alarmed at the rapid rise to prominence of this 'parish organist', and regarded as a snub to Boulanger, the creation of this special, optional class underlines Delvincourt's skill as an administrator. Darius Milhaud became the composition professor, and now Messiaen also had a suitably prestigious post.

Recordings of his music also began to appear in the post-war years. The earliest known commercial recording was a performance of *Les Offrandes oubliées* under Roger Désormière made in 1942.[6] Pathé recorded three 78rpm discs of Yvonne Loriod's performances of three *Préludes* and two pieces from the *Vingt Regards.*[7] Pathé was also responsible for the most remarkable of these early recordings, capturing for posterity a performance of *Trois petites Liturgies*, made by the original performers at the time of première in April 1945.[8] Given the unusual scoring and the length of the work, necessitating nine sides on 78rpm discs, Pathé's undertaking was highly significant.

Messiaen was also beginning to attract very serious attention abroad. The *Liturgies*, *Quartet for the End of Time*, *Visions de l'Amen* and *La Nativité* were all performed in Britain within two years of the end of the war, often with involvement from the BBC. Admittedly there were some snide mutterings within the Corporation in the wake of Messiaen's visit during December 1945, such as the memo marked 'Private and Confidential' sent to the Director of Music by Julian Herbage:

> While I am aware that certain musical circles in France regard [Messiaen] very highly, I recollect that before the war we were extremely doubtful of his qualities as a composer. What we have heard

recently[. . .] seems to indicate that these doubts were fully justified. Naturally we must realize that occasionally we may be "sold a pup" from abroad, but in this case I feel it was very unfortunate that such strong political pressure was put on us to engage Messaien [sic] [. . .]⁹

The 'political pressure' presumably refers to the fact that the French Government played a hand in Messiaen's trip, as they did with a number of other French artists in the wake of the liberation, such as Poulenc, thanks to the enthusiasm of Tony Mayer at the French Embassy in London. Whatever the concerns in some quarters, publicly the BBC feted Messiaen, arranging concerts, broadcasting his music and holding receptions for him.

Elsewhere, Messiaen taught during the summer of 1947 at the conservatoire in Budapest, and in 1948, at the instigation of Luigi Dallapiccola, he made a triumphant tour of Italian towns where concerts were being given in his honour. In the meantime, his music began to find advocates across the Atlantic in America. Leopold Stokowski added *Hymne au Saint Sacrement*, *Trois petites Liturgies* and *L'Ascension* to his repertoire, making the first recording of the latter.¹⁰ An even greater champion was Serge Koussevitzky. He conducted *Les Offrandes oubliées* and *L'Ascension*, and also invited Messiaen to teach composition at Tanglewood in 1949, alongside Copland.¹¹ A particular highlight of Messiaen's first trip to America was the performance of *L'Ascension* on 14 August 1949 in Koussevitzky's emotional farewell concert at the helm of the Boston Symphony Orchestra.¹² With an audience of 15,000, this was the first time that Messiaen experienced his music being presented on a truly vast scale.

Crucially, Koussevitzky gave Messiaen one of the most important commissions of his career: a work for the Boston Symphony Orchestra. What was exceptional about Koussevitzky's instructions was his avoidance of setting parameters: he said simply 'choose as many instruments as you desire, write a work as long as you wish, and in the style you want'.¹³ Presented with this extraordinary remit, the 'atomic bomb of contemporary music' did not disappoint. The product of nearly two and a half years' work, Turangalîla-Symphonie, a ten movement, seventy-five minute work for piano, ondes Martenot and very large orchestra, exploded into the world in December 1949.

As we have seen, Messiaen's meteoric rise in status coincided with a particularly rich vein of creativity of which Turangalîla is only the most extravagant example. During the summer and autumn of 1945 he composed Harawi, an hour-long song-cycle, and Chant des déportés, whilst, if Messiaen's dating is correct, he wrote Cinq Rechants, a twenty-minute virtuosic tour de force for 12 a cappella voices, within a month of completing Turangalîla in November 1948. With these works coming hard on the heels of the wartime triptych of Visions de l'Amen, Trois petites Liturgies and Vingt Regards, it is no wonder that Messiaen later recalled the 1940s as a time when his creative powers felt invincible.[14]

To any casual observer, then, Messiaen's life and career just after the war was the picture of artistic success and achievement. Amidst the performances, the debates, the polarized press reaction to his music, the recordings, the trips abroad and the furore caused by his students at home, one fact was undeniable: Messiaen had arrived.

At the same time that Messiaen was emerging as a major figure, he was becoming enveloped by the central tragedy of his life. During the 1940s, Claire began to manifest signs of early dementia. As early as 1943, at the very time when his career truly began to flourish, Claire's condition was making domestic life difficult enough that friends of Messiaen suggested finding a little studio flat in which he could work.[15] How long it took Messiaen to acknowledge that Claire's problems were serious is unclear, but in 1946 he arranged for her to go to Lourdes. In January 1949, Claire had a hysterectomy. This operation appears to have acted as the catalyst for a more marked decline:

> There was post-operative shock as a result of which she lost her memory, all her memory, and then, little by little, her sanity. It was dreadful, for her above all, but more appalling still for my little boy who didn't understand what was happening.[16]

10. Messiaen c. 1945.

Claire gradually lost the use of all her faculties, including her eyes, her movement and, perhaps most difficult of all, her ability to recognize people.[17] Despite this it was not until 1953, four years later, that Messiaen arranged for her to be admitted to the institution in which she remained until her eventual, rather unexpected death in April 1959. The impact on Messiaen of his wife's appalling condition, which he regarded as a 'tragic martyrdom',[18] was immense, affecting him on every level.

The man who had gone hungry during the fugue exam for the Prix de Rome because he could not open his own briefcase found himself taking on the role of a single parent having to do all of the housework, the cooking, the washing and to prepare Pascal for school. Messiaen also had to try to explain to his son a situation of which he could scarcely have made sense himself. Pascal was barely of school age when Claire's symptoms were becoming noticeable, and by his early teens this tragic illness had effectively robbed him of his mother, without allowing him the opportunity to grieve. Some help must have been forthcoming from relations and friends, not least during the occasions when Messiaen's career took him abroad. Nevertheless, the difficulties faced by both Messiaen and Pascal were immense. For instance, in June 1949, Messiaen visited Darmstadt, then went almost immediately to Tanglewood to teach for five weeks. Once travelling time is added, it is clear that father and son were on occasion apart for significant periods of time. There is also a sense of history repeating itself, for Messiaen's absence from his family for the early part of the war, missing a formative period in his son's life, followed by the mental decline of his wife upon his return is painfully redolent of the experience of Pierre twenty years earlier.

Such domestic difficulties are, of course, merely the readily identifiable, physical manifestations for Messiaen of Claire's illness. To all intents and purposes, Messiaen lost his wife, thus losing in the process a close friend, confidante, supporter and sympathetic fellow musician. In this context, also, Claude Rostand's remarks in April 1945 about fearing for Messiaen's reason must have been particularly hurtful. Nor should it be forgotten that, whereas he avoided mentioning her in later life, Claire was a major influence upon Messiaen's early career.[19] Aside from being cited as second only to his mother in the preface to *Technique de mon langage musical*, Messiaen wrote the *Thème et variations* and, far more importantly, the two great song-cycles of the 1930s, *Poèmes pour Mi* and *Chants de terre et de ciel*, for 'Mi', his wife, Claire Delbos. This is a necessary reminder before adding two further factors that are crucial if we are to begin to understand the complexity of emotions experienced by Messiaen at this time and the full extent of this intensely sad human tragedy.

From around the time that Claire Delbos became ill, the remarkable pianism of Yvonne Loriod began to operate as a compositional catalyst for Messiaen. It is clear that, following the onset of his wife's illness, Messiaen and Loriod grew emotionally close, gradually falling in love. Quite simply, over time, Loriod became Messiaen's close friend, confidante, supporter and sympathetic fellow musician. More than fifty years on, in an age where salacious details are often the first concern, it would be easy to present this situation with a nudge and a wink, but that would overlook the central profound tragedy of Messiaen's circumstances during the decade and a half of his wife's illness. For, by the teachings of the Roman Catholic faith he practised with such ardour, Messiaen was, and must remain, married to Claire Delbos until she died; a development that was far from being a certain consequence of her illness. Breaking the sanctity of that marriage would have been anathema to Messiaen. Any feelings he might have for Loriod must remain unrequited. When Messiaen later stated categorically that he had never had any doubts regarding his faith,[20] it should not be mistaken for meaning that he never had any difficulties with its implications.

This tragic situation, with its complex and conflicting emotions, provides the backdrop not only to the manifold successes outlined in this chapter, but also to the events discussed in the next two chapters. Messiaen retained his strong creative impulse almost throughout this period, but his music did move away from the religious path it had hitherto trodden with resolute certainty and to which it would return in the 1960s. Moreover, his music changed not once but three times. Each of these transmutations can be viewed as a kind of escape: first of all, escape by entering into a surrealist world of myths and dreams, then by shunning the past and concentrating on what is radical and progressive. Finally, Messiaen retreated from society and musical fashion, and instead sought solace in nature.

The three works composed during the surrealist first phase form a triptych, drawing their inspiration from the Tristan myth. Messiaen later stressed that in writing these works, he was not attempting to rework earlier treatments of the myth, such as 'Wagner's *Tristan und Isolde* or Debussy's *Pelléas*, to mention only the two greatest 'Tristans' in music'.[21] Rather, Messiaen's triptych conveys, albeit by differing methods, a distillation of the central concept underpinning the Tristan myth:

> I preserved only the idea of a fatal and irresistible love, which, as a rule, leads to death and which, to some extent, invokes death, for it is a love that transcends the body, transcends even the limitations of the mind, and grows to a cosmic scale.[22]

Given the terrible personal circumstances against which the Tristan triptych was composed, the idea of a love that can only be fulfilled in death is scarcely surprising, especially when it is remembered that, for Messiaen, death was a beginning rather than an end. The illness of Delbos, and his growing affection for Loriod, may have precipitated a period of creativity underpinned by the idea of *Liebestod*. Nevertheless, it should be noted that an early composition, *La Mort du nombre*, covers similar territory. If the myth was already an important feature of Messiaen's hinterland, it was brought centre-stage in his thoughts when he was commissioned to provide incidental music for a production of Lucien Fabre's play of *Tristan et Yseult* which opened at the Théâtre Edouard VII in Paris on 22 February 1945. Messiaen's partly-improvised contribution was recorded on the organ at the Palais de Chaillot on Friday 2 February, between 5 pm and midnight. All that is known to have survived of this incidental music is a short fragment headed '*Tristan et Yseult – Thème d'Amour*' (Tristan and Yseult – Love Theme) and consisting of the music that Messiaen re-used in the summer of 1945 as the main theme unifying the song cycle *Harawi*.[23]

Messiaen was steeped, then, in the various workings of the Tristan myth. Nevertheless, his triptych relinquishes physical human drama and the temporal imperatives of theatrical narrative found either in Gottfried von Strassburg's telling of the story, or Wagner's opera or Fabre's play. Messiaen's three *Tristan* works are neither progressive nor interdependent, with no suggestion that they need be performed in close proximity. Messiaen prefers instead to establish a dream world exploring intense states of mind through the manipulation of its symbolist and surrealist imagery. There are feelings of hope, joy and excitement, but the dreams can also be nightmarish, evoking fear and deep anxiety, whilst throughout love and death are entwined. Death is seen not merely as an inevitable, even desirable, consequence of this intoxicating love but also as a kind of purifying rite of initiation to a higher level of existence, a more profound understanding between the lovers. There is also in this idea of death engendering a stronger bond of love, a direct link with Messiaen's faith. Christ's death not only displays God's love for the world, but is also a necessary prerequisite for the salvation of humanity.

For the composition of *Harawi*, the first panel of the triptych, Messiaen returned to Petichet, where, in happier times, he had written the two earlier Delbos inspired song-cycles, *Poèmes pour Mi* and *Chants de terre et de ciel*. Starting work on 15 June 1945, he completed his 'Chant d'Amour et de Mort' exactly three months later, on 15 September. Not unexpectedly, this hour-long song-cycle is one of Messiaen's darkest compositions. The cycle begins and ends at night-time, and the prevailing colours of the poetry are red, violet and black. The notable exception to this is the frequent references to the green dove ('colombe verte'), which, following the Peruvian folklore whose influence permeates the cycle, acts as a symbol for the beloved. The works of Raoul and Marguérite Béclard d'Harcourt on Andean folklore[24] had aroused Messiaen's interest in Peruvian music, drawing him to the conclusion that it contains 'the most beautiful melodies in the world'.[25] As a consequence, *Harawi* is unique amongst Messiaen's works for containing discernible, though modified, quotations from folk music. Nevertheless, the cascading images of Messiaen's poetry and his intoxicating music, underpinned, like the wartime works, by cyclic themes, banish any hint of a folksong setting from this surrealist masterpiece.

The word *Harawi* is itself a Quechua word ('*Yaravi*' in Spanish) for a love song resulting in the death of the lovers, and Piroutcha (literally 'spinning-top') is the Isolde of this Peruvian Tristan. The name of the man is never divulged for, as in Poèmes pour Mi and Chants de terre et de ciel, it is usually he who is speaking in the poetry despite the cycle being written explicitly for soprano. Subsumed by his feelings for the beloved, this man shows scant regard for the niceties of a more conventional song recital:

> Katchikatchi les étoiles, faites-les sauter,
> Katchikatchi les étoiles, faites-les danser,
> Katchikatchi les atomes, faites-les sauter,
> Katchikatchi les atomes, faites-les danser.
> Les nébuleuses spirales, mains de mes cheveux.
> Les electrons, fourmis, flèches, le silence en deux.
> Alpha du Centaure, Bételgeuse, Aldébaran,
> Dilatez l'espace arc-en-ciel tapageur du temps,
> Rire ionisé fureur d'horloge au meurtre absent,
> Coupez ma tête, son chiffre roule dans le sang!
> Tou, ahi! mané, mani, Tou, ahi! mané, mani, O.
> Roule dans le sang, roule dans le sang! Ahi!

> Katchikatchi the stars, make them leap,
> Katchikatchi the stars, make them dance,
> Katchikatchi the atoms, make them leap,
> Katchikatchi the atoms, make them dance.
> Spiral nebulae, hands of my hair.
> Electrons, ants, arrows, silence halved.
> Alpha Centauri, Betelgeuse, Aldebaran,
> Dilate the rainbow space rowdy in time,
> Ionised laughter rage of clock for absent murder,
> Chop off my head, its figures are rolling in blood!

11. Roland Penrose, *Seeing is believing (L'Île invisible).*

Tou, ahi! mané, mani, Tou, ahi! mané, mani, O.
Roll in blood, roll in blood! Ahi!

The desire for decapitation, delivered in an almost cursory manner both here and in the fifth song, 'L'Amour de Piroutcha', is one manifestation of the influence on *Harawi* of the painting *Seeing is believing*[26] by the

English surrealist Sir Roland Penrose. The picture is portrayed directly in 'Amour oiseau d'étoile', the tenth song, and it is easy to see why Penrose's image of a woman's head, upside down with her neck merging into the night sky and stars, deeply affected Messiaen. This 'symbol of the whole of Harawi',[27] stands as a suitable image and metaphor for the entire Tristan triptych. Messiaen's beloved is part of a broader cosmic existence, and there can be no physical contact. The outstretched hand represents the hand of the picture's viewer and, hence, emphasizes his physical detachment from the woman. All the while, the sleeping town, evoked in the first and last lines of Harawi, remains blissfully ignorant of the unfolding drama, just as the world was unaware of Messiaen's personal difficulties amidst his public successes.

When Harawi was first performed in Brussels, the demanding piano part was played not by Yvonne Loriod but by Messiaen himself. As with Poèmes pour Mi and Chants de terre et de ciel, the singer was Wagnerian soprano Marcelle Bunlet, who had also given the first performance with Messiaen of Delbos's L'Âme en bourgeon on 28 April 1937. On 27 April 1947, almost exactly ten years after that performance, Messiaen accompanied Ginette Guillamat in the first performance of his wife's final set of songs, Trois Aspects de la mort, at the Société Nationale in the Salle de l'École Normale de Musique. This performance cannot have been an easy task for Messiaen, especially given that this short cycle, with its unintentionally prophetic title, opens with a setting of one of his mother's poems, the aptly titled Sans espérance (Without hope). Nevertheless, such sentiments are the antithesis of those found in Messiaen's own music. By the time of the performance of Trois Aspects de la mort, he was immersed in the composition of his boldest work to date, Turangalîla-Symphonie.

If Harawi explores the darker side of Messiaen's interest in the idea of a fatal love, ending in an oblivion recalling the emptiness at the start of Visions de l'Amen, Turangalîla is a gregarious beacon of joy. Gone is the confessional intimacy of the vocal recital, replaced by the public spectacle of a work designed for large concert halls. Rather than singer and pianist, there are now ondes Martenot, piano, and extended orchestra, with expanded brass and percussion. The ten movements of this exotic bundle of energy have an irrepressible *joie de vivre* that seems scarcely credible given the personal backdrop to the work. Messiaen was unabashed in describing Turangalîla as being a work about love, stating with candour that the fifth movement, surrealistically entitled Joie du sang des étoiles (Joy of the stars' blood), represents 'the "peak" of carnal passion'.[28] This guiltless admission is not as surprising as at first it might seem from the dogma-loving Catholic. For Messiaen, human love was 'a reflection – a pale reflection, but nevertheless a reflection – of the only genuine love, divine love'.[29] In addition to stressing that the same concept of an all-consuming fatal love that permeated *Harawi* also underpins Turangalîla, Messiaen freely acknowledged that the feeling of elation is built upon a foundation of sorrow:

> The *Turangalîla-Symphonie* is a love song. It is also a hymn to joy. Not the respectable, calmly euphoric joy of some good man of the 17th century, but joy as it may be conceived by someone who has glimpsed it only in the midst of sadness, that is to say, a joy that is superhuman, overflowing, blinding, unlimited.[30]

It is only in the dream world of the sixth movement, 'Jardin du sommeil d'amour' (Garden of love's sleep) that any sustained oasis of peace can be found in Turangalîla. As Messiaen himself pointed out,[31] if 'Joie du sang des étoiles' is carnal, agitated, frenetic, noisy and even brutal, 'Jardin du sommeil d'amour' is pure, calm and tender. It represents the imprisonment of the sleeping lovers, who are oblivious to the world, even to their confinement, bathed in dappled light recalling Debussy's *Pelléas*. The garden is full of 'new plants and flowers, bright and melodious birds who sing of love'.[32] Trapped by tragic circumstance, Messiaen was able to be with his beloved only in his dreams. Writing later, he made a heartfelt plea: 'Time passes, forgotten. The lovers are outside of time. Don't wake them . . .'[33]

It would be misleading to suggest that *Turangalîla* has anything like the same degree of narrative intent as *Harawi*. Apart from the two central movements, Messiaen is unusually coy about linking movements to specific phrases or images. Instead there are two movements called simply 'Chant d'amour', three which take the symphony's title of 'Turangalîla'; and there is a Développement de l'amour, whilst the whole is framed by an 'Introduction' and a 'Finale'. This is far from being abstract music, but it is not representational in the direct manner of many of the composer's other works, despite the epithets given to its cyclic themes: 'statue', 'flower', 'love' and 'stone'. Nor does the Sanskrit word *Turangalîla* itself provide much insight. It can be split into two elements, 'Turanga', roughly meaning 'tempo', and 'lîla', having connotations of life, creation, rhythm and movement,[34] but this is scarcely more explicit than Messiaen's description of a love song and hymn to joy. He states clearly that the title has nothing to do with its status as a girl's name, or as an Indian rhythm codified by Çarngadeva. Like Ravel's *Pavane pour une infante défunte*, *Turangalîla* was chosen as the title of the symphony primarily because the word makes a pleasing sound.

It might have been thought that, after completing by far his largest work to date in November 1948, Messiaen would have rested. By the time that he finished *Turangalîla*, he had almost certainly decided that he needed to reappraise his musical language. However, he had also received an enticing commission from Marcel Couraud, conductor of the National Choir of Radio France, to write a work for his virtuoso group of twelve mixed voices L'Ensemble Vocale. Messiaen might have been expected to wait until the spring, or even the summer before embarking on the new work. Instead, it appears that he began work straight away. There is some doubt as to whether he completed *Cinq Rechants* by the end of December 1948, but it seems likely that, at the very least, he sketched the bare bones of his ideas for the work even if it was not completed until some way into 1949. The parameters of the commission provide a clue to Messiaen's impatience, for whilst complete freedom of text and style was allowed, the basic stipulation was that the piece should be a love song.[35] In other words, Couraud's commission provided the impetus for a further Tristan work, making a triptych. Perhaps aware that his music was on the verge of fundamental change, Messiaen may have recognized the necessity of completing *Cinq Rechants* in as close a proximity to *Turangalîla* as possible.

In *Cinq Rechants* Messiaen returns to the Peruvian folklore of *Harawi*, combining it on this occasion with the mediaeval 'alba', a troubadour song about the parting of lovers at dawn. Like *Harawi*, references to various Tristans combine with onomatopoeic phonetics, and Messiaen's own brand of surrealist French and semi-invented words. Whilst the surrealistic poems of *Harawi* have their interpretative challenges, the hodgepodge of fragments that make up the text of *Cinq Rechants* is a stream-of-consciousness of an entirely different order. Nonetheless, the effect is thrillingly beguiling. The voices jump from languorous lyrical passages to sudden bursts of energy, simultaneously creating an addictive, totally convincing sound world and a feeling of dislocation from reality. *Cinq Rechants* may be part of the same intoxicating brew of influences and inspiration as the previous Tristan works, but there are also hints of a new asceticism in the music and the work concludes with the words 'dans l'avenir' ('into the future'). Messiaen was about to attempt to escape his personal circumstances in a new way.

There can be little doubt that the impetus behind the Tristan triptych is, at least in part, autobiographical. As with *Poèmes pour Mi* and *Chants de terre et de ciel*, *Harawi* is written with Claire in mind. It is Messiaen's last song-cycle, for he would never again return to the genre so closely associated with his first wife. It would be fruitless to draw any firm conclusions about the remaining two *Tristan* works, except to observe that the identity of the beloved is ambiguous, an ambiguity that presumably stems from Messiaen's own confusion regarding his feelings. Nevertheless, the central heartfelt poem of *Harawi*, 'Adieu', which describes the 'solemn separation, before the definitive separation of death',[36] stands as a eulogy, conscious or otherwise, to a healthy Claire:

> *Adieu toi, colombe verte,*
> *Ange attristé,*
> *Adieu toi, perle limpide,*
> *Soleil gardien.*
> *Toi, de nuit, de fruit, de ciel, de jour,*
> *Aile d'amour.*
> *Adieu toi, lumière neuve,*
> *Philtre à deux voix.*
>
> *Étoile enchaînée,*
> *Ombre partagée,*
> *Dans ma main mon fruit de ciel, de jour,*
> *Lointain d'amour.*
>
> *Adieu toi, mon ciel de terre,*
> *Adieu toi, désert qui pleure,*
> *Miroir sans souffle d'amour,*
> *De fleur, de nuit, de fruit, de ciel, de jour,*
> *Pour toujours.*

> Farewell to you, green dove,
> Saddened Angel.
> Farewell to you, limpid pearl,
> Guardian sun.
> You, of night, of fruit, of heaven, of day,
> Wing of love.
> Farewell to you, new light,
> Two-voiced potion.
>
> Star enchained,
> Shared shadow,
> In my hand my fruit of heaven, of day,
> Distant love.
>
> Farewell to you, my heaven on earth,
> Farewell to you, desert who cries,

Mirror without the breath of love,
Of flower, of night, of fruit, of heaven, of day,
Forever.

Notes

1. Benson, *South Bank Show: Messiaen.*
2. Related by Virgil Thomson in an insightful article devoted to Messiaen for the *New York Herald Tribune*, 23 September 1945 and reproduced in the programme for the first performance of *Turangalîla-Symphonie*. How the pacifist Messiaen felt about this label can only be speculated.
3. *Chant des déportés* was sandwiched between the symphonic fragments from Debussy's *Le Martyre de Saint-Sébastien* and Fauré's *Requiem*.
4. The second performance was given by the BBC Symphony Orchestra and Chorus under Andrew Davis at the Royal Festival Hall on 22 March 1995.
5. The body whose approval was needed in order to gain the consent of the government minister responsible for such appointments.
6. Orchestre de l'Association de Concerts Gabriel Pierné, Roger Désormière (cond.), Paris, 1942, Association Française d'Action Artistique; AA6. This is an exceptionally rare recording, having been transferred neither to LP nor to CD, and it does not appear to be in the collections of the Bibliothèque nationale de France, the British Library or the Library of Congress.
7. 'Le baiser de l'Enfant-Jésus' from *Vingt Regards* on PDT 113; nos. 5, 'Les sons impalpables du rêve', 1, 'La colombe', and 3, 'Le nombre léger', from the *Préludes* on PDT 132; 'Regard de l'Esprit de Joie' on PDT170. Pathé also recorded Loriod playing works by Bach and Chopin around this time.
8. Pathé PDT 190/4 S (78 rpm discs, 9 sides). This extraordinary document was issued on CD in March 1998 by Dante Productions (LYS 310).
9. BBC Written Archive Centre, memo dated 15 January 1946, in 'RCONT1 Olivier Messiaen, Composer 1945–1962'.
10. This recording is now available on CD from Cala (CACD 0533).
11. Messiaen's statement that *Cantéyodjayâ* was composed at Tanglewood between 15 July and 15 August 1948 (Disc notes for Adès CD 203142)

must be a memory slip as the archives at Tanglewood are clear that the composer first attended in 1949, returning in 1975. Similarly, claims that he attended in 1947 are erroneous.

12. Following his retirement Koussevitzky gave several further concerts with the BSO in 1950 as 'Conductor Emeritus', including music by Henry Barraud who, as head of Radio France, had commissioned *Chant des déportés* from Messiaen in 1945.

13. Samuel, *Music and Color*, p. 156.

14. Hill, *Messiaen Companion*, p. 7.

15. I am extremely grateful to Peter Hill and Nigel Simeone for invaluable information clarifying the chronology of Claire's illness.

16. Massin, *Une poétique du merveilleux*, p. 172.

17. Goléa, *Rencontres*, pp. 150–1.

18. ibid, p. 151.

19. Messiaen's understandable reluctance to speak about his first wife, and especially about her illness, has caused problems for biographers. Until recently there was almost total ignorance regarding Claire Delbos, to the extent that it was only with the research of Nigel Simeone and Peter Hill that light has been shed on these sad events.

20. See, for instance, Samuel, *Music and Color*, p. 17.

21. Samuel, *Music and Color*, p. 30.

22. ibid.

23. Nigel Simeone, 'Tristan et Yseult – Thème d'Amour', programme booklet to concert given at the Messiaen 2002 Conference, Sheffield on 22 June 2002. Simeone discovered this fragment in November 2001.

24. Specifically *La musique des Incas et ses survivances* (Paris: Paul Guethner, 1925).

25. Goléa, *Rencontres*, p. 149.

26. Also known as *L'Île invisible*.

27. Goléa, *Rencontres*, p. 156.

28. Programme note for first performance.

29. Samuel, *Music and Color*, pp. 30–1.

30. Messiaen, *Traité II*, p. 151.

31. ibid, p. 275.

32. ibid, p. 275.

33. ibid, p. 275.
34. Goléa, *Rencontres*, p. 84.
35. Similar commissions later resulted in works by other members of La Jeune France, Daniel-Lesur's *Cantique des Cantiques* (1952) and Jolivet's *Epithalame* (1953).
36. Messiaen, *Traité III*, p. 295.

5 For now we see through a glass darkly 1949–52

[Boulez] was furious . . . like a lion that had been flayed alive, he was terrible.[1]

'Today will be a big day in music.' Serge Koussevitzky was speaking on Friday 2 December 1949 before the first performance of *Turangalîla-Symphonie* under Leonard Bernstein,[2] and, although it may have been tinged with showmanship, Koussevitzky's prophecy was both perceptive and accurate. *Turangalîla* has progressed from courting controversy in its early outings to becoming an established fixture in the concert repertoire, and a rival to *The Rite of Spring* as a work showcasing the prowess of orchestras. In the same way as Stravinsky's ballet, *Turangalîla* became a totem for Messiaen's music among supporters and detractors alike, casting a long shadow over the understanding and misunderstanding of his later works.

After the première in Symphony Hall, Boston, at 2.30pm that Friday afternoon, *Turangalîla* was repeated at the same venue on Saturday evening, 3 December, and then presented at Carnegie Hall, New York, the following Saturday. These first performances were significant events. Short passages of the rehearsals were broadcast, with Bernstein explaining aspects of the music, John Cage held a reception and dinner in Messiaen's honour,[3] and the concerts attracted widespread press interest. Reactions to the first performances were polarized. Among the press, Irving Kolodin, critic of the *New York Sun*, was

SIXTY-NINTH SEASON · NINETEEN HUNDRED FORTY-NINE AND FIFTY

Seventh Program

FRIDAY AFTERNOON, DECEMBER 2, *at* 2:30 *o'clock*

SATURDAY EVENING, DECEMBER 3, *at* 8:30 *o'clock*

LEONARD BERNSTEIN, *Conducting*

MESSIAEN............................Turangalîla-Symphony, for
Piano, Onde Martenot, and Orchestra

    I. Introduction
           Modéré, un peu vif
   II. Chant d'amour 1
           Modéré, lourd
  III. Turangalîla 1
           Presque lent, rêveur
  IV. Chant d'amour 2
           Bien modéré
   V. Joie du sang des étoiles
           Un peu vif, joyeux et passioné

INTERMISSION

   VI. Jardin du sommeil d'Amour
           Très modéré, très tendre
  VII. Turangalîla 2
           Piano solo un peu vif; orchestre modéré
VIII. Développement de l'amour
           Bien modéré
   IX. Turangalîla 3
           Modéré
    X. Final
           Modéré, avec une grande joie

Piano Solo: YVONNE LORIOD
Onde Martenot Solo: GINETTE MARTENOT

(First Performance)

BALDWIN PIANO   RCA VICTOR RECORDS

This program will end about 4:20 o'clock on Friday Afternoon,
10:20 on Saturday Evening.

12. Programme for the first performances of *Turangalîla-Symphonie*.

the most positive, describing the music as 'a gaudy patchwork of pleasure and delight', and concluding that the concert was 'a really arousing experience'.[4] Nevertheless, most reaction was at the opposite end of the spectrum and, as Poulenc observed in a letter to Henri Sauguet, Messiaen 'was unmercifully slated by all that lot and was generally detested by the musical milieu as a whole'.[5] Cyrus Durgin led the critical opprobrium in the *Boston Globe* complaining that '. . . in the two or three million notes that Mr. Messiaen put to paper with sublime persistence, the only offense is to the ears . . . [Turangalîla] is not the most acrid music ever heard . . . but it is the longest and most pointless music within memory.'[6] In the *Boston Post* Warren Storey Smith cast doubt about Koussevitzky's assertion of Turangalîla's historical import, countering with a prophecy of his own: 'Will we hear all this again, save for this evening's performance? I doubt it.'[7]

Reactions to Turangalîla were equally divergent when it was performed on the other side of the Atlantic. As Poulenc related in a letter to Milhaud on 6 September, the European première, given on 25 July 1950 at the Aix-en-Provence festival, caused tempers to flare even amongst friends:

> At the end of Messiaen's *atrocious Turangalîla-Symphonie* . . . in front of an astonished crowd, Roland [-Manuel] and Arthur [Honegger] set upon each other; as for Georges [Auric] and me, that was a real drama. Georges was green, still unwell from a mixture of flu and a frozen melon, and I was red as a beetroot. For seven minutes we said dreadful things, Georges defending Messiaen, while I was at the end of my tether about the dishonesty of the work, written to please the crowd and the elite, the bidet and the baptismal font, all in the awful tradition of Dukas and Marcel Dupré. People surrounded us as if they were at a cock-fight.[8]

Normally supportive of Messiaen's music, Poulenc had already written to him on 1 August to assure him that there was nothing personal in his indignation: 'You can't have failed to have been told, many times over, that I don't like your Symphony, which is true. On the other hand, since nobody except Paul Rouart has told you how much your *Rechants* delighted me this spring, I want to reassure you that my behaviour, in the present case, is strictly temporary, based solely on an aesthetic disagreement.'[9] Eleven years later Poulenc wrote another letter about *Turangalîla*, but this time he wished to admit that he had been wrong about the work, prompting heartfelt gratitude from Messiaen: 'I was infinitely touched by your letter. Before the nobility of spirit, the frankness, the affection and the artistic integrity of such a gesture, words are powerless . . . I thank you with all my heart, and much more than I know how to say.'[10]

In Britain, there was considerable debate within the BBC about whether or not the European première warranted a broadcast. Edward Lockspeiser, the biographer of Debussy, worked for the BBC's Overseas Music Department advising on French music. He had already examined the *Cinq Rechants*, judging that 'a performance would hardly warrant the great amount of work which would have to be spent on it – unless it falls into the hands of a fervent admirer of Messiaen, which few of us are'.[11] By 12 May, Lockspeiser had spoken to Roger Désormière about *Turangalîla*, and concluded that 'we can expect the new symphony [. . .] to say in an uninhibited way everything the composer wants to say about everything, that it will be full and pretty involved, pretty lairy and noisy, significant & sensational'.[12] Mr [B.] Douglas[13] felt that 'a considerable number, perhaps the majority of its listeners, will be bored by this work'[14] but Mr [P. C.] Crossley-Holland[15] was an enthusiastic advocate of broadcasting *Turangalîla*: 'Here is a life-sized outlook on life & what sounds like a life-sized work.'[16] In the end, though, the European première was not broadcast on the BBC. It was not until a studio performance by the LSO under Walter Goehr in 1953 that *Turangalîla* was eventually heard in Britain, prompting a distinctly sniffy response from W. R. Anderson in the *Musical Times*: 'Messiaen's glorification of small ideas, and the use of so much fancy-percussion, make me doubt very much if there is anything really big in him.'[17] When the same forces finally gave the first concert performance of the symphony in Britain at the Royal

Festival Hall on 12 April 1954, the broadcast provoked Robert Simpson[18] to fire off a memo of understated fury the next day to his BBC colleagues: 'If there is any danger of the Turangalila-Symphonie being broadcast again I will make a report on it; otherwise I think the subject is better left alone.'[19] According to Alexander Goehr, son of Walter and later a Messiaen pupil, the event was responsible for the producer, Leonard Isaacs, losing his job.[20] After the concert there was a gathering at Felix Aprahamian's house in Muswell Hill. Messiaen initiated some clapping games, then Loriod played the entirety of Boulez's Second Piano Sonata, 'which was, in the confines of the drawing-room, a stupendous noise. I was, for the second time that evening, completely overwhelmed, not least because when she had finished playing, the piano was covered with blood.'[21]

Right from the first performances in December 1949, the question of whether, and in what way, the ten movements of *Turangalîla* constitute a symphony has arisen repeatedly. However, it is more pertinent to ask why does this work alone amongst Messiaen's orchestral offerings attract the epithet 'symphony'? It might be thought that the twelve-movement *Des canyons aux étoiles. . .* (1971–4) and the eleven-movement *Éclairs sur l'au-delà. . .* (1988–91) have at least as much reason to be called symphonies. The answer derives at least as much from the genesis and gestation of *Turangalîla* as from its intrinsic musical nature. What neither the audience nor the critics can have known in 1949 is that Messiaen did not set out to compose a seventy-five minute work in ten movements. His initial response to Koussevitzky's remarkable commission was to write a much more conventional symphony, lasting just under half the length of the finished work, with just four movements and no mention of *Turangalîla*. The four movements in question would eventually become the 'Introduction', 'Chant d'amour II', 'Jardin du sommeil d'amour' and 'Final'.[22] In other words, Messiaen originally wrote a symphony on traditional lines, comprising a first movement, scherzo, slow movement and finale. It was only after completing this original conception that Messiaen added the three movements that share the name of the symphony,

'Turangalîla'. Whereas the initial four movements are characterized by an overwhelming ebullience, with an emphasis on melody, the three 'Turangalîla' movements which were now interspersed between them often have the sense of peering into the workings of a particularly complicated clock. Having incorporated three movements containing overt compositional number-crunching, Messiaen clearly felt that the balance of the symphony was wrong. He added another two movements, a further 'Chant d'amour' and a 'Développement de l'amour' reinforcing the central idea that he had taken from the Tristan myth of 'an irresistible love'. The 'Développement', with its climactic unfoldings of the 'love' theme, each more passionate than the last, acts as a development section for the entire symphony, progressively cranking up the emotional intensity. Nevertheless, something else was still needed. The resulting movement is the most famous of all: 'Joie du sang des étoiles'. This furious headlong *moto perpetuo* provides a foil at the heart of the symphony for the sustained reverie of the slow movement, 'Jardin du sommeil d'amour', much greater than that given by the 'Chant d'amour' in the initial four-movement version of the work. It is not surprising that, as the last movement to be composed, 'Joie du sang des étoiles' encapsulates the effervescent spirit of *Turangalîla* as a whole, even if, in retrospect, it seems remarkable that it was not part of Messiaen's original conception. There is a sense that 'Joie du sang des étoiles' was the movement that he needed to write all along during the pyramid-like genesis of the symphony. In purely musical terms, its position can seem puzzling for it whips up an even greater frenzy than the 'Final'. However, as Messiaen explicitly stated, 'Joie du sang des étoiles' is about carnal love,[23] the physical union that, whilst an important factor, would make a poor conclusion to a work celebrating an all-embracing, transcendent vision of love.

On 9 December 1948, Messiaen noted in his diary 'Symphony finished and *good* in all respects'.[24] Even for a composer with the self-belief of Messiaen, some reassurance was needed before sending *Turangalîla* to Boston. He had not written anything substantial for full orchestra since *Poèmes pour Mi* a decade earlier. Given the developments in his compositional technique, and the importance of Koussevitzky's commission, it is natural that he should not only want to check what the music actually sounded like, but also get some feedback from fellow composers and students. Messiaen arranged for three movements of his symphony, the third, fourth and fifth, to be performed under the title *Trois tâla* at the Théâtre des Champs-Elysées on the mornings of Saturday 14 and Sunday 15 February 1948.[25] With no less a figure than André Cluytens conducting the Orchestre de la Société des Concerts du Conservatoire, this was no mere run-through. The event warranted a short review in the *Guide du Concert*, which noted that the *Trois tâla* 'caused quite a stir' and, after mentioning various difficulties, concluded that 'Messiaen is a man on the move'.[26]

However, the response from one member of the audience was not exactly encouraging. Boulez reacted with contempt, reputedly describing it to Messiaen as being like 'bordello music'. This typically brusque response was symptomatic of Boulez's drift away from his former *maître* at this time. For several years, Boulez had been publicly critical of aspects of Messiaen's music. These were not the old charges, that the music went too far in this or that direction, was too dissonant or too complicated, to which Messiaen had become accustomed. Rather, Boulez was berating his former teacher, in often patronizing terms, for not being progressive enough: '[For] Messiaen, ... whose harmonic character would irritate even the most indulgent, method is still at the stage of a grid filled in, for better or for worse, with a mass of chords. [...] when Messiaen writes a rhythmical canon, for example, it is immediately underlined by an avalanche of chords, for no reason at all.'[27] This blunt evaluation could only have hurt. Messiaen, the radical composer and trail-blazing pedagogue, the beacon of academic liberalism in the otherwise dourly traditional Paris Conservatoire, was now being upbraided by his former student.

All of this at a time when his musical fluency was at a peak and when he had achieved a victory for progress at the Conservatoire with the creation of his own special class in analysis. Nevertheless, the transfer from private meetings arranged by word of mouth to a timetabled class was a risk. Whatever assurances were given by the Conservatoire's director, Claude Delvincourt, Messiaen must have been aware that he risked losing the freedom to explore through his teaching whatever seemed appropriate at any particular time. The new analysis class could never have the same frisson of anti-establishment excitement as the informal meetings at the house of Guy Bernard-Delapierre, which themselves had grown out of the first few clandestine classes at Mme Sivade's salon during the Occupation. Was the blessing of the Conservatoire a vindication of Messiaen's pedagogical approach or a sign that he was losing his radical edge? As early as 1945, several of Messiaen's *flèches*, including Boulez, had gone to study with the Schoenberg disciple René Leibowitz. After a brief infatuation, Boulez left Leibowitz, attacking him thereafter as a charlatan – a charge he never even remotely suggested with respect to Messiaen. Other students, though, stayed with Leibowitz who, as the most prominent advocate of what Schoenberg disciples regarded as the true approach to serialism, was happy to cultivate antipathy to Messiaen. The extent of the hostility is reflected by the attitude of Max Deutsch, another Schoenberg pupil operating in Paris. When Alexander Goehr arrived in Paris in the mid-1950s wanting to study both with him and with Messiaen, Deutsch told him 'You have to choose. If you come to me, you can't go there'.[28]

Messiaen was being pressured by his former and current students. During the time that he was composing *Turangalîla*, the younger generation was beginning to show signs of turning the serial approach to composition, invented by Schoenberg and developed by Webern, into a new orthodoxy for the postwar musical world. It is against this backdrop that Messiaen's decision to add the three 'Turangalîla' movements into what had, until that point been a relatively conventional symphony, should be seen. As the most overtly progressive movements in the symphony, they could almost be seen as three studies in the kinds of musical approach that fascinated his most talented students. If he was ambivalent about the attempted revolutions of the new generation, Messiaen was not part of the *ancien régime*.

For all its originality, *Turangalîla* closes a chapter in Messiaen's life. It may be the work that grabbed the headlines for decades after, and it may have provided many with their first experience of being bowled over by Messiaen's intoxicating blend of grand romantic gestures and intellectual rigour. Nevertheless, to echo Debussy's famous evaluation of Wagner's influence, far from heralding the dawn of a creative era, *Turangalîla* should be viewed as a magnificent sunset. Whilst it contains many important technical advances, in terms of expression it is not the springboard for the works of the following decade or more, but the culmination of all that came before. For some, the sheer heart-on-sleeve public emotionalism of Messiaen's symphony was already distinctly antediluvian in the brave new world being constructed by the post-war generation. The young artists who had witnessed the horrors of the war did not wish to embrace the traditions that had helped to produce that global catastrophe.

Messiaen's impetus for the new broom approach was more personal. The surrealist dream world of the *Tristan* triptych could no longer be sustained. The decline in the condition of his wife, Claire, that followed her operation in January 1949 seems to have been the point in Messiaen's mind when he acknowledged the extent of her mental decline. His comments to Brigitte Massin about Claire's illness imply that it started with the operation rather than this being one point in a much longer deterioration. It is surely no coincidence that the most obvious shift of musical thinking in Messiaen's career occurs either side of January 1949. In the wake of the operation, grim reality appears in place of surrealistic fantasy, with clear, rational thinking underpinning each work. Having no commissions to fulfil, the time was ripe to experiment in order to find a way forward rather than dwelling on the past. By the time that the Boston and New York critics got their teeth into *Turangalîla*, Messiaen had already entered a new phase of creativity. Displaying extraordinary artistic ruthlessness, he now excised from his stylistic palette large tranches of the idiosyncratic musical language he had spent more than two decades developing. The turmoil in his home life meant that there could be no monumental grand designs. Although he continued to operate at the same extraordinary level of invention as during the previous six years, Messiaen simply could not find the necessary time and space for writing unsolicited orchestral works that he had done in the early 1930s. Rather, he produced a succession of solo pieces, some for piano, others for organ, in which he did not start afresh, but chose to isolate and develop the progressive elements that already existed within his music. In the words of Boulez, rather than his 'omnipresent harmony', Messiaen now concentrated on 'the more anarchic intervals'.[29]

During the summer of 1949, Messiaen composed, or began work on, a remarkable series of pieces. First of all, whilst making a brief visit to the summer school at Darmstadt in June, he conceived a piano study, *Mode de valeurs et d'intensités*. Then, during his five week sojourn at Tanglewood in July and August he composed a kind of anarchic piano *fantaisie* entitled *Cantéyodjayâ*, a further piano study, *Neumes rythmiques*, and noted ideas for a new organ cycle, *Messe de la Pentecôte*. The conscious grandiosity of *Turangalîla* is replaced in these works by an unprecedented expressive concision. *Cantéyodjayâ* is the first example of Messiaen composing the kind of musical collage that would become characteristic of his later works. The turnover of events in this manic stream of consciousness is relentless, with a succession of ideas seemingly falling over each other to be heard, including several rough and ready versions of new techniques. There are also fragmentary echoes of the *Tristan* triptych and the score is littered with invented Franco-Sanskrit captions, such as '*doubléafloréalîla*', suggesting, as Paul Griffiths has observed, a private game.[30] Nonetheless, whilst containing some of the same *joie de vivre* as *Turangalîla*, far from being a continuation, *Cantéyodjayâ* is more of an exorcism of Messiaen's musical past.

Cantéyodjayâ may have been a necessary stylistic purgative for Messiaen, but it was not actually heard in public until 1954.[31] Far more important for Messiaen's immediate reputation were *Mode de valeurs et d'intensités* and *Neumes rythmiques*, which were soon sandwiched by two pieces entitled *Île de feu* (Isle of fire) to form a set of *Quatre Études de rythme* (Four rhythmic studies). As early as 1945, Messiaen made a reminder to himself in his diary to 'Make series from Tempo',[32] reflecting his wish to apply Schoenberg's serial method to aspects of composition other than pitch. By the following year his ambitions were becoming broader, with an entry noting 'Develop timbres, durations and nuances along serial principles'.[33] Aspects of these ideas can be found in parts of Turangalîla, but it was not until the summer of 1949 that Messiaen was able to turn his attention properly to the problem.

The resulting Mode de valeurs et d'intensités is constructed from three distinct modes, each having twelve chromatic pitches (at fixed register) and twelve durations whilst seven dynamic levels (piano, mezzo forte, etc.,) and twelve levels of attack (staccato, accented, etc.,) are distributed across the three modes. Each note is an individually tailored sound, created from a unique combination of these parameters so that the modes form a kind of musical periodic table. Having thus greatly restricted his room for manoeuvre, Messiaen then utilizes his musical elements with complete freedom. Far from sounding tightly organized, the piece gives the impression of randomness, though the mist of apparent chaos occasionally clears just enough to make it apparent that there is reasoning behind Messiaen's placement of each sound. The flexibility that Messiaen elicits from his seemingly rigid resources is his willingness to ignore the rules underpinning the canonical application of Schoenberg's serial method. The importance of Mode de valeurs, though, is that it explodes all pre-existing notions of how the notes of music should relate to each other, with there being no continuity of melody, rhythm or dynamics. Instead, each individual sound stands in its own right. Four years after attracting the sobriquet 'Atomic Bomb of contemporary music', Messiaen had achieved the musical equivalent of splitting the atom.

For many years it was thought that Mode de valeurs was written after Cantéyodjayâ, which contains a simpler version of the same technique in one of its episodes. This is for the simple reason that Messiaen had said so, stating that Cantéyodjayâ was written during his sojourn at Tanglewood in July and August 'several weeks before the Mode de valeurs et *d'intensités*.[34] Not surprisingly, given his erratic domestic circumstances, Messiaen evidently became confused about the complicated chronology of this period. Leaving aside his repeated erroneous statements that *Cantéyodjayâ* was composed in Tanglewood in 1948 rather than 1949, the score of *Mode de valeurs* is marked 'Darmstadt 1949'. What Messiaen had forgotten was that at the time of this first trip to Darmstadt, the summer school was held in June rather than September, as became the norm from a couple of years later. Assuming that Messiaen remembered *where* he composed a piece more accurately than *when* it was written, this means that *Mode de valeurs* was conceived, at the very least, in June 1949, that is several weeks *before* he wrote *Cantéyodjayâ*, and the finishing touches were put on the famous study the following winter. The importance of this is that, rather than *Cantéyodjayâ* being a burst of creativity containing the kernel of the idea developed in *Mode de valeurs*, the 'rhythmic study' was exactly that, a study exploring a new technique, which was then applied within a broader compositional form in *Cantéyodjayâ*. Writing in 1958, Messiaen was proud of being 'the first' to develop the idea of a 'super-series applied to all the elements of music'.[35] He soon became dismissive, though, regarding the 'three pages' of *Mode de valeurs* as perhaps 'prophetic and historically important, but musically, it's three times nothing',[36] whilst *Cantéyodjayâ* is conspicuous by its absence from later writings and even some work lists. Nevertheless, the three-part heterophony of *Mode de valeurs* suggests a symbolic kinship with the 'Le mystère de la Sainte Trinité' from *Les Corps glorieux*; the inscrutable nature of quasi-serial techniques would be put to good use in later works as analogies for the more impenetrable manifestations of the divine.

If *Mode de valeurs* is the most famous of the *Quatre Études*, *Neumes rythmiques* is equally audacious, radically re-interpreting the mediaeval concept of musical neumes (the little clumps of notes found in plainchant). Like *Cantéyodjayâ* it is a mosaic of musical fragments. However, whereas the earlier work is a mosaic on the structural level, with the many contrasting sections jostling for attention, *Neumes rythmiques* achieves this quality *within* the 'neumatic' portions of music. In fact, the piece consists of just three types of music, two of which are gradually expanding rhythms that take it in turns to interrupt the 'rhythmic neumes'. These neumes consist of distinctive gobbets of sound, which are presented in varying combinations (although the neumes themselves are almost never varied). Perhaps most striking about *Neumes rythmiques*, though, is that within a year of completing the Tristan triptych, Messiaen is thinking almost exclusively in terms of timbre and rhythm rather than harmony. It is not necessary to be a virtuoso analyst to sense that the menacing pounding at both ends of the keyboard – an eerie effect made all the more uneasy by Messiaen's deliberate restriction of the dynamic – acts as one of the structural linchpins of *Neumes rythmiques*. Having stripped his music of the last vestiges of tonality, it is the relationship between different qualities of sounds that is now the main preoccupation of Messiaen's music. He is exploring ways to make coherent sense of his apparently disjunct fragments without the aid of a clear harmonic structure.

Whilst the developments of *Mode de valeurs* and *Neumes rythmiques* grab the attention in the *Quatre Études*, the *interversion* passages of the fourth piece, *Île de feu II*, are far more profound in their long-term consequences for Messiaen's music. Inserted between the fiery impulsions that dominate the piece, this is another innovation given a trial run in *Cantéyodjayâ*, although the seeds of the technique date back at least as far as *Vingt Regards*. Derived from serial procedures, the idea of *interversion* is even more subversive of Schoenberg's initial principles than *Mode de valeurs*. Rather than varying his series by inverting it or reversing it, Messiaen explodes it from within, thus destroying any notion of a fundamental sequence of notes or a theme as the foundation for the work. Nonetheless, unlike *Mode de valeurs* or *Neumes rythmiques*, the *Île de feu* pieces show Messiaen already trying to break away from the abstraction that was becoming part of the new creed for the younger generation of composers. The inspiration for both pieces came from Papua New Guinea, or rather from what Messiaen learnt about it from Pierre Tallec, a former Governor of the French colony and friend of Messiaen, who attended the class at the Paris Conservatoire and regularly acted as assistant, pulling stops for him at the Trinité.[37]

The consequences of the technical innovations in the *Quatre Études*, especially *Mode de valeurs*, and *Cantéyodjayâ* were far-reaching for the younger generation of composers. The epithet *études* is apt, for the pieces propose solutions to structural problems concerning a number of composers at the time. Messiaen's quasi-serial experiments opened the door to total serialism, but the techniques themselves would not have been seized upon with such zeal were it not for the totally new sound-world that resulted from their application.

Messiaen recorded the *Quatre Études de rythme* in May 1951, courtesy of the recently formed UNESCO. The rigours of recording in the pre-tape era took their toll on Messiaen. After playing *Île de feu II* no less than eighteen times in succession, he was left for weeks with cramps in his hands.[38] The resulting set of two 78rpm discs was distributed by Pathé, and it is a sign of the times that the recording of these jewels of the very latest trends in modernism was announced in an advert that also promoted not only Dinu Lipatti playing Mozart, but also the latest offerings by Edith Piaf and Charles Trenet. The 78s of the *Quatre Études* are the only known recordings of Messiaen performing any of his own works for solo piano, but they confirm the lessons of his organ recordings and various commercial and broadcast performances of *Visions de l'Amen*, *Poèmes pour Mi*, *Harawi* and *Quatuor pour la fin du Temps*. It is too simplistic to attribute deviations from the written score or any imprecision purely to technical deficiencies on Messiaen's part. He may not have possessed the fearsome pianism of Yvonne Loriod, but he was, nonetheless, an extremely accomplished performer. Even in a piece like *Mode de valeurs*, Messiaen's recording is a re-creation attempting to capture and convey its spirit. His quasi-fantaisie account of *Mode de valeurs* confirms that, like Debussy's *Études*, this is more than an arid technical exercise. That Messiaen does not always differentiate between his twelve means of attack, or that the lack of a third pedal on his Érard piano cuts the durations of the long bass notes significantly short, does not nullify the effectiveness of the piece. In Messiaen's performance of the Études, it is easy to see what prompted the Cologne music critic Herbert Eimert to coin the term 'star music'.[39]

Messiaen did not attend Darmstadt in 1951, but his influence was still felt. The journalist Antoine Goléa took along the recording of the Quatre Études and played them during his lecture on new developments in French music. In the audience was the twenty-two-year-old Karlheinz Stockhausen, who had befriended one of Messiaen's former students, the Belgian composer Karel Goeyvaerts. The two young men had already performed and discussed the second movement of Goeyvaerts's Sonata for two pianos, to the evident bemusement of Theodor Adorno. Written a year after Mode de valeurs, the sonata draws upon similar principles to those underpinning Messiaen's study. Despite close acquaintance with the techniques involved, the recording of Messiaen's Études were a revelation for Stockhausen. In some corner of the Marienhöhe at Darmstadt he got Goléa to play the discs over and over again, listening with fascination. Stockhausen resolved to go to Paris to study with Goeyvaerts's former maître. Undeterred by a complete lack of French, the young German composer turned up in Paris in January 1952 and, helped through the formidable Conservatoire administration by Goeyvaerts, joined the classes of both Messiaen and Milhaud.

Messiaen stated repeatedly that Stockhausen was very unhappy in his class. In January 1984 he recalled that in 1952 he had been obliged to analyse sonata form, particularly in relation to Beethoven:

> From 1956 I was king in my little academic universe, and there, from 1956–1979, I could do whatever I wanted. What I wanted to cover was Stockhausen, Boulez and Xenakis themselves and the whole of ultra-modern music (including musique concrète and electronic music); but also Monteverdi, Gesualdo and Claude le Jeune; Mozart, Wagner, Debussy and Stravinsky as well as Schoenberg, Berg and Webern; the Middle Ages with its plainchant, Adam de la Halle and Guillaume de Machaut; ancient and exotic things, Greek metre, the Indian decî-tâlas, Balinese music and Japanese gagaku.

Alas! Stockhausen never knew these happy times! When he came to me, not only was I immersed in fugue and sonata form, but I had made a firm decision never to have disciples, and had absolutely forbidden myself to talk about my own personal researches. So Stockhausen was very unhappy in my class. I treated him kindly and with the greatest possible respect, since I knew for certain that I was dealing with a real genius who had to be guided towards his true path. After a year he left me and went to Herbert Eimert, with whom he was initiated into electronic music. Then he left Eimert, to soar up with his own wings. In fact, Stockhausen did not need a teacher. The few musical encounters he has had in his life were merely springboards for his future works.[40]

These self-deprecating protestations seem to have been misplaced. Although Stockhausen only attended the Messiaen class for about a year (he lasted just a few weeks with Milhaud), he has spoken warmly of both Messiaen and his class:

Many things I knew already from my studies in Cologne. But most of it I knew without it mattering to me: it was dead . . . In many respects Messiaen did the opposite of what I wanted. He never tried to convince me. That made him a good teacher. He did not give instruction in composition, but showed how he understood the music of others and how he worked himself.[41]

This self-effacing approach was crucial for the development of another of Messiaen's most celebrated pupils; Iannis Xenakis. A member of the Resistance during the Second World War who had been injured by a shell fragment in 1944, Xenakis had been forced during the later period of civil war, in 1947, to leave his native Greece.[42] Xenakis had not followed anything like a traditional musical grounding when he presented himself to Messiaen in 1951. Trained in architecture and mathematics, and having worked with Le Corbusier, Xenakis's desire to forge a path as a composer had been met only with discouragement from Honegger and Boulanger. His attempts at composition had not been well received and, when he first consulted Messiaen, he asked whether he should restart his musical education from scratch, 'enter a harmony class, a fugue class, and so on'. A strong believer in the necessity of the thorough grounding that the Conservatoire system gave its students, Messiaen's usual instinct would have been to encourage traditional forms of study. He pondered Xenakis's predicament for a few days before telling him: 'No. You are already thirty, you have the good fortune to be Greek, to have studied mathematics, to have studied architecture. Take advantage of these things, and make them your music.'[43]

At the same time that he was giving Xenakis renewed confidence in his compositional path, Messiaen was continuing the developments of the *Quatre Études* and *Cantéyodjayâ* by writing for the organ for the first time in over a decade. In *Messe de la Pentecôte* and *Livre d'orgue* Messiaen gave a thoroughly modern perspective to existing genres. Whilst the *Messe* is specifically intended for use at Mass on Pentecost Sunday, and the Classical French term *Livre d'orgue* suggests a suite of movements more suited to a concert context, the latter contains several liturgical movements and the former is certainly not without austere, even abstract, passages. Even if he had meant it at the time, by the early 1950s Messiaen could no longer sustain the claim that he had made when applying for the post of *titulaire* organist at the Trinité that 'the pattern of [the liturgy], and the instrument itself, are not suitable for modern music'.[44] In these two cycles, there is still the emphasis on exploring new rhythmic techniques begun in the *Quatre Études*. What is striking, however, is the extraordinary range of sounds that Messiaen produces, for he evidently no longer felt that 'one must not disturb the piety of the faithful with wildly anarchic chords.'[45] Whatever the more conservative members of the faithful felt, Messiaen's growing status as a composer, an organist and a pedagogue meant that these works were of interest to more than some small band of initiates. The forum for the first performance of the *Livre d'orgue* in France (the première was in Stuttgart to inaugurate the organ at the Villa Berg) was the Concerts du Domaine Musical, which were run by Boulez. Expecting a modest, though respectable audience, Boulez put out fifty chairs at the Trinité and opened a side door. In the event, nearer two thousand people turned up and a disorderly crush ensued, engulfing both the composer and the Prefect of Police, André Dubois, who was attending privately as a devotee. Messiaen lost two buttons from his overcoat and only managed to get inside after explaining that there would be no *Livre d'orgue* if he could not gain admittance.[46] In Messiaen's hands, the organ had moved from the margins of musical experience to the forefront of progressive compositional thought. In terms of registration, he was thinking the unthinkable, breaking all the usual conventions of how stops should be combined. Listening to Messiaen's own recording of *Messe de la Pentecôte*, made in the mid-1950s, it is possible to grasp the feral nature of this music at the time. Goehr recalls that 'it sounded like electronics'[47] and Messiaen was truly opening up new worlds of sound.

Given this fascination with manipulating sound, it is only natural that Messiaen should have wanted to explore the possibilities being opened up by the advent of magnetic tape and the development of *Musique concrète*. One of his former students, Pierre Henry, had already been working with Pierre Schaeffer in developing this entirely new approach to creating music, and both Messiaen and Boulez embarked upon studies using the new medium early in 1952, whilst Stockhausen joined the fray later in the year. All three composers were intrigued by the possibility of manipulating recorded sounds to go beyond the limitations of conventional instruments. For Schaeffer, who was interested in creating aural canvases from familiar sounds, the approach of this triumvirate was perplexing:

> It was really strange; when Messiaen came into the studio he said 'I would like next to no sounds' – those were his words. When Stockhausen came, he said, 'I shall work with a single sound.' And Boulez came and wanted to make a study on a single sound . . . And they had to come to *me* with this desire, in a situation where I had discovered exactly the opposite approach.[48]

Whereas the studies by Boulez and Stockhausen each last for just a few minutes, Messiaen's piece, *Timbres-Durées*, is a more ambitious experiment lasting over a quarter of an hour. While it would now be a

simple task with computers to arrange and assemble the various fragments of sound that make up this study in rhythm, this would have
been a time-consuming and laborious task in 1952. The mind boggles
at the thought of Messiaen attempting to negotiate the intricacies of
advanced tape-editing. In the event, Pierre Henry was drafted in to
realize the finished work, although the composer doubtless oversaw
every step of the process. The result of Messiaen's and Henry's efforts
was first heard at a concert of *Musique concrète* organized by Pierre
Boulez on 21 May 1952. This strangely compelling, and at times
distinctly jaunty, piece was also heard at least twice in America, for
Boulez sent Cage some discs with all of the pieces from the May
concert. Cage subsequently organized *Musique concrète* events in
Columbia, on 22 December, and at the University of Illinois. It is a
pity that Messiaen did not hear the latter, for Cage created a primitive
version of surround sound for *Timbres-Durées*, playing it simultaneously
on eight tape-machines, each linked to a speaker, and adjusting the
volume controls so that the music flew around the room. As it was, it
did not take Messiaen long to decide formally to withdraw *Timbres-
Durées*: a unique occurrence in his output. It is not difficult to understand why he should do this, for there is a feeling of Messiaen
struggling to manipulate a brand new technology when he could
achieve similar or better results far more adroitly using conventional
instruments.

By withdrawing *Timbres-Durées*, Messiaen was not simply admitting
that 'I don't have a gift for it',[49] or even that he could never be good at
Musique concrète, but was tacitly recognizing that, for him, the way
ahead was not going to become clearer just by changing the medium.
Nor would it be discovered simply by exploring the musical concerns
of his students, especially Boulez. There is a sense, in the late 1940s, of
the pupil becoming the *maître*, of Boulez actively reversing his relationship with Messiaen. In retrospect, the older composer found neither
Boulez's departure from his classes, nor his subsequent public and
private admonishments, especially surprising, essentially viewing
them as an inevitable part of a young genius's path of discovery.

The attacks must have been upsetting at the time as is clear from the fact that, on at least one occasion, Boulez felt the need to buy Messiaen a present, an African xylophone, in order to atone for any hurt caused. That Messiaen ultimately retained the respect and affection of Boulez, when so many others from the younger man's formative years were spurned, is perhaps the biggest tribute to his qualities as teacher, composer and human being. Crucially, from an early stage, their relationship went beyond the teacher-student relationship of the classroom:

> He [Boulez] was living in the rue Beautrellis at the time [. . .] and my
> father lived on the quai Henri-IV (which is also in the fourth
> arrondissement). So we used to take the métro together, me to have
> lunch with my father and he to go home. And we used to talk on the
> métro. And, from what he's told me since, these talks guided him
> much more than the class did.[50]

By the early 1950s, there is a sense of mutual support and encouragement between the two men. Boulez had become, in the words of Alexander Goehr, 'a kind of embarrassed defender of Messiaen'.[51] On 4 May 1952, Messiaen and Boulez gave the first performance of the latter's *Structures Ia* for two pianos during a concert organized by UNESCO at the Comédies des Champs-Elysées. In many ways, this performance marked the closest convergence between the two composers. In *Structures Ia*, Boulez explores the possibilities of total serialism, the application of Schoenberg's organization of pitch to all the other compositional parameters. In effect, it is a more extensive and rigorous application of the ideas first explored in *Mode de valeurs*, and Boulez acknowledges the debt owed to Messiaen's experiment by using the mode from his former *maître*'s work as the basis of the series in *Structures Ia*. That Messiaen and Boulez gave the première together could only underline to any onlooker the aesthetic kinship now shared by the two composers who would respectively come to be viewed as the godfather and torchbearer of the post-war avant-garde. They were now exploring similar ideas, whether they be the extension of serialism or, as demonstrated at another concert two and a half weeks later, the possibilities opened up by *Musique concrète*. However, the path that Boulez was forging with such determination was only a cul de sac for Messiaen. Interesting and intellectually stimulating as he found the experiments of the *Quatre Études*, or the more abstruse pages of *Messe de la Pentecôte* and *Livre d'orgue*, he was never going to remain comfortable for long with an approach to music that strives to be objective and, almost inevitably, abstract. Just as Boulez had needed to break from the overwhelming personality of his *maître*, now Messiaen moved away from the musical concerns of his fiery protégé to a direction more in tune with his own creative personality. His response to the problem of how to progress in the monkish creative climate of the 1950s was unique. In order to move forward, he turned to the oldest musicians on the planet. Having opened the door to total serialism for his students and watched them gallop through, Messiaen quietly closed it after them and went out into the garden to listen to the birds.

Notes

1. Messiaen, 'Entretien avec Claude Samuel', ECD 75505.
2. Harold Rogers, 'Bernstein Leads 10-Movement "Turangalîla"', in *Christian Science Monitor*, 3 December 1949, 13.
3. Jean-Jacques Nattiez (ed.), *The Boulez-Cage Correspondence*, trans. Robert Samuels, (Cambridge: CUP, 1993), p. 48.
4. Irving Kolodin, 'The Music Makers', in *The New York, N. Y. Sun*, Monday, 12 December 1949.
5. Sidney Buckland (ed. and trans.), *Francis Poulenc, Echo and Source, Selected Correspondence 1915–1963* (London: Victor Gollancz, 1991), p. 180.
6. Cyrus Durgin, 'Turangalîla, or Love in the East Indies, or a Messiaen Afternoon' in the *Boston Globe*, Saturday, 3 December 1949.
7. Warren Storey Smith, 'Symphony Concert' in *The Boston Post*, Saturday, 3 December.
8. Myriam Chimènes (ed.), *Francis Poulenc: Correspondance 1919–1963* (Paris: Fayard, 1994), p. 695.
9. Chimènes, *Poulenc: Correspondance*, p. 690.

10. Letter dated 28 October 1961, Chimènes, *Poulenc: Correspondance*, p. 983.
11. BBC WAC, memo dated 25 October 1949 in 'RCONT1 Olivier Messiaen, Composer 1945–1962'.
12. BBC WAC, 'RCONT1 Olivier Messiaen, Composer 1945–1962'.
13. Assistant Music Programme Organiser – Third Programme.
14. BBC WAC, 'RCONT1 Olivier Messiaen, Composer 1945–1962'.
15. Assistant Music Programe Organiser – Home Service.
16. BBC WAC, 'RCONT1 Olivier Messiaen, Composer 1945–1962'.
17. W. R. Anderson, 'Round about Radio' in *Musical Times* (Vol. 94, August 1953), 359–60.
18. Assistant to Third Programme Music Organiser.
19. BBC WAC, 'RCONT1 Olivier Messiaen, Composer 1945–1962'.
20. Goehr, *Finding the Key* (London: Faber and Faber, 1998), p. 42.
21. Goehr, *Finding the Key*, p. 44.
22. Information on the genesis of *Turangalîla* kindly provided by George Benjamin and Paul Crossley.
23. Messiaen, *Traité II*, p. 235.
24. Peter Hill, 'Messiaen in the 1950s', lecture given at Berkeley on 29 September 2002. The score gives the date of composition as 17 July 1946–29 November 1948.
25. Confusingly, the three movements eventually labelled *Turangalîla* were originally called 'Tâla' by Messiaen. Given the contradictory evidence over the genesis of the symphony, it is possible that Messiaen used 'Tâla' as a multi-purpose epithet for movements from the project.
26. *Guide du Concert*, vol. xxviii, nos.23–25 (12, 19 and 26 March 1948), p. 254, cited Simeone, 'An exotic Tristan in Boston' in Richard Barber (ed.), *King Arthur in Music*, p. 109.
27. Pierre Boulez, 'Propositions', in *Polyphonie*, 2 (1948), 65–72, reproduced as 'Proposals' in *Stocktakings from an apprenticeship*, trans. Stephen Walsh (Oxford: Clarendon, 1991), p. 49.
28. Alexander Goehr, unpublished interview, Cambridge, 4 July 1996.
29. Marks, 'Messiaen at 80', programme broadcast by BBC2 on 10 December 1988.
30. Paul Griffiths, *Olivier Messiaen and the Music of Time* (London: Faber and Faber, 1985), p. 147.
31. The first performance was given by Yvonne Loriod in Paris on 23 February 1954 at the Concerts du Domaine Musical.

32. Hill, 'Messiaen in the 1950s'.

33. Peter Hill, 'The performance history of Messiaen's *Quatre Études de rythme*', paper given at the Messiaen 2002 Conference, Sheffield, 20–23 June 2002.

34. Disc notes for Adès CD 203142.

35. ibid.

36. Samuel, *Music and Color*, p. 47.

37. Peter Hill, private communication.

38. Hill, 'Interview with Loriod', p. 296.

39. Cited in Karlheinz Stockhausen, *Stockhausen on Music*, compiled Robin Maconie (London: Marion Boyars, 1991), p. 35.

40. Michael Kurtz, *Stockhausen – a biography*, trans. Richard Toop, (Faber & Faber: London, 1994), p. 49.

41. Karlheinz Stockhausen, *Texte zu eigenen Werken – zur Kunst Anderer, Aktuelles*, vol. ii (Cologne, 1964), p. 144, cited Kurtz, *Stockhausen*, pp. 47–8.

42. He was born in Romania of Greek parents, and spent his formative years in Greece.

43. Matossian, *Iannis Xenakis*, p. 58.

44. Letter to the curate at La Trinité, 8 August 1931, in Massip (ed.), *Portraits*, p. 11.

45. ibid.

46. Felix Aprahamian, private communication.

47. Goehr, unpublished interview.

48. Michael Kurtz, 'Interview mit Pierre Schaeffer', *Zeitschrift für Musikpädagogik*, 33 (January 1986), pp. 16 ff, cited Kurtz, *Stockhausen*, p. 55.

49. Samuel, *Music and Color*, p. 59.

50. Messiaen, 'Entretien avec Claude Samuel', ECD75505.

51. Goehr, unpublished interview.

6 A natural retreat 1951–9

> There are a thousand ways of probing the future. . . I only wish that
> they would not forget that music is a part of time, a fraction of time,
> as is our own life, and that Nature, ever beautiful, ever great, ever new,
> Nature, an inextinguishable treasure-house of sounds and colours,
> forms and rhythms, the unequalled model for total development
> and perpetual variation, that Nature is the supreme resource.[1]

Messiaen had long been fascinated by nature, in particular, birds
and their songs. He spoke fondly of his experiences of sunrises and
sunsets as a teenager in the Aube countryside during his summer visits
to his grandmother and aunts in Fuligny. It was on these trips that he
first tried writing birdsong down. It was even earlier than this, as a
toddler in Ambert, that Messiaen encountered 'the revelation of
nature',[2] and it was here too that his interest in birds began to manifest
itself: 'My parents liked to tell how one day, when I was in the countryside with my father, it was in the Puy-de-Dôme, suddenly there were
some larks singing. I abruptly put down my piece of bread and
indicated that he must listen. I was three, apparently.'[3] As an adult,
Messiaen would continue to draw attention to the marvels of birdsong.
He recalled in *Technique of my Musical Language* that Dukas used to say
'Listen to the birds. They are great masters.'[4] It was advice that
Messiaen took very much to heart, for the influence of birds can be
felt throughout his œuvre. Birds appear in many guises within his
music, from a single melodic line to a five-octave harmonization, and

from an individual species to a chorus of a dozen or more. Birds and their songs are used as soloists, as decoration, as malleable musical material, as dramatic protagonists and as symbols of divine purpose. In relativist terms, Messiaen's achievement is remarkable. Most of the precedents for the musical transcription of birdsong, composers such as Josquin, Daquin, Rebel, Rameau, Beethoven, Liszt, Wagner or Mahler, simply produce stylized babbling. Messiaen was not quite the first composer actually to listen to the birds, to try incorporating something more sophisticated than a few trills. Equally fascinated by nature, Ravel gave prominent parts for birdsong in a number of his works. When writing the opera *L'Enfant et les sortilèges*, for instance, he regularly went for long night-time walks in the woods, listening to the birds, with the result that the mesmerizing scene where the child is transported into the forest includes a nightingale transcription that would not be entirely out of place in a score from Messiaen's maturity.

Ironically for a composer whose music would become a kind of sonic aviary, the first instance of a bird in Messiaen's music has nothing to do with birdsong. 'La Colombe', which opens the piano *Préludes*, is an attempt to capture not the sound of a dove, but its spirit. It is with the works of the mid-1930s, such as *La Nativité*, that the influence of transcribed birdsong begins to appear. At this stage, these are simply stylized melodic shapes within the flow of the music. By the *Quartet for the end of Time*, Messiaen is prepared to call the movement for solo clarinet 'Abyss of the birds', and indicate elsewhere that certain passages should be 'like a bird'. In the preface to the score, Messiaen even gives an indication of the species for the first time, saying of the first movement that 'a blackbird or a solo nightingale improvises'. The catalyst for this deeper enthusiasm for birdsong appears to have been his time spent as a soldier stationed at Verdun in the early days of the war. Étienne Pasquier recalled how, at Messiaen's request, he arranged the rota for keeping watch so that they could listen to the dawn chorus together:

'Look. A faint glimmer, over there. It's dawn,' Messiaen would say. Little by little, light began to appear. 'Listen carefully. Once the sun comes out, pay attention.' The moment was still. Then, all of a sudden, we heard 'Peep!' A small cry of a bird, a bird giving the pitch, like a conductor! Five seconds later, all the birds started singing together. Like an orchestra! 'Listen to them!' said Messiaen. 'They're giving each other assignments. They'll reunite tonight, at which time they'll recount what they saw during the day.' So, every time Messiaen had his night watch, I would go with him, and it would start all over again. 'Tweet! Peep!' A few seconds would go by. Then, suddenly, the whole orchestra of birds would be singing! It was deafening. Then the singing would stop, but later, like a genuine military regiment, the birds would return in the evening to report what they had observed.[5]

Following the *Quartet*, birds make regular, if relatively modest, flights into Messiaen's works of the 1940s, usually with their stylized songs providing filigree decoration, as in the slow movement of *Turangalîla*, 'Jardin du sommeil d'amour'. By the early 1950s, birdsong had already become a notable feature of Messiaen's musical landscape, so that its inclusion in the two organ works, *Messe de la Pentecôte* and *Livre d'orgue*, is not in itself remarkable. What is noteworthy is the significant increase in avian activity, with a movement in each work dedicated to birdsong, whilst it is a major feature of several other movements. Just as the dove is a symbol of the Holy Spirit in mediaeval art, the birds in these organ works are used as an allegorical device to express the two mysteries at the heart of Messiaen's faith: Communion and Easter. Birdsong begins to move centre-stage in these works, both musically and symbolically. In March 1952, in response to a request for a test piece for the flute competition at the Conservatoire, Messiaen wrote *Le Merle noir* (The Blackbird), his first work explicitly based upon the song of a specific bird. The flute in this little miniature, one of just a handful of chamber works in the composer's output, presents the song of the blackbird upon an abstract pedestal of serialism in the piano part. The boundaries of the phases of Messiaen's creativity are not clear-cut, but *Le Merle noir* can be viewed nonetheless as the fulcrum between the quasi-serial techniques of the *Quatre Études* and the ornithological extravaganzas to come. Messiaen was on the verge of making the natural world the exclusive source of his musical inspiration for the remainder of the decade. Furthermore, from the composition of *Le Merle noir* in 1952 until his death forty years later, every single work that Messiaen composed included material derived from birdsong.

For this to happen, though, Messiaen needed a teacher, since he was making his transcriptions 'without being able to determine the name of the bird that was singing'.[6] 'Deeply mortified' by his ignorance, he turned to Jacques Delamain, a noted ornithologist, writer and producer of Cognac. In April 1952, the month after he composed *Le Merle noir*, Messiaen visited la Branderaie de Gardépée, Delamain's large estate in the Charente district. Walking around the deliberately unkempt grounds, no doubt rejuvenated periodically by the Delamain family Cognac, he received his first lessons in recognizing the characteristic features and habits of different species of bird. The following Spring, he undertook further researches at Orgeval, near St Germain-en-Laye, and these expeditions acted as the catalyst for the step-change in Messiaen's use of birdsong. It is from this point that each transcription changes from being a vague *oiseau* to being labelled in his music as a specific species, notated in a specific place, and sometimes on a specific date. This more thorough approach bore its first fruit with a work for solo piano and orchestra. Originally called *Printemps* (Spring), reflecting not only the season when he undertook his birdsong researches in both 1952 and 1953, but also the fact that it marks a new departure, Messiaen soon opted for a more specific title: *Réveil des oiseaux* (Awakening of the birds). After the portrait of a single feathered protagonist in *Le Merle noir*, Messiaen's enthusiasm following his stay with Delamain resulted in a work for no less than thirty-eight species, presented without any other musical material. Beginning at midnight and concluding at noon, *Réveil des oiseaux* is built from an alternation of piano cadenzas and ensemble to create 'a completely truthful work'.[7] As if in riposte to Cocteau's claim among the fripperies of *Le Coq et l'arlequin* that 'the Nightingale sings badly',[8] Messiaen devotes the entire opening piano cadenza to this bird. It is a passage that, as an inevitability by this stage, was intended to exploit the prodigious talents of Yvonne Loriod. Faced with a work that so fundamentally reinvented the notion of what constituted a piece of orchestral music, even she, despite having already performed numerous new works by a remarkable diversity of composers, struggled at first to grasp what Messiaen was trying to achieve. In September 1953, having committed the intricacies of the solo part to memory, she played it to him. Despite being note-perfect, Messiaen told a crestfallen Loriod that she had completely misunderstood the music. Her response was to get her mother to drive her to the woods near Orgeval to experience the dawn chorus for herself. When next she played to Messiaen, he was in raptures.[9] The composer may have been pleased with his soloist, but the first performance at Donaueschingen on 11 October 1953 was not a great success, leaving the audience bemused. At this stage, Messiaen's enthusiasm was patently not infectious so far as the public was concerned. The limp reception of *Réveil des oiseaux* may have been a disappointment, but other worries awaited Messiaen at home.

Two weeks after the first performance of *Réveil des oiseaux*, he had to dash to Neussargues, where the neighbours had become concerned about Claire. She underwent tests, first for cancer, then, in November, at the Salpêtrière hospital, which specialized in neurology. When the results of the investigations came at the beginning of December, the news was shattering; Claire had been ill for a long time, with a slow-moving, progressive infection resulting in 'cerebral atrophy, incurable'.[10] Finally, she was admitted to a sanatorium at La Varenne. Messiaen visited Claire devotedly. He had not given up all hope of, if not a miracle, then some kind of improvement. He got her violin mended and took it to her, hoping that she might be able to play it, but she did not know what it was or what to do with it. At the same time, Pascal was proving troublesome. Messiaen clearly loved and cared for him deeply, but, having not had the most conventional childhood himself, he was perhaps not best equipped to deal with a teenager on his own. A workaholic by nature, Messiaen spared no effort in trying to provide for Pascal. It is easy, from the outside, to see that an adolescent son who had already lost his mother to mental illness was unlikely to view his father's labours positively, but it is difficult to know what else Messiaen could have done given that income was unpredictable. Pascal's marriage to Josette Bender on 2 August 1958 encapsulated the rift between them. Messiaen gave his written permission and generously bought the couple an apartment, at 62 boulevard de Belleville, Paris 20ᵉ. He did everything except attend the wedding. Nonetheless, from the 1960s onwards, their relationship improved markedly, with Pascal and Josette often visiting Petichet during the summer.

Family, notably Pierre and Marguérite, and friends helped as best they could during Claire's illness. For Pierre, the parallels between the experiences of his first marriage and that of his son cannot have been lost. War caused both Pierre and Olivier to be absent from their families when their sons were in their early years. Both Cécile and Claire suffered declines in mental health coinciding with, if not caused by, the anxieties of wartime. For both generations father and son found it difficult to relate to each other. That said, there is a world of difference between the 'profound melancholy' of Cécile and Claire's loss of her mental faculties, followed by physical disability.

Messiaen and Claire had been married for twenty-one years when she entered the nursing home. Her illness had been an increasing problem for about half of that time. Now that she was gone from the apartment, it must have been painfully obvious that Claire would never be coming back. As early as 1943 Messiaen had tried to find quiet places to compose, away from the disruptions that Claire's illness caused at home. Now that she was no longer there to distract him, he fell silent. In the poetic notes that accompany some of his later birdsong portraits, such as *Catalogue d'oiseaux* or *La Fauvette des jardins*, the word 'silence' occasionally appears, separated from the surrounding text and denoting a much longer period of time in the unfolding events than the several seconds for which the music pauses. Similarly, when looking through a chronological list of Messiaen's works, 1954 is a blank year in the catalogue. To put this in context, it is worth

13. Villa du Danube.

remembering that years in which he did not produce any music at all
are extremely rare. In the year of his national service, Messiaen managed to complete the transcription of *L'Ascension* for organ. In the year
that Pascal was born and depriving him of sleep, he still wrote the half-
hour-long *Fêtes des belles eaux*, a short Communion motet, *O Sacrum
Convivium!*, and orchestrated *Poèmes pour Mi*. Even when he was a

prisoner of war, he produced the *Quartet for the end of Time*. Now, though, with Claire in a nursing home and Pascal being 'difficult', Messiaen reached his lowest ebb. Any respite that his teaching might have provided from his morbid domestic circumstances was shattered in April, when Claude Delvincourt, the visionary director of the Conservatoire, was killed in a car crash. Then, on 6 May, his deputy at the Trinité, Line Zilgien, died of cancer.

Messiaen composed nothing during 1954. He had no commissions pending and no prospect of any commissions in the future. Not that he needed such incentives, for, at this point, only a handful of his pieces had been written to a specific request. Nonetheless, after the surge of interest during the 1940s, things were decidedly quiet. Even if he wanted to compose for his own satisfaction, it was far from clear what kind of work Messiaen should or could write next. He had turned decisively away from the fascination with post-Webern serialism that had become the obsession of the younger generation, in favour of birdsong. The problem was that, far from being a compositional panacea, *Réveil des oiseaux* raised more questions than it answered. Messiaen had created a bold new kind of musical work using birdsong, and nothing but birdsong, as his material, creating a soundscape of a dawn chorus. He now faced the problem that his experiment, while a fascinating and punctiliously researched success in its own terms, did not have the impact of other works. Like much great music, Messiaen's mature works make an impression even if the performance is less than ideal. By contrast, *Réveil des oiseaux* needs an exceptionally fine performance in order to succeed musically. With the many strands of birdsong, it is difficult to provide aural signposts through the work. *Réveil des oiseaux* is not just a random jumble of lines, but, for such a harmonically based composer as Messiaen, having material that is primarily melodic soon becomes restrictive.

Nonetheless, his birdsong researches continued undaunted. In 1955, Boulez asked Messiaen to write a work for small orchestra for the Domaine Musical. Despite ornithological excursions that year to the Sologne region and in his beloved Petichet, accompanied to the latter by his now near-constant companion, Yvonne Loriod, Messiaen decided against birds native to France for the new work. Getting down to work early in October after returning from his summer jaunts, he used recordings instead, supplemented by visits to the bird market in Paris, to make notations of birds from North and South America, China, Malaysia and India.

The resulting *Oiseaux exotiques* (Exotic birds) answers the questions posed by *Réveil des oiseaux* with elegant simplicity. First of all, Messiaen makes no attempt to create a work that could be regarded as ornitho-logically realistic. With calls and songs from several continents, Messiaen combines and juxtaposes birds that would never be heard together in the wild. Secondly, having rejected the purist approach with the fundamental concept of the work, it is not so hard to include elements that are not birdsong. These are relatively modest – a few bits of unpitched percussion, and some supporting chords – but the effect is profound. Most important of all, perhaps, is that the birds are no longer restricted to melodic lines. Many are now given harmonies. In fact, several are more harmony than melody. This makes it much easier for Messiaen to colour the songs so that they fit into an overall musical identity. This does not mean, as is commonly asserted, that his assertions of accuracy and fidelity in transcribing birdsong are falla-cious. To state that Messiaen's notations of birdsong are heard through the filter of his musical sensibility is to make no more a profound (still less damning) observation than that the portraits of birds that adorn the covers of the seven scores for *Catalogue d'oiseaux* are seen through the eyes of the artist, André Béguin. Just as an artist, however realistic or naturalistic, is seeking to portray their subject in a way that conveys something more than, or at least different from, a photograph, Messiaen's transcriptions are not attempting the same thing as a recording, however closely the composer tried to come to capturing the notes and timbre of each species. When he did use the objective medium of magnetic tape, in *Timbres-Durées*, Messiaen felt the need to change the sounds taken from nature beyond all recognition in an attempt to create viable music.

14. Aerial photo of the lakes at Petichet, c. 1950.

Whatever the nature of the material, there was no doubt from the first performance of *Oiseaux exotiques* on 10 March 1956 that Messiaen had succeeded in using birdsong to write a piece of music. The pianism of Loriod is still the star feature, but it is more integrated into the ensemble, which itself is much more modest, using a distinctive combination of winds with tuned and metallic percussion. More importantly, Messiaen has recaptured his knack of providing striking sounds that make the listener sit up and take notice, such as the trumpet fanfares after the longest piano cadenza or the relentless hammer-blows of the Himalayan Laughing Thrush, first heard near the beginning and repeated to devastating effect at the end. *Oiseaux exotiques* rapidly gained a place among the modest list of *avant-garde* hits.

Having established that it was possible to create a successful musical work using birdsong, Messiaen now had the bit between his teeth. He had no commissions to fulfil following the completion of *Oiseaux exotiques*, but, with his fluency rejuvenated, he carried on composing regardless, turning his attention once again to native French birds. He embarked upon a series of field trips around France, including to

15. Marcel Couraud, Messiaen, and Jeanne Loriod, after a performance of *Trois petites Liturgies*, Scuola di San Rocco, Venice, 20 September 1957.

Sologne, Provence and Brittany in 1956. These expeditions provided Messiaen with the material for a new cycle of piano pieces, the first six of which were complete by 30 March 1957, when they were performed by Yvonne Loriod.[11] Work was brought to an enforced halt not long after this trial run as Messiaen fell extremely ill in the Spring with jaundice and gallstones.[12] On his return to health, he continued with his researches, going to, amongst other places, Perpignan and Gardépée, followed in 1958 by Banyuls and a return to Perpignan. A further seven pieces were now added to the six given in March 1957, the resulting collection standing as one of his greatest masterpieces: *Catalogue d'oiseaux*.

The title, with its suggestion of some objective kind of list, is really a misnomer. The series of thirteen nature portraits that make up the *Catalogue* present the main protagonist not only in the context of other birds from the region, but also the surrounding habitat. Messiaen had

16. The glaciers of the Meije viewed from La Grave.

already drawn inspiration from the dramatic Alpine sights to the east of Grenoble and Petichet along the Romanche river. Travelling along the awesome gorge of the Infernet, with its vertical walls of rock rising hundreds of feet above the narrow mountain pass, it soon becomes clear what stirred Messiaen to write 'Les Mains de l'abîme' from *Livre d'orgue*. As a composer who loved the dramatic power that comes from juxtaposing extreme opposites, he could not fail to be roused by La Grave, just a little further upriver to the east, but about 3,000 feet higher and itself overlooked by the dazzling brilliance of the glaciers of the Meije towering a further 4,500 feet. So important was this breath-taking view to *Livre d'orgue* that a picture adorns the cover of the score (although the dull monochrome does nothing to convey the blinding light often produced by the glaciers). This spectacular topography becomes the point of departure for *Catalogue d'oiseaux*, with the opening 'Le Chocard des Alpes' (Alpine Chough). Messiaen had written music depicting the mountains and gorges, and he had written music using birdsong. The logical step was to bring the two together. As if to complete this sense of taking stock, Messiaen utilizes quasi-serial methods to depict the rocky scenery. After this he goes much, much further, with the remaining pieces of *Catalogue d'oiseaux* taking wing in every sense. Messiaen paints on to his aural canvas the landscape, the fauna, the changing light, the smells, other creatures and the colours to create a vast celebration of the variety of nature, with the birds taking pride of place.

As with any great masterpiece, *Catalogue d'oiseaux* works on many levels. Messiaen reinvents his parameters with each of these nature portraits, so that each has its own form, its own way of presenting the musical material, its own way of telling its story. And stories they are, for in *Catalogue d'oiseaux* Messiaen treats his birds, and even the plants and rocks, anthropomorphically, often imbuing them with character-istics and motifs, so that the music conveys not only what they look and sound like, but the feelings that they induce in the observer. Nowhere is this more vivid than in the fifth piece, 'La Chouette hulotte' (The Tawny Owl), where his preface likens the calls to 'the scream of a murdered child'. Elsewhere, the rugged, harsh calls of the mountain birds are infused with the characteristics of their habitat, whilst the clipped flamenco-like strutting of the 'Le Traquet stapazin' (The Black-eared Wheatear), has as much to do with its red plumage and black eye markings, which reminded Messiaen of a Spanish nobleman attending a masked ball, as its song. Nor are such sentiments restricted to the birds. The rocks depicted in 'Le Merle de roche' (The Rock Thrush) suggest to the composer's febrile imagination 'a cortège of cowled ghosts in stone, bearing the corpse of a woman whose hair trails on the ground'.[13] In other pieces Messiaen's feelings about the unfolding musical events are conveyed in a distinct *souvenir* passage. For instance, in 'Le Loriot' (The Golden Oriole), the song of the protagonist is heard much more slowly towards the end, as an idealized memory with a tender, glowing harmonization.

Lasting more than two and a half hours and posing a gargantuan challenge to the pianist in terms of both virtuosity and interpretation, Messiaen knew that complete performances of *Catalogue d'oiseaux* would be a rarity. Nonetheless, from the symmetrical arrangement of the thirteen pieces within seven books, the interrelationships between pieces or books, and the progression of the means of expression, it is clear that *Catalogue d'oiseaux* is more than just a collection of disparate nature portraits: it is a cycle. For instance, there is a broad geographical progression, starting towards the south-east of France, high in the mountainous habitat of 'Le Chocard des Alpes' and ending at the north-west tip, on the island of Ushant off the Brittany coast. Then there is the web of connections between pieces, a portion of which can be seen quite easily from the central three books. Lasting about half an hour, the single piece in Book Four, 'La Rousserolle effarvatte' (The Reed Warbler), is easily the longest of *Catalogue d'oiseaux*, forming the hub of the cycle. The time-scale is circadian, covering twenty-seven hours in the life of the marshes in the Sologne region, starting and ending at night, with the clear implication that this snapshot merely typifies the kind of activities occurring day after day. This is balanced, on the one hand, by the two nocturnal pieces that form Book Three, and, on the other, by the two light-infused portraits of Book Five. Set in the soporific stillness of a hot July day in Provence, 'L'Alouette calandrelle' (The Short-toed Lark), the motionless opening piece of Book Five, mirrors the tender caresses of 'L'Alouette lulu' (The Woodlark) in Book Three, itself an assuaging antidote to the nightmare of the preceding 'La Chouette hulotte'.

Claire's illness was an ever-present cloud, and, by the late 1950s the effects of this unceasing burden were becoming visible, as Alexander Goehr recalls:

> He looked neglected. That was before the era of the coloured shirts. He wore a blue suit and a white shirt. Always the same. We used to joke whether it was always the same one or whether he had several. I remember there was a performance of his in Donaueschingen and he said he couldn't go because he had «embêtements avec la blanchisserie» [trouble with the laundry]. It was really because he was trying to look after himself, and he couldn't. You met him in the street sometimes and he'd stare at you as one in his own world.[14]

A television interview with Messiaen, made following the première of Varèse's *Déserts* and its attendant *scandale*, is notable as much for his wild hair as his fiery discussion of the music. A man who disliked modern cities, and who stated that living in Paris killed his mother,[15] Messiaen was now finding life in the capital increasingly oppressive. Although he was forward-thinking as a composer, in his day-to-day life he shared his mother's 'horror of modern progress, of anything mechanical',[16] and his field trips to collect material for *Catalogue d'oiseaux* offered his only respite from the difficulties of life, both domestic and professional. Goehr movingly evokes the despondent mood that even pervaded Messiaen's class at the Conservatoire:

> Face to face with his sometimes obstreperous students and opinionated hangers-on, he was even reduced to tears. We sat in silence for long periods, especially after an aggressive attempt by one of us to argue with him. Here we were, before one of the most perfect musicians of our times, combative and argumentative, in tense, unbroken silence. And he would say, 'Gentlemen, let us not argue like this. We are all in a profound night, and I don't know where I am going; I'm as lost as you.'[17]

This was an extraordinary admission coming from the *Maître* who could trace a path through centuries of music history. Turning to nature had helped Messiaen find a way forward with his own music, but he was troubled by the puritanical approach being espoused by the younger generation of composers, observing that 'most musicians of the day deny inspiration, declaring it to be romantic and outmoded'.[18] More informally, he said about the summer school for new music at Darmstadt '*Ils sont tous fous*' (they're all crazy).[19]

In the context of this sea of troubles, it is possible to speculate about the subtext to some of Messiaen's compositional choices in *Catalogue d'oiseaux*. The cycle opens with a quasi-serial passage recalling the experiments of the early 1950s, which proved to be a cul de sac for Messiaen, but that soon became *de rigueur* at Darmstadt. The serialism with which cosmopolitan musical thought was obsessed became Messiaen's point of departure for his journey into nature, only to reappear in the horrific evocation of night in 'La Chouette hulotte', which is the only piece to have any of its action set close to Paris. From the harsh opening, the listener is immediately transported to the radiance of 'Le Loriot', which, as a pun on the name of the work's dedicatee, Yvonne Loriod, contains both some of the most tender and some of the most virtuosic music in the entire cycle. At the other end of *Catalogue d'oiseaux*, it is striking that the desolation permeating the final piece, 'Le Courlis cendré' (The Curlew), makes an unusual ending to a work by Messiaen. It is set on the island of Ushant, in Finistère, literally the end of the earth and a place so bleak that, in the winter, the sheep have to be tied together to prevent them being blown away. Far more in keeping with Messiaen's usual practice would be to conclude the cycle with the triumphant flourish representing 'the joy of the blue sea' that ends the penultimate piece, 'Le Traquet rieur' (The Black Wheatear). Instead, *Catalogue d'oiseaux* peters out into the silence of 'cold, black night' with a dribble of surf. The cycle ends in gloom, about as far away as it is possible to go in France both from Messiaen's beloved Dauphiné, where it began, and from Paris. Even as *Harawi* dissolves into the stars of night, Messiaen allows a quiet, assuaging cadence, but here there is nothing to lift the spirits. It is hard to escape the sense that 'Le Courlis cendré' is a coda to the escape that *Catalogue d'oiseaux* provided for Messiaen. In its final pages, the natural world is rudely interrupted by the mechanized boom of the foghorn from the lighthouse at Créac'h. It is a sign that Messiaen's period of escape has come to an end; sooner or later he must return to the city.

Yvonne Loriod gave the first complete performance of *Catalogue d'oiseaux* at the Salle Gaveau on 15 April 1959. For some years she had regularly accompanied Messiaen when he visited Claire. The two women got on well, as far as Claire's limited faculties allowed, with Loriod helping her to walk around the ward, sometimes taking her out into the garden.[20] Messiaen's closest friends knew about the extent of Claire's illness, but, generally, he preferred not to talk about it:

> For a long time, Messiaen kept these terrible things to himself, and when asked about his wife, he limited himself to vague answers about her illness, and that she had been a very fine artist before falling ill. Later, when he could no longer hide the truth, he spoke of her as a saint, owing to her long and tragic martyrdom.[21]

On 22 April 1959, seven days after the first perfomance of *Catalogue d'oiseaux*, Messiaen noted in his diary 'Mie died at 10 o'clock in the morning . . . Inform Pascal, Alliet, Marguérite and Alain'.[22] Despite, or perhaps because of, her lengthy illness, Claire's death was unexpected. After a decline spanning more than a decade and a half, she had been released from her torment. She was fifty-two years old. Her funeral took place three days later on 25 April at the church of Bourg-la-Reine and she was buried in the local cemetery.[23] By coincidence, as Antoine Goléa relates in a moving passage of *Rencontres avec Olivier Messiaen*, the composer was due to attend a rehearsal of one of the song cycles inspired by his relationship with Claire:

> Colette Herzog was due to sing *Chants de terre et de ciel* a few days later in a concert at the École Normale de Musique. She had asked Messiaen to come to a rehearsal, something he had gladly agreed to do. This rehearsal was due to take place at 4 o'clock in the afternoon. The day before, Colette Herzog – who gave me this account herself – received a telephone call from Messiaen. Full of apologies, he asked her, with exquisite courtesy, if it would be possible to change the rehearsal time to an hour later. The next day, Messiaen arrived at 5.10 p.m. and

apologized again [. . .] I was there; I had known since that morning that Claire Delbos had died forty-eight hours earlier. He had come straight from the cemetery. He didn't talk about it, of course. His face was extremely pale, but also seemed to show a sort of deep peace. He appeared tranquil and relaxed. He slightly gave the impression of arriving from another world. Having made his apologies, he began the rehearsal and worked with Colette Herzog and her pianist in the most rigorous and concentrated way for two hours [. . .] For him, the person who had just died had left the accursed earth, where she had been so ill, for the heaven which she so richly deserved.[24]

Messiaen and Mi had been married for nearly twenty-seven years. As husband and wife, pianist and violinist, both composers, they had supported and encouraged each other in their early years as professional musicians, through the disappointments and the successes, through the upset of miscarriages and the joy brought by the birth of Pascal. They experienced enforced separation early on, in the guise of national service, only for that to be a comic prelude to the more testing separations first of Messiaen's capture by the Germans, then of Claire's mental illness. Violinists will be grateful that she inspired the Thème et variations, but the song-cycle is the medium in which she most clearly acts as muse, and Poèmes pour Mi, Chants de terre et de ciel and Harawi stand as a threefold testament and celebration of Messiaen's love for Claire Delbos. With her death, he could at last move on from the intense pain and heartache of having a wife who was physically alive, but whose mind had long since ceased to function. He kept a few cherished photographs of Claire in his work desk:[25] evidence, were it needed, that he neither forgot nor lost his affection for her. Nonetheless, Messiaen would barely mention Claire, and he never composed for voice and piano again.

Notes

1. Olivier Messiaen, *Conférence de Bruxelles, prononcée à l'Exposition Internationale de Bruxelles en 1958* (Paris: Alphonse Leduc, 1960), p. 14.

2. Samuel, *Music and Color*, p. 33.
3. Massin, *Une poétique du merveilleux*, p. 24.
4. Messiaen, *Technique*, p. 34 (single vol. edn, p. 38).
5. Rischin, *For the End of Time*, pp. 10–11.
6. Samuel, *Music and Color*, p. 91.
7. ibid, p. 131.
8. J. Cocteau, *Oeuvres complètes IX* (Genève: Editions Marguerat, 1950), p. 16.
9. Peter Hill, private communication.
10. PHNS, p. 209.
11. Hill, 'Messiaen in the 1950s'.
12. ibid.
13. Preface to the score.
14. Goehr, unpublished interview.
15. Massin, *Une poétique du merveilleux*, p. 52.
16. Pierre Messiaen, *Images*, p. 144.
17. Goehr, *Finding the Key*, p. 56.
18. Messiaen, *Conférence de Bruxelles*, p. 11.
19. Goehr, unpublished interview.
20. PHNS.
21. Goléa, *Rencontres*, pp. 151–2.
22. Hill, 'Messiaen in the 1950s'. 'Mi' and 'Mie' were used as interchangeable spellings by Messiaen. Alliet was Messiaen's dentist, and a family friend.
23. Hill, 'Messiaen in the 1950s'.
24. Goléa, *Rencontres*, pp. 151–2.
25. Nigel Simeone, private communication.

7 The statue remains on its pedestal 1960–9

> I wanted to renew the tradition, but also to prove that the Latin texts
> are very beautiful and that their unintelligibility adds to their
> mystery. The statue remains on its pedestal.[1]

It is tempting to regard Messiaen's life after Claire passed away as
being, if not easy, then blissfully devoid of major upset or trauma,
either artistically or domestically. The central drama of his life, Claire's
long debilitating illness, was over. The three remaining decades saw
Messiaen gaining ever wider international recognition and acceptance
as one of the major figures of the twentieth century, bestowed with
honours and composing a series of valedictory triumphs of ever
greater proportions. As a broad narrative this is not wildly inaccurate,
but no life is so lacking in nuance, and Messiaen is no exception. These
years were not without their personal trials and tribulations. For all
that the masterpieces of his maturity seem to have the immutability of
a mountain range, an impression cultivated by the composer, their
creation was often beset by delays, doubts and second thoughts.

Inevitably, there is a sense of the shackles being broken following
the death of Claire. After the unusually desolate conclusion to *Catalogue
d'oiseaux*, Messiaen's next work, *Chronochromie*, was a phenomenally
bold assertion of his credentials as a radical exponent of progressive
musical thought, the godfather of the avant-garde, with his biggest
orchestral canvas since *Turangalîla*. As was inevitable by now, sounds

depicting the natural world, including not only birdsong but also evocations of rock formations and an extraordinary transcription of an alpine torrent, are very much to the fore. Messiaen's working title, 'Postlude',[2] implies that his original intention may have been to produce a boisterous epilogue to *Catalogue d'oiseaux*. If this was the plan, he quickly changed his mind, for *Chronochromie* presents the natural world in an entirely different way, as an abstract collage of 'found' objects, rather than painting a specific scene. Moreover, rhythmic machinations form the backbone of *Chronochromie* to an extent not seen since the revolutionary experiments of the *Études de rythme*, *Messe de la Pentecôte* and *Livre d'orgue*. The work is divided into seven sections, formed around the ancient Greek literary idea of related strophe and antistrophe sections (Messiaen incorporates two of each), a contrasting 'Épode' with the whole being framed by a forthright Introduction and Coda. Anyone expecting the big tunes and juicy harmony of *Turangalîla* was in for a shock. Each of the two movements in *Chronochromie* entitled 'Strophe' has a band of permutating rhythms and chords forming a continuously changing web of sounding-colours over which sings a flock of assorted birds. In fact, these movements mark a massive expansion into orchestral terms of the basic idea, though not the techniques, underpinning 'Liturgie de cristal' (*Quartet for the end of Time*) and 'Soixante-quatre durées' (*Livre d'orgue*). In each case there are two distinct strata; on the one hand, a tightly organized, mechanized, mysterious, dazzling band of coloured rhythm, and, on the other, the freedom of birdsong.

Each of the first performances of *Chronochromie* caused uproar; at Donaueschingen on 16 October 1960 and at the French première on 13 September 1961 as part of the Besançon festival, audiences were audibly divided. The first performance in Paris, on 13 February 1962 at the Théâtre des Champs-Elysées, caused a full-scale *scandale* on a par with the infamous opening night of *Le Sacre du printemps*. Messiaen later recalled that 'there were only enemies in the audience. At the end of the work, everyone took to booing, and when I rose to greet the conductor, Antal Dorati, a furious listener leaned out of his box and I had to stoop to avoid – narrowly – a knuckle-blow to the head'.[3] The boldness of the gestures and quickfire pace of the unusual new sounds produced by rhythmic permutations undoubtedly contributed to the growing fury of some. However, Messiaen's rhythm-games are noticeable by their absence from the movement that provoked the greatest protests, the 'Épode'. This could be regarded as Messiaen's most extreme orchestral aviary, for it consists of nothing more than violins, violas and cellos, each with its own line of birdsong. For many, this assault on the traditional homogeneity of the string section was the final straw.

Not that the protests of city-dwellers were going to dampen Messiaen's enthusiasm. On one birdwatching trip to the Île de Rouzic in April 1960, when he was in the midst of work on *Chronochromie*, he literally risked life and limb to record the sights and sounds of the numerous seabirds. His *cahier* became spattered with a mixture of blood and seawater when he slipped on the rocks, gashing his leg.[4] Undeterred, he continued to make his notations until he realized that the light was fading and, even more alarming, noticed that the tide had come in, covering the beach where his boat had landed. Disoriented in the gloaming, Messiaen followed the cries of the birds. Finally, he heard the shouts of the anxious boatman, who had raised the alarm, and saw the lights of countless launches heading towards the island. The two men returned to the mainland to find Loriod and the boatman's wife distraught and in tears.[5]

During the Spring of 1961, Messiaen and Loriod undertook a more sedate trip, spending three weeks after Easter travelling from the Dordogne to Provence. Upon returning to Paris, their thoughts finally turned to marriage.[6] When Claire died in 1959 Loriod had been in Karlsruhe, returning to Paris on 25 April to find a pale-faced Messiaen waiting for her at the Gare de l'Est: 'Something terrible has happened: Claire has died, on Wednesday; I've just come from the burial.' He went on to make a heartfelt plea: 'You must not leave me now, you who are young and so full of life.'[7] Two years to the day after Claire's funeral, Messiaen and Loriod finally made the decision to get married. After circumstance had kept them apart for so long, it might be thought that they would have a lavish wedding. Nothing could be further from the truth. The religious ceremony on 3 July 1961 was not at the Trinité, but Sainte-Geneviève-des-Grandes-Carrières, close to Loriod's apartment on the rue Marcadet.[8] In addition to the couple themselves, only nine people attended; the priest Abbé Aubin, Loriod's parents and two sisters, Pascal and Josette, the composer (and former student) Jacques Charpentier and his wife Danièle. Like an episode in the life of Saint Francis, the service was gate-crashed by a tenth guest, a nightingale, whose rousing song ensured that the event was not entirely bereft of music.[9]

Despite this ornithological blessing, Messiaen and Loriod decided to keep the marriage secret for the time being. This was not difficult for they continued to live apart until early 1964. Neither Loriod's apartment on the rue Marcadet, nor Messiaen's house on the villa du Danube was large enough for both of their needs; a problem that was eventually solved by buying additional apartments adjacent to Loriod's. Extensive complications also surrounded Claire's estate, preventing Messiaen selling up, severely restricting his finances and, inevitably, generating substantial legal fees. These remained unsettled until April 1964. Nevertheless, such practicalities do not explain concealing the marriage. Two years was hardly an indecent scramble, and demonstrated due respect to Claire. However, it seems that the couple, whose relationship had been the catalyst for much speculative gossip, felt, in all innocence, that more time was needed in order to avoid unseemly rumour. Years later, Messiaen was still muddying the water by saying of his first tour to Japan 'Yvonne and I had just married, and in a way it was our honeymoon'.[10] In fact, although Mrs Fumi Yamaguchi, the organizer of the trip, visited Paris in June 1961 to discuss arrangements with Messiaen,[11] this 'honeymoon' did not take place until a year later.

Japan made a big impression on Messiaen and Loriod, to the extent that for sometime afterwards they 'thought only of sleeping on a tatami and eating sukiyaki and tempura'.[12] As someone long attracted to the Orient from afar, Messiaen was captivated by the sights and sounds of Japan; the landscape, the birds, traditional Japanese music,

17. Messiaen's Paris home from the early 1960s until his death, rue Marcadet, Paris 18ᵉ.

and the culture. Moreover, after the hostility and insults that his music had attracted since the war, culminating in the furious scenes at early performances of *Chronochromie*, Messiaen could not be other than overwhelmed by the enthusiasm and respect shown to him in Japan. From their arrival into Tokyo on 20 June 1962 to their departure on

24 July, the Messiaens were treated as celebrities, with virtually their every move being filmed by Japanese television and a tremendous welcome wherever they went. Moreover, Mrs Yamaguchi ensured that, as well as the numerous concerts, interviews and receptions, their schedule included opportunities for sightseeing and, most importantly, time to go and listen to the local birds.[13] The trip to Japan also bore musical fruit once the Messiaens finally got to Petichet in mid-August, having been busy at the Aspen festival and given concerts in Montreal in the meantime. Composing at great speed, Messiaen produced a series of musical postcards of Japan, grouping them as *Sept Haïkaï*. The longest movement, 'Les Oiseaux de Karuizawa', resulted from three days spent early in the trip on the nature reserve at Karuizawa, where Messiaen was assisted by two former students, Sadao Bekku as interpreter and Mitsuaki Hayama spraying the innumerable mosquitoes with insecticide.[14] Birdsong collected during a visit to Mount Fuji became the third movement's 'Yamanaka-Cadenza'; the second movement depicts the park at Nara; a boat trip to Miyajima, passing the large red *torii* in the sea is the subject of the fifth movement; and at the centre is a depiction of the acidic sounds of Gagaku.[15] If the sounds and the sights come from Japan, they are heard through the prism of Messiaen's creative personality: 'The *Haïkaï* are performed in Japan, but I don't know if they like the *Haïkaï* especially, because when they're asked if it's Japanese, they say, "it's Japan seen by Messiaen".'[16] Nonetheless, right from his earliest works, the silences in Messiaen's music have little to do with the usual western connotations of absence. Rather, Messiaen's silences would be recognizable to Japanese musicians as 'Ma', what Takemitsu has described as a 'living presence' in the music which is as important to the whole as the notes being played.

The most poignant part of the Japanese trip, a visit to Hiroshima, was not included in *Sept Haïkaï*. The Messiaens were met at the station by a choir of girls singing French folk-songs. Respects were paid at the memorial to the dead before visiting the church, in which, as Fr. Ernest Goossens their host, explained, everything was a donation from somewhere in the world. Their recital was enthusiastically received and, on their departure, the girls' choir sang again, chasing after the train.[17]

Back in France, Messiaen had a comical run-in with the taxman. In April 1962, he had been featured in *Paris-Match*: another example of his growing celebrity. The photographer had the idea of borrowing some paintings by Robert Delaunay, the artist that Messiaen preferred 'over all others',[18] from Sonia Delaunay and displaying them in the composer's house as a backdrop to some of the photographs. Messiaen's tax inspector, a kind man by nature, saw the article and telephoned the composer to ask why he had not declared these admirable pictures.[19] The cause of Messiaen's enthusiasm for Delaunay's pictures is not difficult to fathom. To start with, despite being on the cusp of abstract painting, his titles are often evocative; with pictures such as *Rythme – Joie de vivre* (see front cover illustration), they could have been chosen specifically with Messiaen in mind. The composer recalled that 'Delaunay appealed to me because he worked more with colour than with line',[20] and the arresting juxtapositions in his canvases can be regarded as a visual equivalent to the aural impact of much of Messiaen's music.

Such observations tell only part of the story, though, for the composer went further, stating that Delaunay is 'very close to what I see when I hear music'. Colour had featured in Messiaen's descriptions of his music for many years. In the preface to the *Quatuor pour la fin du Temps*, for instance, he spoke of the piano's 'cascades of sweet orange-blue chords', the score of *Catalogue d'oiseaux* is littered with kaleidoscopic descriptions of plumage, sunrises or sunsets, and the idea of musical colour is inherent in the title of *Chronochromie*. Messiaen now went a step further, beginning to talk about what he saw when he heard music; not just poetic allegory or descriptions of scenery, but the specific colours produced by specific chords in his mind's eye. Whether or not he had synaesthesia, the medical condition where two senses become entwined, so that one might see smells, is difficult to ascertain. It is a poorly understood phenomenon, and few synaesthetes (or doctors) have the composer's musical sensitivity. Messiaen said on some occasions that he did, but in later life insisted that he was not synaesthetic. What can be said with confidence is that he thought that colour was tremendously important, and that for Messiaen the word related to a panoply of specific identifiable sound-colour relationships rather than being the vague shorthand used to describe any music with timbral variety:

> Each sound-complex has a well-defined colour. This colour can be reproduced in any octave, but will be normal in mid-range, diffused towards white (that is, lighter) rising to a higher register, and toned down by black (that is, darker) when descending to a lower register. By contrast, if we transpose our chord semitone by semitone, it will change colour at each semitone. Take, for example, a sound-complex which gives a group of colours: ash, pale green, mauve [. . .] transpose one semitone higher, it will become emerald green, amethyst violet and pale blue. If we transpose it up another semitone, it will give oblique bands of red and white, on a pink background with black patterns.[21]

Related to Messiaen's sensitivity to colour is the increasing extent to which each piece is defined by its orchestration and its form. There is no set ensemble and no prescribed instrumentation for the music of his maturity, and it is a rarity to find two works with the same number of movements. Now, in *Couleurs de la Cité céleste*, Messiaen began marking the colours of some chords in the score, not as a description of something else, but as a characteristic of that particular sonority. As he later explained, 'the brass should, if I dare say, "play red"; the woodwinds should "play blue", and so on'.[22] Messiaen believed passionately that this relationship between sound and colour was one that could be seen and heard by everyone. However, there was an additional benefit, for by referring to chords in terms of colours, Messiaen put all harmonies, from common triads to twelve-note complexes, on to an even footing that made their common musical labels redundant. He was thus able to side-step the entire dogmatic debate of the time about what was and was not appropriate material for a composer; he was composing neither tonally, nor atonally, nor modally, but using different areas of colour. Music and colour had been entwined for Messiaen throughout his life, but, from this point on, colour joined rhythm and birdsong as a recurrent theme of lectures, speeches and interviews, attracting both bemusement and amusement. Nonetheless, his emphasis on the timbral aspects of music was profoundly influential on the new generation of composers in the 1970s, such as Grisey and Murail, who became known as 'Spectralists'.

In addition to marking the beginning of Messiaen's active proselytising about the 'sound-colour relationship', *Couleurs de la Cité céleste* is also the work in which, for the first time since the furore surrounding *Vingt Regards* and *Trois petites Liturgies*, his faith returned to the concert hall. The last three decades of his life are dominated by religious monuments, including his *magnum opus*, *Saint François d'Assise*, his largest choral work, *La Transfiguration*, and two orchestral works lasting more than an hour, *Des canyons aux étoiles* … and *Éclairs sur l'au-delà* … .. It is remarkable, therefore, to think that if he had died in

18. Pierre Boulez, Messiaen and Yvonne Loriod during the recording of *Couleurs de la Cité céleste* for Erato, Notre-Dame du Libon, January 1966.

1962 Messiaen's name would not necessarily have been synonymous with religious works, having produced nothing outside the more private world of the organ loft for nearly twenty years. He would have argued, and did argue that, since God is in everything, all of his music was about God. However, if all of his works are religious, some of them are more explicitly religious than others, and it is the absence of the latter which is significant in this period. It would be too simplistic to attribute this silence to a single cause. Rather, a combination of factors appears to have sapped Messiaen's capacity for faith-based works. It would have been remarkable if the vitriolic criticisms during *le cas Messiaen* did not cause Messiaen to reflect upon the best approach to expressing his faith in music, just as the complaints of 'elderly ladies' during the early years of his tenure at the Trinité caused soul-searching about how best to reconcile serving the parish community with his artistic instincts and integrity. Furthermore, Stephen Broad has recently drawn attention to the vigorous post-war aesthetic debate within the Catholic Church, culminating in the early 1950s with condemnations from the Vatican of the 'so-called modern movement' and the denunciation by Pope Pius XII of 'works which astonishingly deform art and yet pretend to be Christian'.[23] Messiaen may also have had difficulty at first in seeing how birdsong could have a significant role in a religious work. Finally, Claire's illness, with all that it brought, must also have played its part: directly in terms of the type of work Messiaen felt capable of composing, and indirectly with domestic disruption making large-scale planning very difficult.

By the time that he began work on *Couleurs* in 1963, the experience of *Chronochromie* had demonstrated his music's capacity for generating controversy regardless of its subject matter. *Chronochromie* had also enabled Messiaen to give a prominent role to birdsong in a work that was not exclusively *about* birds. It is hard, also, to resist the conclusion that, following his marriage to Loriod, Messiaen had regained much-needed domestic stability, thus enabling his faith to return centre-stage in his music. If such a sentiment crossed his mind Messiaen may have felt that he had tempted fate. July 1963 saw him making plans for a full summer of composition, including packing 'the new chords discovered for Haïkaï'.[24] On 18 July, shortly before they were due to depart for Petichet, Loriod fell critically ill and was admitted to hospital, receiving two blood transfusions. A week later she had a hysterectomy. Any chance of the couple having children had gone, and five days later Messiaen must have feared that he would lose Loriod as well, for on 30 July she suffered an embolism.[25]

Against this anxious background, he began to compose *Couleurs*. The inspiration came from chapter 21 of Revelation, with its descriptions of the city wall, the foundations of which 'were garnished with all manner of precious stones'. Messiaen had made a note in his diary to write a work on the 'wall of many colours' in September 1960, when he was completing *Chronochromie*.[26] He was himself a collector of precious stones, but *Couleurs* also has a clear musical ancestor in Dukas's *Ariane et Barbe-bleu*. In particular, Messiaen repeatedly expressed his admiration for: 'the amazing scene of the gemstones ... Each stream of gemstones is represented by a variation in Ariane's theme, in a particular orchestration and tonality. Thus Dukas was able to link orchestration and tonality to the colour of the stones ...'[27] The birds make their, by now obligatory, appearance in *Couleurs*, with species from several southern hemisphere countries such as New Zealand, Brazil, Venezuela and Argentina making appearances. Whilst most of these had to be notated, like many of the species in *Oiseaux exotiques*, from recordings or seeing the birds in zoos or bird markets, the Argentinian birds were transcribed during a teaching and concert tour to Buenos Aires made in June 1963. As well as God's musicians, *Couleurs* also includes the music of the Church in the form of plainchant. Heard through Messiaen's apocalyptic prism, the four Alleluias used in *Couleurs* could not be further removed in spirit from the common misperception of plainchant as music sung by mournful monks. They appear as mighty chorales on the winds, or form vibrant, clanging processionals on metallic percussion, the effect, as the composer himself suggested in the preface to the score, being akin to 'a rose window of dazzling and invisible colours'.

In the Autumn of 1963 Messiaen received his most prestigious commission to date; a request from André Malraux, the Minister of Culture, for a work to commemorate the dead of the two World Wars. Typically, rather than a War Requiem, Messiaen produced a work concentrating upon resurrection, taking its title, in Latin, from the end of the Nicene Creed: *Et exspecto resurrectionem mortuorum* (And I await the resurrection of the dead). Written for an ensemble of winds and percussion, with lower brass dominating, *Et exspecto* begins with a 'De profundis', the cry from the depths of Psalm 130, but rapidly turns its attention to the after-life. The five movements of the work are hewn from the same rock as *Couleurs*, but the effect is, if anything, even more imposing. *Et exspecto* was composed with the resonant acoustics of cathedrals in mind, and Messiaen also expressed a desire to hear it 'in the high mountains at La Grave, facing the Meije glacier, in those powerful and solemn landscapes that are my true homeland'.[28] Unusually for a mature work, it features just two birds, the Calandra Lark and the Amazonian Uirapuru. The latter is a prime example of the composer transforming local folklore into a Christian symbol. By tradition the Uirapuru is heard at the moment of death (though Messiaen managed to notate it without mishap), so in *Et exspecto* it represents 'an inner voice – Christ's – waking the dead from their sleep and giving the signal for imminent resurrection'.[29] *Et exspecto* concentrates upon the qualities of individual chords, notes and sounds, displaying an organist's ear for the musical space needed when operating in a large acoustic. From the initial cavernous notes of the contrabassoon and saxhorn, via the dramatic moments focusing on the sonorities of the gongs and tamtams, to the relentless strides of the great multitude of the resurrected, the gestures are simple, powerful and devastatingly effective.

   Et exspecto was first heard in a semi-private performance on Friday 7 May 1965 before an invited audience in a prestigious venue of Messiaen's choosing: 'Malraux, who had commissioned the work, said to me "Messiaen, where do you want the first performance?". I replied, "In the Sainte-Chapelle, Minister" because I wanted to have the sun shining through the windows at eleven in the morning, with gold and blue, and red and violet reflections shining on the instruments and the audience. And I got it!'[30] The first fully public airing, on 20 June, the feast of Corpus Christi, was bathed in light from another famous set of stained glass windows, on this occasion those of Chartres Cathedral. The performance, attended by President de Gaulle, followed the celebration of Mass. The orchestra, under Serge Baudo, was placed in the chancel, and every corner of the cathedral was packed. In the score, Messiaen is also glowing in his praise for a third performance, 'in these concerts of the Domaine Musical created by Pierre Boulez, where one hears the most beautiful performances of contemporary music from France and the world'. Messiaen's one-time student was rapidly becoming one of his most valued interpreters.

Like *Et exspecto*, Messiaen's next project was very much a work of the mountains: 'It was in clear weather, while looking at Mont Blanc, the Jungfrau and the three glaciers of the Meije in Oisans, that I understood the difference between the small splendour of snow and the great splendour of the sun – that is also where I could imagine the extent to which the site of the Transfiguration was awesome.'[31] The end of his 1961 diary mentions a 'work for chorus and orchestra on the Transfiguration',[32] but the composer later recalled that he had been considering a work on the subject for 'perhaps twenty years, ever since the day when I heard, in a little country church in the Dauphiné, in Motte-d'Aveillans, an old priest deliver a sermon on light and filiation'.[33] The resulting fourteen-movement oratorio, *La Transfiguration de Notre-Seigneur Jésus-Christ*, became Messiaen's most ambitious project to date, occupying his thoughts throughout the latter half of the 1960s.

Unusually, there is a substantive set of documents and correspondence revealing significant details of the work's genesis.[34] It was commissioned in June 1965 by Mme Maria Madalena de Azeredo Perdigão on behalf of the Calouste Gulbenkian Foundation, Lisbon, to mark the tenth anniversary in the following year of the death of its founder. Messiaen agreed to write a 45-minute work: 'for five soloists, large orchestra and mixed chorus . . . the choir will vocalize without words'.

Messiaen then spent the summer of 1965 hard at work following a nine-movement plan for the piece.[35] Given that the completed oratorio has a monumental demeanour and certitude that gives every impression of having appeared, fully formed in tablets of stone, the differences between Messiaen's original conception and the finished work are remarkable: the former having two fewer instrumental soloists, five fewer movements, a time-scale of about half the eventual length and, crucially, no text for the chorus. The latter reflected Messiaen's desire to avoid having to write: 'a poem in French, translating it into Portuguese, adapting the translation to the accents of the music, etc., etc'.[36] In a letter sent on 18 June Mme Perdigão proposed a solution that neatly circumvented such difficulties: a Latin text.[37] However unwittingly, it seems that she, to borrow a phrase that Messiaen used about his role with his students, revealed the composer to himself. Messiaen took up the idea with enthusiasm, for in addition to the linguistic practicality of Latin, the language was totemic of the transformation occurring at this time in the Catholic Church.

By the mid-1960s, Messiaen's faith had endured throughout many trying episodes. In marked contrast to the sharp vacillations in artistic or political thought, the teachings of the Catholic Church gave Messiaen a constant, immutable bedrock which provided the foundation for his entire philosophy. His faith had been tested at a relatively early age by the loss of his mother, and it had shown no sign of wavering while he was a prisoner of war. Messiaen had been confronted with the difficulties posed by Church teaching during Claire's illness. Now his faith produced another challenge. On this occasion, though, the questions came from the Church itself through the radical re-evaluation initiated by the Second Vatican Council.

The first documents of Vatican II were promulgated on 4 December 1963 and made profound liturgical reforms, with the active participation of the congregation being encouraged wherever possible, and the introduction of the vernacular into services. In addition to providing the catalyst for an unexpected reassessment of his faith, Vatican II had a profound impact on Messiaen's musical life, particularly his duties at the Trinité. A side-effect of using native languages in services was that, if not sounding the death-knell, it effectively downgraded plainchant. As well as drawing the attention of many young composers to this rich source of material, Messiaen regarded plainchant as the only true liturgical music; a music, moreover, that he believed should be sung in Latin. Messiaen's predilection for Latin was underpinned by aesthetic and esoteric reasons. Like Stravinsky, he felt that there were benefits in using a 'dead' language for devotional purposes: 'I'm in favour of Latin. Not because I like it especially, but because I think that Latin puts a certain distance between the listener and the person pronouncing the words. It puts them on another level, on the level they ought to be on – that is, the spiritual level.'[38]

For some, the adjustment in thinking required by Vatican II was too much. Langlais, initially supportive, soon turned his back on the reforms.[39] For Messiaen, the idea of abandoning his duties or of challenging the wisdom of the Church was anathema. There is no suggestion that he was against Vatican II, if such a simple position were possible for such a complex process. In the same breath as he praised Latin, he went on to observe that 'the fact that the vernacular has been adopted is a very very good thing [...] because it allowed many people who had never read the Bible to hear texts of which they were previously unaware'.[40] However, there is a sense in *La Transfiguration* of Messiaen making a discreet statement of concern about what might be lost to the Church amidst the evident gains. As such, it can be thought of as Messiaen's reaction to (rather than against) the challenge of Vatican II.

La Transfiguration is a vast liturgy for the concert hall which determinedly cultivates the mysterious and transcendent at every level. The fourteen movements of the finished work are divided into two groups of seven, or septenaries. The first dwells upon the theme of light, the physical aspect of the transfiguration story. The second septenary, which is twice as long despite having the same superficial structure, is concerned with the theological concepts of filiation and affiliation, the kinship of Jesus to the Father and, by extension, all humanity. The text (drawing not only upon Scripture and the missal, but also the writings of Saint Thomas Aquinas), the language and, of course, the music, are all put at the service not of explaining, but of actively meditating upon this most symbolic of episodes in the New Testament. Messiaen's efforts to ensure that every word of the text is audible, despite the fact that they use a language which he chose for its very unintelligibility, typifies the transcendent approach of *La Transfiguration*.

In musical terms, this gigantic oratorio is a reconciliation of past and present. Messiaen's response, when faced in the late 1940s with a combination of personal trauma and artistic pressure, had been negative, in that he rejected many key elements of his musical language. Anyone listening blind to *Trois petites Liturgies*, *Mode de valeurs et d'intensités* and *Réveil des oiseaux* could be easily forgiven for not recognizing that they are by a single composer, let alone that they were written within the space of ten years. On encountering changes in the 1960s to liturgical traditions which he thought were immutable, Messiaen resurrected the elements that had been rejected from his music. Crucially, this was not at the expense of the developments made in the interim, for the divergent styles found in Messiaen's music before and after 1949 are brought together in *La Transfiguration* to form an omnifarious whole, thus initiating the stylistic inclusivity of his later years. The oratorio commands a very large stage indeed, for the entirety of (Messiaen's) creation is marshalled in praising the glory of God: allusions to plainchant follow ritualistic tolling of bells, cello melodies nestle alongside enormous chorales, aviaries of birds sing above abstruse rhythmic procedures, and intricate chords dissolve to reveal major triads. As such, what became a ninety-minute oratorio for seven instrumental soloists, 'très grand' choir and orchestra is the first of Messiaen's monumental acts of homage in which he draws upon the entirety of his, by now substantial, compositional resources, the full palette of musical colours.

As Messiaen himself acknowledged, the formal scheme of *La Transfiguration*, with its sequences of Gospel recitation, meditative movements and chorales, is redolent of Bach's Passion settings. Parallels are also clear in the cantatas, notably the first that Bach wrote for Leipzig, *Die Elenden sollen essen*, BWV 75. Like *La Transfiguration*, it has fourteen (a special number for Bach) movements presented in two groups of seven, the two parts exploring different theological perspectives raised by the Gospel text. Not that his approach to the structural organization of the oratorio is the only way in which Messiaen inherited the great Lutheran's mantle. In cantata movements such as 'Du sollst Gott, deinen Herren, lieben', the opening chorus of BWV 77, Bach set himself apart from his contemporaries by imbuing every aspect of the music, from the use of canon (a metaphor for the law) to the ten-fold entry of the trumpet reflecting the ten commandments, with a theological symbolism. Similarly, it is possible to see in each of Messiaen's religious works how the music is governed at multiple levels by the subject matter, often in ways that are only apparent from a close examination of the score. *La Transfiguration* is, in many ways, the supreme example of this theologically symbolic compositional approach, from the choice of particular birds via the pervasive influence of the numbers three and seven, to the use of particular modes and rhythmic devices in a manner directly analogous to Bach. Nowhere is the primacy of the theology more apparent than in the end of the work. The thirteenth movement 'Tota Trinitas apparuit', provides the climactic peroration of the entire oratorio with the presentation of nothing less than the Trinity on the blazing consonance of E major. This is really the conclusion of *La Transfiguration*, an impression confirmed by Messiaen's original nine-movement scheme. However, the concept of an 'end' becomes immaterial in view of the eternal nature of its subject matter. More than a mere coda, the 'Choral de la Lumière de Gloire' recreates the overwhelming E major climax of 'Tota Trinitas apparuit'. In doing so, Messiaen seems to fly in the face of musical 'common sense', with the effect being akin to Beethoven adding a movement to his fifth symphony. However, this is a transcendent work. We are beyond the restrictions of reason and are now in eternity, where the rules about such repetition cease to apply.

In 1965, this was still a long way off. The summer was clearly productive, for Messiaen felt able to write to Mme Perdigão on 31 October to say that he had composed eight of the work's projected nine movements. Despite this, concerns were beginning to emerge about meeting the tight deadline, as he had yet to begin the orchestration and he was now in the midst of the new term at the Conservatoire and also had concerts looming in Liège, Brussels, Dijon and Metz. Nonetheless, Messiaen was confident enough of finishing the work by mid-April that he even told Mme Perdigão that she could announce the title.[41] After endless snags, a conductor, Manuel Rosenthal, and the orchestra of the ORTF[42] were lined up for the première on 5 June and Philips arranged to record the work; even the hard-to-pin-down Mstislav Rostropovich agreed to be the cello soloist. Mme Perdigão confirmed the arrangements in a letter to Messiaen on 7 February 1966: 'All this had been difficult to arrange, but at last all is done'.[43] Her confidence was misplaced. In a phone call with Messiaen on 14 March she learned that there were problems with both the orchestra and Rosenthal, the latter threatening to withdraw unless he could have more rehearsal time. However, this was the least of her concerns, for Messiaen also informed her that he was not going to finish the work in time. Like all composers, some of Messiaen's works had been completed within a whisker of rehearsals starting. This time, though, he had completely miscalculated; it is only possible to guess at the mounting anxiety, guilt and embarrassment during the course of the winter in the mind of the normally methodical and reliable composer. Having broken the unpleasant news to the redoubtable Mme Perdigão, he set himself to ride out the storm. In response to a strongly worded letter from the understandably 'dismayed' Mme Perdigão reiterating the arrangements and commitments entered into by all parties, Messiaen sent a spirited defence on 19 March of what had become his firm decision to pull out:

When Serge Koussevitzky commissioned my *Turangalîla-Symphonie* he gave me six years: two for researching, two for composing and two for orchestration. For a work which is just as massive, you have given me nine months. . . . It would have been a tour de force to have completed even half the work under these circumstances. I should explain to you that I have made a first sketch, with music and Latin words, which in many places consists of just the melodic line alone. To go more quickly, I am putting to one side my search for counterpoint, harmonies, orchestral timbres. Between October and December I have written the music for the ninth movement, and when I wanted to undertake the orchestration, I had to start with all these little scraps which consist of just a melodic line. In part they are finished, but since most of the music has yet to be orchestrated, I would only be able to deliver a representative fragment. Moreover, in the course of my work I have discovered a formal imbalance: the piece lacks a development at the centre and a true finale. There are two pieces to add for which I have written no music at all yet.[44]

Leaving aside Messiaen's wilful amnesia about having agreed to the nine-month timescale, this extraordinary letter puts a completely different perspective on his confident proclamation at the end of October 1965 that he had finished the music for eight of the movements. Most fascinating, though, is the admission of a problem with the structure of the work. Messiaen's doubts about the 'formal imbalance' seem to have emerged once he had completed the ninth movement in December, for in a letter dated 17 January 1966 he told Jacques-Bernard Dupont, Director General of the ORTF, that: 'The work needs to last a minimum of $1^1/_2$ hours, so I've asked for a delay of three years for the composition and the orchestration.'[45] No doubt weighing up various options in the meantime, it is not especially surprising that Messiaen refrained from telling the formidable Mme Perdigão of his concerns for two months.

In 1966, the same year that he so spectacularly failed to deliver *La Transfiguration*, Messiaen was finally appointed Professor of Composition at the Paris Conservatoire. It was two decades after Boulez had launched his ill-fated petition in favour of his *maître*. In reality, the position made relatively little difference to his basic approach to teaching, for his class always centred on the analysis at the piano of music ranging from plainchant to the most recent music. Being an official composition class simply meant that Messiaen included the works of his students within his teaching time. Before this, students would occasionally wait after the class to ask for his comments on one of their works. What comes across from the testimonies of numerous students is the humility with which Messiaen approached his task. Alexander Goehr recalled: 'I showed him this orchestral piece, which was performed at Darmstadt, and he read it. He was very good. He read terribly well and he immediately put his finger on this, that or the other. But I remember at the end he apologized, saying "Excuse me, I am an older man. I can't write this sort of music".'[46] This may simply reflect Messiaen's state of mind when Goehr was a student in the mid-1950s, but the self-effacement was typical of his approach throughout his teaching career:

> My role, apart from the daily musical analyses, was to step aside, to forget what I liked myself to try to discover what they would like and to help them find their own voice. So, with each pupil I used to 'change my jacket' and I tried to become the pupil to see what we must do – what was bad, what was good for him – exactly like being a confessor or a doctor.[47]

Some indication of Messiaen's style as a teacher can be found in the posthumously published *Traité de Rythme, de Couleur et d'Ornithologie*. Initially conceived in 1949 as a treatise on rhythm, it grew to encompass the composer's thoughts on colour, birdsong, plainchant, Debussy and many other favoured areas for discussion in his class at the Conservatoire. Given the substantial proportions of so many of his musical works, it will come as no surprise that, as books by composers go, the *Traité* is a heavyweight in the most literal sense quite apart from the content. In contrast to his earlier, much, much smaller treatise *Technique de mon langage musical*, the two volumes of which ran to a mere 128 pages, the seven *Tomes* of Messiaen's *Traité* total 3,289 pages or $9^3/_4$ inches of shelf space. As a composer Messiaen was always good at openings. It is necessary only to think of the string onslaught that begins the *Turangalîla-Symphonie*, the initial horn glissando of *Oiseaux exotiques*, or the descending gongs that introduce the 'Récit Évangélique' movements of *La Transfiguration* to realize that he thought very carefully about the start of his musical works. It comes as no surprise, then, to find that he is equally adroit at grabbing attention when wearing his pedagogical hat. Thus, the *Tome* of the *Traité* dedicated to birdsong begins with the dinosaurs, and *Tome VII*, which examines harmony and colour, begins with H. G. Wells's *Invisible Man*.

Despite the often revelatory insights that he had into the works of other composers, and although he was quite happy to discuss at great length the compositional techniques that he employed, Messiaen was unable or unwilling to answer questions regarding compositional decisions in his own music; why a phrase should be in a particular place, or why a rest should be a specific length; the process of taking the techniques and turning them into individual pieces of music. According to Goehr: 'Once or twice, when I dared ask him such questions, he would just look at you with complete blankness, as if you didn't exist. Just look straight through you as if he hadn't heard what you had said.'[48] Messiaen's strength as a teacher came from an openness to new modes of thought allied to his phenomenal memory. The etymology of a chord in Debussy might be traced in a path encompassing Monteverdi, Mozart and Musorgsky before observing its descendants in Stravinsky, Boulez and Murail, all illustrated as they occurred to him by examples played by Messiaen at the piano. Perhaps his greatest asset was his refusal to become jaded: the fresh-faced eagerness both to discover new experiences and to look anew upon the familiar that is the mark of a great pedagogue.

By the end of 1966, a new arrangement had been agreed for *La Transfiguration*, with the work now being scheduled for 1969, the centenary of Calouste Gulbenkian's birth. Having briefly existed in a twelve-movement version,[49] the oratorio now resembled its final form, with fourteen movements arranged into two 'septenaries', although with six rather than the eventual seven instrumental soloists. It was not until the following summer that Messiaen could devote serious time to the work. A remarkable diary entry at the end of June 1967 confirms that, by this time, orchestration was becoming a more integral part of the compositional process, frequently adding to and modifying Messiaen's original ideas:

> In T[ransfiguration], especially in 'Terribilis' and in the third and fourth 'Récit Evangélique', use *speeds* ('allures'): undulations with differing rhythms, faster and slower trills with rhythms and chords of colours; *blocks* ('masses'): the same sonority multiplied by itself in different octaves. During the pauses, change timbres, change harmonies, evolving into complex chords. Low sounds pianissimo, with speeds and blocks, high sounds in rapid counterpoint with hundreds of wild staccato notes in rapid demisemiquavers, pizzicato, or the sound of xylophones, or the sound of rain, or the crashing of rocks, or crackling of burning wood etc. [. . .] Choral voices superimposed in complex sonorities pianissimo, with mouths closed and open.[50]

By the time that he was working on the orchestration of *La Transfiguration*, Messiaen had become an establishment figure. In the middle of the 1950s he had reached perhaps his lowest ebb, with Claire having entered the nursing home, commissions proving hard to come by and the incredible creative momentum of the 1940s largely having dissipated. Now he had a settled home life and prestigious commissions filling his in-tray. With their monumental spirit resulting in music designed for large spaces, *La Transfiguration* and *Et exspecto* might be thought of as 'De Gaullist' works redolent of the Napoleonic *spectacles* of composers such as Cherubini and Le Sueur (Berlioz's teacher). *Et exspecto* in particular is the archetype of state recognition. For his part, the normally politically reticent composer signed an appeal in 1965 supporting the re-election of Charles de Gaulle.[51] His appointment in 1966 as Professor of Composition at the Paris Conservatoire officially recognized his influence on the younger generation of composers for the first time. The following year saw the creation of a piano competition bearing Messiaen's name at the

Festival de Royan. Then, in December 1967, Messiaen was elected to the music section of the Académie des Beaux-Arts, being formally installed on 15 May 1968.[52] It is ironic that the man who had attracted some of the most radical artists of the 1940s and 1950s, and whose class had been described by Boulez as having 'a whiff of sulphur', should have been welcomed into the bastion of the establishment at the very moment that students were erecting barricades and challenging de Gaulle's governance of the country.

The reaction to his music at the Festival de Royan in April 1968 was symptomatic of Messiaen's change in status. Prophetic of the events of the following month, the young audience that year was particularly querulous. The concert on 7 April began with the world première of a choral work by Xenakis, *Nuits*, which, with its forthright manner, strange new vocal timbres and references to political prisoners, sent a frisson through the audience. This was followed by a selection of Messiaen's piano works, performed by Michel Béroff,[53] and the *Cinq Rechants*. Messiaen's pieces were applauded, but, when he was called forward, several voices began yelling 'Xenakis! Xenakis!'. As they left the theatre, Messiaen ruefully observed to Claude Samuel: 'You see, twenty years ago they whistled at the *Rechants* because they found them too modern. Now they whistle because they find them not modern enough . . .'[54]

The student uprising in the Spring of 1968 severely disrupted teaching at the Conservatoire. It also upset Messiaen's usual summer plans as the exams were postponed, causing the autumn term to be re-scheduled for 1 September rather than 1 October. Mme Perdigão was sympathetic and uncommonly relaxed about the delays that this would cause to Messiaen's progress on *La Transfiguration*. In an update at the end of September, the composer revealed that he had just two movements left to orchestrate, 'Terribilis est locus iste' (XII) and 'Tota Trinitas apparuit' (XIII) (neglecting to mention that the former was texturally one of the most complex and the latter one of the longest), confidently predicting that the work would be finished by January 1969.[55] At long last, on 23 February 1969, he wrote to Mme Perdigão with: 'great news: my work is completely finished. To be exact, it was finished on 21 February.'[56] The next few months were dominated by preparations for the première on 7 June, for which he insisted upon a minimum of thirty rehearsals for the choir. There was a panic at the end of April when the scores for the conductor, Serge Baudo, were lost on a flight to Lisbon; they eventually surfaced in Dakar.[57] The Messiaens flew to Portugal on 1 June, with Loriod playing in concerts that night and the following evening in Coimbra and Lisbon respectively. After all the difficulties encountered during the lengthy gestation of *La Transfiguration*, disaster almost struck at the final hurdle when Rostropovich, suffering from food-poisoning, failed to turn up to the première. While the increasingly restless audience of 9,000 waited, unaware of the missing soloist, Mme Perdigão sought out the feverish and bedridden cellist in his hotel room and, with due compassion, persuaded him that staying put was not an option. The concert went ahead and the work was a triumph, prompting a half-hour ovation and Messiaen to note jubilantly in his diary that it was: 'un success absolument formidable!!!!!'.[58]

Having spent four years working on his largest work to date, Messiaen now produced his longest organ cycle thus far in the space of just two months; August and September 1969. The *Méditations sur le Mystère de la Sainte Trinité* has a similar spirit of synthesis to the oratorio, and there is a sense in which it is fulfilling the same function of taking stock, but for the world of the organ loft rather than the concert hall. The first piece opens with the rugged angularity of *Livre d'orgue*, but there are also passages of extreme tenderness, notably the last section of the fifth piece, of a kind not heard since the works of the 1930s. The sense in which *La Transfiguration* and the *Méditations* are companion pieces goes beyond size and musical content, for they explore similar theological territory – filiation and the Trinity respectively. In both cases, Messiaen draws directly upon Aquinas, the arch-theologian of the Church. In *La Transfiguration* this is straightforward, for Aquinas's words can be sung. In the *Méditations*, Messiaen created a musical cipher, a 'communicable language' into which he translated the words, thus maintaining the deliberate 'unintelligibility' which made Latin so attractive for the text of La Transfiguration. In the preface to the score, he described this as a kind of game, one which had the added benefit of creating a significant amount of new musical material.

The Messiaens were away from Petichet for just over two weeks at the beginning of September 1969, most of which was taken up with a trip to Iran, during which Et exspecto was performed 'in front of the Padana of Darius in Persepolis. It was at night, with the stars and all the statues – I mean the bas-reliefs which decorate the Padana's double turn staircase. It's one of the great monuments of Antiquity, and for me a very, very great musical memory.'[59] The Messiaens had examined the bas-reliefs between the rehearsal and the concert: 'That's when I heard the song of a bird that must have been in the rocks in front of the Padana of Darius [. . .] I transcribed the song, but I wasn't able to catch a glimpse of the bird [. . .] no one was able to identify it; so, in desperation, I called it "bird of Persepolis".'[60] This bird, which he later identified as a kind of bulbul, appeared in the seventh of the *Méditations*.

Given the time spent in Iran, followed by a concert trip to Ghent, the speed at which the nine pieces of the *Méditations* were composed may at first seem astonishing. It can be explained in part, of course, by the fact that organ music needs just three staves whereas much of the time spent on La Transfiguration had been dedicated to the orchestration. However, the *Méditations* is also an example of a concrete link in Messiaen's output between organ improvisations and a subsequent composition. It was his talent for improvisation that prompted Jean Gallon, his harmony teacher, to steer Messiaen towards the organ in the first place. For much of his time at the Trinité he played at four services each Sunday, adapting his improvisations to the nature of the music being used. Whereas for the High Mass he only played plainchant, the usual fare at the eleven o'clock Mass was Classical and Romantic music. The third Mass, at midday, was reserved for modern music, while the much briefer service of Vespers involved only short improvisations. He would often produce 'pastiche voluntaries – faux

Bach, faux Mozart, faux Schumann, and faux Debussy – in order to continue in the same key and style as the piece just sung'.[61] He was not greatly enthused by playing hymns, especially with their prevalence following Vatican II. However, the seriousness with which he took his duties can be seen from the fact that playing for the Profession of Faith by the boys of the Lycée Condorcet in June 1972 took precedence over attending the sessions for the recording of *Poèmes pour Mi* sung by Felicity Palmer with Pierre Boulez conducting the BBC Symphony Orchestra.[62] For a special Mass on 10 March 1969 commemorating the centenary of the death of Berlioz, Messiaen improvised on themes by his fellow Dauphinois, including the 'Evocation' from *La Damnation de Faust*.[63] Not that he only improvised at the organ. There were plenty of informal occasions, when Messiaen was among friends, that he improvised at the piano. One such occasion was on 20 October 1968 when, having presented Langlais with the Légion d'Honneur in his capacity as a member of the Institut, Messiaen entertained the assembled guests by improvising on the piano for a long time.[64] Despite playing the piano in numerous concerts, the only known occasion when he improvised in public on the instrument was in a charity recital with the violinist Angel Reyes given on 3 July 1949 during the crossing to America for his first trip to Tanglewood.[65] Aside from this event, Messiaen became increasingly reluctant to improvise publicly anywhere other than at the console of the *grand orgue* at the Trinité, as is clear from a letter written to Felix Aprahamian on 15 December 1983. Messiaen is trying to explain why, having consented during a hasty telephone conversation the previous evening to improvise at a concert in London, he must change his response to '"non" définitif et absolu':

> When Tournemire improvised in a concert, it was good. But the improvisations were much more beautiful during Masses at Sainte Clotilde, when he had the Blessed Sacrament in front of him. I think I resemble him somewhat in this respect. I improvise much better during a Service, on my organ at the Trinité. In a concert my gifts desert me and my imagination disappears.[66]

19. Messiaen at the organ of the Trinité, playing Tournemire, 1973.

According to Messiaen, the *Messe de la Pentecôte* was 'the result of twenty years of improvisations',[67] its composition becoming a matter of necessity as he realized that: 'they were tiring me out, that I was emptying all my substance into them. So I wrote my *Messe de la Pentecôte* [. . .] followed by *Livre d'orgue*, which is a more thought-out work. After that, as it were, I ceased to improvise.'[68] In fact, Messiaen began improvising again several years later, but it is no surprise that the mental demands of this instant creativity were taking their toll at the time when Claire's illness took a turn for the worse. The two works were originally conceived in 1949 as a single entity, and the *Messe* has passages of distinctly premeditated number-crunching, while the more thought-out *Livre d'orgue* also contains passages of whimsical spontaneity. The effect of Messiaen's organ playing can also be felt in less direct ways than improvisations feeding compositions. The mosaic structures and superficially fragmentary nature of his music in the latter half of his career are reminiscent of an experienced organist in a large church allowing the acoustic to clear while changing registration.

The organ at the Trinité was given a major overhaul during the first half of the 1960s. The instrument was restored in time for the centenary of the church itself, prompting Messiaen to prepare a celebration on 23 November 1967 at which he would improvise in response to a sermon by Monsignor Charles, the rector from the Sacré-Coeur renowned for his preaching. The subject of this evening, advertised as *Le Mystère de Dieu*, was, appropriately enough for the venue, the Trinity, prompting Mgr Charles and the composer to decide that the sermon should be in three parts, each followed by an improvisation from Messiaen.[69] It was also agreed that each improvisation would end with a very clear cue for the understandably anxious Mgr Charles: the series of seven repeated notes followed by a long held note that make up the call of the yellowhammer.[70]

This motif underlines the close correspondence between the improvisations and the *Méditations*, with four of the work's movements ending with the yellowhammer. In fact, as with his playing for other special events, Messiaen prepared his contributions, with pencil sketches for the outline of each improvisation.[71] That Messiaen's improvisations were sometimes so meticulously primed might appear to be contradictory to the entire notion of music created in the moment. An analogy can be found in public speaking: perhaps a priest who, like Mgr Charles, is noted for his sermons. Preaching on a run-of-the-mill Sunday, on a subject particularly close to his heart, he might need no notes at all. For other subjects, he may use an aide-mémoire of the themes that he wishes to pursue. For important occasions, these notes are likely to be more extensive, sometimes being nothing less than a script. However, if he were to publish his sermons, much more care and rigour would be applied to the placing of each and every word. In the same way, Messiaen did not regard improvisations as being compositions, even though some of his organ pieces bear a close resemblance to this music of the moment: 'out of an improvisation grew a work that is completely written out. And I myself meditated a great deal on the mystery of the Holy Trinity.'[72] Even though meticulously prepared, Messiaen's teaching occupied a similar position, for it was primarily an oral experience rooted in the fluid interaction of the class environment. It is no surprise, therefore, that he spent more than four decades working and endlessly revising the *Traité*, leaving it written, yet unfinished, at his death. The few 'lectures' by Messiaen that were published in his lifetime, not to mention entire swathes of his 'conversations' with Claude Samuel, are notable for their carefully crafted, *ex cathedra* tone; they are a world away from the fluid interaction in his class at the Conservatoire. The fact is that all of the works by Messiaen, from *Le Banquet céleste* to *Concert à quatre*, and all of the thousands of words about his music and that of others in the *Traité*, in *Technique*, and in countless interviews and writings, account for very little of his musical and pedagogical activity. The majority of the music created by Messiaen was ephemeral. The composer of enduring monuments depicting the celestial city spent the majority of his time building musical sand-castles, washed away by that day's tide.

Notes

1. Samuel, *Music and Color*, p. 146.
2. PHNS, p. 233.
3. Samuel, *Music and Color*, p. 197.

4. PHNS, p. 236.
5. Traité V, vol.ii, p. 603.
6. PHNS, p. 239.
7. ibid, p. 229.
8. The civil wedding took place two days earlier.
9. PHNS, p. 241.
10. Samuel, *Music and Color*, p. 99.
11. PHNS, p. 245.
12. Samuel, *Music and Color*, p. 99.
13. Messiaen, 'Entretien avec Claude Samuel', ECD75505.
14. PHNS, pp. 246–7.
15. The ancient traditional music of the Japanese Court.
16. Messiaen, 'Entretien avec Claude Samuel', ECD75505.
17. PHNS, pp. 250–1.
18. Samuel, *Music and Color*, p. 43.
19. Massin, *Une poétique du merveilleux*, p. 85.
20. Samuel, *Music and Color*, p. 45.
21. Olivier Messiaen, *Conférence de Notre Dame*, Paris: Alphonse Leduc, 1978, p. 10.
22. Samuel, *Music and Color*, p. 139.
23. Stephen Broad, 'Messiaen and modern *art sacré*', paper given at the Fourth Biennial Conference on Twentieth-century Music, Brighton, August 2005.
24. PHNS, p. 253.
25. ibid, p. 253.
26. ibid, p. 254.
27. Samuel, *Music and Color*, p. 167.
28. ibid, p. 142.
29. ibid, p. 141.
30. Messiaen, 'Entretien avec Claude Samuel' ECD75505.
31. Preface to the score of *La Transfiguration*.
32. PHNS, p. 264.
33. Samuel, *Music and Color*, p. 145.
34. For a full account, see Nigel Simeone, 'Towards "un success absolument formidable": the birth of Messiaen's *La Transfiguration*', *Musical Times* (Vol. 145, Summer 2004), 5–24.
35. PHNS, p. 265.

36. ibid.

37. ibid, p. 266.

38. Messiaen, 'Entretien avec Claude Samuel' ECD75505.

39. See Jacquet-Langlais, *Ombre et lumière*, pp. 218–27.

40. Messiaen, 'Entretien avec Claude Samuel' ECD75505.

41. PHNS, p. 267.

42. Office de radiodiffusion-télévision française.

43. PHNS, p. 269.

44. ibid, p. 270.

45. Simeone, '*La Transfiguration*', p. 15.

46. Goehr, unpublished interview.

47. Marks, 'Messiaen at 80', programme broadcast by BBC2 on 10 December 1988.

48. Goehr, unpublished interview.

49. Nigel Simeone, private communication.

50. PHNS, p. 275.

51. ibid, p. 263.

52. Messiaen's inaugural speech is reproduced in Christopher Dingle and Nigel Simeone (eds), *Olivier Messiaen: Music, Art and Literature* (Ashgate, forthcoming).

53. Winner of the inaugural Concours de Piano, Olivier Messiaen.

54. Samuel, *Permanences*, p. 325.

55. Simeone, *La Transfiguration*, p. 21.

56. PHNS, p. 279.

57. ibid, p. 281.

58. ibid.

59. Messiaen, 'Entretien avec Claude Samuel' ECD75505.

60. Samuel, *Music and Color*, p. 127.

61. ibid, p. 25.

62. PHNS, p. 292.

63. ibid, p. 280.

64. Jaquet-Langlais, *Ombre et lumière*, p. 262.

65. PHNS, p. 186.

66. Nigel Simeone, *Bien Cher Félix . . .: Letters from Olivier Messiaen and Yvonne Loriod to Felix Aprahamian* (Cambridge: Mirage Press, 1998), p. 51.

67. Samuel, *Music and Color*, p. 118.

68. ibid, p. 25.

69. ibid, p. 125.

70. PHNS, pp. 275–6.

71. Another set of improvisations for which pencil sketches survive are those which accompanied a 1979 recording of his mother's *L'Âme en bourgeon*; Erato STU 71104.

72. Samuel, *Music and Color*, p. 125.

8 A Passion for opera 1970–83

I said to myself 'I'm going to be seventy years old. I have a right to be extravagant'.[1]

Having not written an explicitly religious work for the concert hall between completing the *Vingt Regards* in 1944 and starting work on *Couleurs de la Cité céleste* in 1963, Messiaen spent the remainder of the 1960s composing music that is not just religious, but unashamedly, and assuredly theological. These works did not provoke the kind of furore that surrounded the *Trois petites Liturgies*, or, for that matter, *Chronochromie*. The tumultuous reception that greeted the first performance of *La Transfiguration* was repeated in Paris and London. In marked contrast to the vacillations and even hostility within the BBC hierarchy over *Turangalîla* in the 1950s, *La Transfiguration* was given the honour of opening the 1970 Proms. Birdsong had featured in each of these works, and the piano had been given a starring role in *Sept Haïkaï*, *Couleurs de la Cité céleste* and *La Transfiguration*. Now Messiaen put Aquinas to one side and wrote his first solo piano piece and his first nature portrait since completing *Catalogue d'oiseaux* in 1959.

The new work, *La Fauvette des jardins* (The Garden Warbler), is both a pendant to, and progression from, the great birdsong cycle. There is an affinity with 'La Rousserolle effarvatte', the centrepiece of *Catalogue d'oiseaux*, that goes beyond mere length, for both pieces begin and end at night, and Messiaen later intimated that 'If age didn't prevent me from thinking about a second *Catalogue d'oiseaux*, La Fauvette could be the central piece of a new cycle.'² A thirty-five minute, single movement piano work of complex design and extreme virtuosity would be a major undertaking for most composers, but *La Fauvette des jardins* appears to have been a relaxation for Messiaen after the labours of *La Transfiguration* and, to a lesser extent, the *Méditations*. With the action centred on the countryside around his summer home in Petichet, the sense is of a holiday piece. It was here, at four o'clock on the morning of 6 July 1970, and again on the following day, Messiaen notated the song of the work's protagonist: the garden warbler.³ *La Fauvette* is a musical portrait of the scene from Messiaen's window in which he solves anew the challenge of composing music from nature, by marking the passing of time through the changing colours of the reflections on Lake Laffrey.

La Fauvette also captures a passing era. When Messiaen first bought his land in Petichet, it was a self-contained little village community, a brief staging post for travellers along the route Napoléon. By 1970, Lake Laffrey and the adjoining Lake Petichet were already becoming increasingly popular with day-trippers from Grenoble, with the birds having to compete with the noise from water sports. *La Fauvette* remains unfettered by any such incursions, the only human presence being that of the onlooker experiencing a sample of the natural odyssey played out day after day and captured by Messiaen's music and accompanying programme:

> . . . Five o'clock in the morning. Daybreak brings silver to the leaves of the ash, revives the scents and colours of the mauve mint and green grass. A blackbird twitters. The Green Woodpecker erupts in laughter. On the far side of the embankment, by Lake Petichet, a Skylark rises into the heavens, coiling its jubilation around a shrill dominant. The Garden Warbler tries out a new song: its rapid vocalises, its tireless virtuosity and its ceaseless tide of invention seem to make time stand still . . .

The cosy, family album of *La Fauvette* – cosy, that is, for everyone except the pianist – stands as a testament to all the summers that

Messiaen spent in his little piece of the Dauphiné countryside. In the midst of writing it, Messiaen made an entry in his diary outlining a piano concerto 'of the mountains', featuring more of his favoured scenery such as the grand Serre and Jungfrau.[4] His next work did indeed depict a mountainous landscape, but the setting of *Des canyons aux étoiles* . . . (From the canyons to the stars) is a world away from the green fields and blue lake of Petichet; portraying instead the spectacular orange and red rock formations in the canyons of Utah. It is a work written for the United States, but emphatically celebrating its natural wonders rather than the America of skyscrapers. Messiaen was reluctant at first to accept the commission, which came from Alice Tully, patron of the Musica Aeterna Orchestra:

> To change my mind, Miss Tully invited me to a lavish dinner. I remember an immense cake crowned with pistachio frogs spewing *crème Chantilly*. It was extraordinary, yet I remained unswayed until, during the meal, Miss Tully recounted how, after an invitation from a maharajah, she'd taken a trip to India simply to shake the paw of a lion. When she found herself nose to nose with the lion, the maharajah and his whole court ran away, but she shook its paw. That lion was her friend. You can imagine the amazement at the dinner table. [. . .] I was reminded of the story of Androcles, who was spared in the arena by a lion he had cared for as a cub. I reread Chrétien de Troyes's *Chevalier au lion*, which is a similar story. In sum, this woman who had undertaken a trip to India to meet a lion she had never met moved me. It was all so extraordinary that I accepted the commission.[5]

This took place during a hectic six-week concert tour of North America in the Autumn of 1970. On 6 October, while the Messiaens were in Calgary, word came that Loriod's mother, Simone, had died. They had dined with her and Loriod's father, Gaston, in Paris at the Critérion restaurant just nine days earlier. Now, to add to their distress, their American schedule made it impossible to return for the funeral.

When eventually they did get back to Paris, Messiaen was approached to write 'a *Symphonie théologique* for Solti and the Orchestre de Paris'.[6]

20. Rafaël Kubelik and Messiaen, in Munich for the first German performance of *La Transfiguration* on 10 June 1971.

This did not materialize, but *Des canyons* effectively combines the idea from the summer of a mountain-inspired piano concerto with a work of faith. Messiaen spent the summer of 1971 working on it, his packing list in the diary including 'books on astronomy, books and my notes on birds of the USA, books on Utah, Arizona and Islands',[7] the last presumably reflecting the prominent inclusion of several Hawaiian birds. Nevertheless, only so much could be taken from books. Upon accepting the commission Messiaen had been emboldened to ask for a trip to be arranged for research in the field, and a visit to Utah was scheduled for the beginning of May 1972. This ended up being the culmination of two busy months of which all but twelve days were spent in the USA. Back in 1970, it was agreed that the first performance of the *Méditations* would be at the Basilica of the Immaculate Conception in Washington on 20 March 1972. Since this involved a rare performance on anything other than his beloved Trinité organ, Messiaen wanted plenty of time to work on the registrations, arriving in Washington on 11 March. The US première of *La Transfiguration*, also in Washington, was on 28 March, with three further performances over the following days, and recording sessions for the oratorio were planned for the end of April. In between, the Messiaens gave concerts on both coasts, fitted in a trip to a canyon to notate birdsong, and, on 14 April, made their brief return to Paris.[8] Unusually, Messiaen missed the Holy Week and Easter services at the Trinité, Easter Sunday (2 April) being marked at Carnegie Hall by the fourth of the performances of *La Transfiguration*.

After all this activity, the Messiaens made the arduous journey to Bryce Canyon, flying to Salt Lake City and then four hours by car:

> But when one is in the canyon, it's extraordinary, it's divine! It's totally deserted and wild. As always in the United States, the solitude is a bit organized: a sort of inn stands at the entrance of the canyon and offers a few small, simple 'cowboy-style' rooms with showers and kitchen. The tour of the canyon itself must be made on foot [. . .] It's not dangerous, and the marked trails keep one from getting lost [. . .] So we set off alone, my wife and I, in the canyon. It was marvellous, grandiose; we were immersed in total silence – not the slightest noise, except for the birdsong. And we saw those formidable rocks tinted with all possible shades of red, orange, and violet, those amazing formations created by erosion: the shapes of castles, towers, bridges, windows, columns! We took walks in the canyon for more than a week, and I transcribed all the birdsongs. I also took note of the fragrances of the sagebrush (an aromatic plant growing there in great quantity), the dizzying height of the chasms and the beautiful shapes and colors of the canyon, while my wife recorded the birdsongs and took hundreds of photos.[9]

Given his love of the dramatic gorges of the Infernet to the east of Grenoble, and the recurrent theme of the abyss in his music, it was scarcely surprising that Messiaen should be so inspired by the American canyons. From Messiaen's perspective, to misquote Oscar Wilde, we are all in the abyss, but some of us are looking at the stars.

21. Messiaen at Cedar Breaks, Utah, May 1972.

The Messiaens also visited two other canyons, Cedar Breaks and Zion Park, and the culmination of each of the three parts of *Des canyons* is a movement inspired by one of the spectacular landscapes encountered during May 1972. Each of these movements is an amazing *tour de force*. Their impact is all the more astonishing for the fact that, in addition to the solo piano, the composer was limited to a mere forty-three instrumentalists in order to squeeze onto the modestly proportioned stage at the Alice Tully Hall in New York's Lincoln Center. Messiaen retained substantial woodwind, brass and percussion sections, but confined himself to just thirteen strings. He completed the short score of *Des canyons* by December 1972, with several movements already being in full score, but the restricted ensemble posed 'terrible problems of instrumentation [. . .] it was really a technical ordeal'.[10] The result is an object lesson in orchestration, a task not completed until the summer of 1974, for the piece effortlessly conveys the monumental grandeur of the landscapes, yet everything can be heard in this ensemble of soloists, even in the most overwhelming tutti. As implied by the title, there is a clear sense of progress in the work, from the remarkable Spartan evocation of the opening 'Le Désert', to the verdant richness of the concluding 'Zion Park et la cité céleste'. The vibrant final pages, with their sustained string chords, are reminiscent of the end of 'Le Jardin féerique' from *Ma Mère l'Oye*, perhaps reflecting the fact that Messiaen had taken Ravel's piano works to Petichet for relaxation during the summer of 1972.

In addition to drawing Mahlerian power from his chamber-sized orchestra, Messiaen also includes two birdsong movements for the piano alone, 'Le Cossyphe d'Heuglin' (White-browed Robin) and 'Le Moquer polyglotte' (Mockingbird), and a striking movement, 'Appel interstellaire' for the solo horn. The last of these was originally written in 1970 for the Royan Festival as a 'tombeau' in memory of the gifted Canadian composer, and former Messiaen student, Jean-Pierre Guézec. Although it was composed before Messiaen even received Alice Tully's commission, the half-valvings and alternate fingerings of 'Appel interstellaire' typify Messiaen's instrumental approach in *Des canyons*. It is the work in which his continual absorption of advanced techniques and fascination with new instrumental possibilities are most apparent. As in so many of Messiaen's pieces, the performer must be careful not to lose sight of the spirit of the music in endeavouring to master the technical challenges. During the rehearsals for a performance conducted by Kent Nagano, the soloist was taking an overly literal approach to some of the effects in 'Appel interstellaire':

> The horn player was doing precisely what is in the score, following every zigzag and jagged mark. Messiaen said 'No, no, this isn't it. Try to interpret it like the wind.' He was giving all kinds of examples.
> Eventually he said, 'Try to think of your favourite pet, think of a dog.' So, we all thought of a dog. He said 'The dog is sound asleep. Think that you are watching the dog have a dream, that the dog is chasing a rabbit in its dream. Imagine the dog getting so excited in its dream that its feet begin to move and its nostrils begin to flare, and then, if you listen carefully, the dog will start to utter little moans as he is chasing this rabbit. That's the sound I want!'[11]

The first performance of *Des canyons* on 20 November was a huge success with the public in the packed Alice Tully Hall. However, as Messiaen ruefully observed later: 'The New York critics clearly didn't understand a thing. The theological aspect, the astronomical effect, the ornithological content, my admiration for the red-orange colour of the rocks in Bryce canyon – all that escaped them completely. I wonder if they could understand that the beauty of America is not concentrated only in the New York skyscrapers.'[12]

In towns and cities, artists are remembered through statues and street names, but *Des canyons* led to Messiaen being honoured by a small part of the landscape it celebrates. Thanks to the efforts of Julie Whitaker, a Utah schoolteacher inspired by *Des canyons*, Lion's Peak (White Cliffs) in Parowan Creek Canyon was renamed Mount Messiaen on 5 August 1978.

Messiaen's next project, the opera *Saint François d'Assise*, was to be his biggest musical monument of all. Written on a scale unprecedented even for Messiaen, it is the summa of summas, his magnum opus and, as he increasingly believed, his swan-song. The composer had been pondering the subject of Saint Francis for many years. He first visited Assisi in 1959, having attended a performance of the *Trois petites Liturgies* at Perugia on 29 September.[13] He returned in April 1970, making detailed notes in his diary on the frescoes that adorn

the Basilica of Saint Francis, where he also attended Mass.[14] A trip to Florence in May of the following year was equally influential, for the Messiaens visited the Museo di San Marco, with its unrivalled collection of paintings by Fra Angelico.[15] The depictions of angels made a particularly deep impact, and the composer based the Angel's costume upon Fra Angelico's 'silver-chest' *Annunciation*, with its large wings coloured with bold stripes of blue, yellow, black and green, offset by a circle of dark blue. It is an image that inspired more than decisions about costumes, for it 'haunted' Messiaen throughout the composition of *Saint François*. On 1 July 1971 Messiaen wrote a reminder in his diary to respond to the request for an opera for 1975 from Rolf Liebermann, general manager of the Paris Opéra.[16] As with Alice Tully the previous year, Messiaen initially resisted Liebermann's request, and, once again, a meal played a key part: 'He then invited me to the Élysée Palace and, ceremoniously, at the end of dinner, in the presence of Georges Pompidou, he said to me: "Messiaen, you will write an opera for the Opéra de Paris!" I couldn't refuse in front of the President of the Republic.'[17] President Pompidou was not a passive observer in this artistic courtship, having asked the Ministry of Cultural Affairs to help persuade Messiaen. In fact, the composer neither refused nor agreed at the meal, remaining silent, but a diary entry on 15 October recorded that he needed to choose a subject and write a libretto.

In retrospect, Messiaen's reluctance might seem surprising, as might the fact that he had not already written a work for the stage. His childhood had been dominated by a love of theatrical works, from the productions of Shakespeare in his cellophane-encrusted toy theatre, and trying his own hand at writing drama, to playing through operas by Mozart, Berlioz and Wagner. All of this was crowned by the impact of Debussy's *Pelléas et Mélisande*, which, along with his other favoured operas, became part of the staple diet in his class at the Conservatoire. According to George Benjamin, *Poèmes pour Mi* was at one stage envisaged as an opera,[18] while in the late 1940s, Messiaen announced that his next work would be an opera. This was just the first of a number of abortive projects, many of which, such as his aspiration to set Claudel,[19] barely even got onto the drawing board. In 1949, Messiaen was commissioned to write a ballet, *Le Nef des fous* (The Ship of Fools) for the 1951 season at the Paris Opéra, and in 1966 he noted in his diary a plan 'to write a new piece for the six Percussions de Strasbourg[20] – a ballet', but neither work was composed. Most extraordinary of all was his idea in January 1965 to compose a '*spectacle complet*: singers, speaking, dance, orchestra, electronic tape, film and television', adding 'I will write the scenario, the text and the music myself'.[21] This last comment helps to explain why Messiaen refused permission for several other ballet projects, for he patently needed to be closely involved with every aspect of the creative process. In the case of Patricia Malavard's proposed ballet to *Visions de l'Amen*, he consented to the entire choreography being published in pictorial form alongside the music, but would not allow it to be danced. Messiaen explained that the music was 'essentially theological and immaterial', and could never be represented by the human figure, declaring that 'the drawings of Patricia Malavard must be viewed in an exclusively symbolic sense'.[22] Eventually a ballet of *Turangalîla*, with choreography by Roland Petit and sets by Max Ernst, was mounted at the Palais Garnier in June 1968. At the first rehearsal with the orchestra Messiaen was clearly in good spirits, despite problems with the ondes Martenot. Étienne Pasquier, who was in the orchestra, later recalled that: 'the equipment was badly adjusted and created a horrible racket. We all had broken eardrums. At the intermission, I went into the lobby with Messiaen, and he said to me: "Boy, what a racket I'm making! That must be why they criticized Debussy. He didn't make enough noise."'[23] The technical glitches were remedied and the ballet was a great success, Messiaen recalling in 1983 that it was 'absolutely excellent'.[24]

Despite all of this, Messiaen's reluctance to accept Liebermann's commission was due to his feeling that he 'didn't have the gift' for a stage work.[25] This echoed his own assessment of *L'Ensorceleuse*, his unsuccessful Prix de Rome cantata, in a letter to Langlais dated

3 August 1931: 'My cantata was good as music, but poor as theatre; the judgement was fair'.[26] Although opera formed part of the staple diet of his teaching, Messiaen told Claude Samuel in 1967 that he thought that 'at the present time it is practically dead'.[27] Furthermore, when Liebermann first approached Messiaen in 1971, the composer was still embroiled in a lawsuit surrounding the ballet of *Turangalîla*. It is an episode that would have been laughable were it not for the fact that, despite reassurances from all and sundry, Messiaen lost. In the early 1950s, Hubert Devillez, who was, in Claude Samuel's damning characterization, 'a literary-political pseudo-personality',[28] made persistent attempts to get a scenario for a choreographic representation of *Turangalîla* accepted by the Paris Opéra. Messiaen 'wanting quickly to forget this episode, was unwise enough to thank and congratulate the librettist-postulant in writing'.[29] Despite there being no contract between them, and only the most tentative overtures towards a collaboration, this letter was enough for the courts eventually to decide in favour of Devillez's assertion of his intellectual rights.

Messiaen had always written his own texts for his vocal works and, especially after the Devillez affair, he was not about to look elsewhere for a librettist. He cited Wagner as his model, and *Saint François* can be viewed in terms of an all-encompassing *Gesamtkunstwerk*. As well as the music and the libretto, the finished scores contain lengthy descriptions of each character's costume, suggestions for the deportment and gestures of the principals, an outline of the décor for each tableau and various stage directions.

Messiaen was not initially fixed upon Saint Francis as his subject, considering the story in Luke's Gospel of the pilgrims on the road to Emmaus. An echo of this idea remains in the first tableau of *Saint François*, 'La Croix', with its dialogue between François and Frère Léon (Brother Leo) while walking along a road. In the end, a combination of factors made it almost inevitable that Messiaen would choose Saint Francis as his subject. The Saint's affinity with nature, and in particular birds, was especially significant, but, even more importantly, Saint Francis is widely considered to have been the man who most resembled Jesus in his manner of life. Furthermore, the infliction of the Stigmata on the Saint enabled Messiaen to come close to a work setting the most crucial events of the Gospels: 'My dream was to write a Passion or a Resurrection of Christ, but I thought that I wasn't worthy of it and, above all, that such images aren't presentable on the stage'.[30] The music of 'Les Stigmates' (No.7) and 'La mort et la nouvelle vie' (No.8) provide a tantalizing hint of what such a work might have sounded like. Nonetheless, the mind boggles at what proportions a setting by Messiaen of the eighty-two verses of John's account of the Passion (to take the shortest) might have taken, given the result of his tackling just nine Gospel verses for *La Transfiguration*.

In February 1972, Messiaen and Liebermann came to an agreement for a 'large-scale opera' for the centenary of the Palais Garnier in 1975. This would be a tight deadline given that he had also agreed to the commission for *Des canyons*, and, as in his initial thoughts for *La Transfiguration*, Messiaen envisaged a work in which the protagonists would speak rather than sing. It is not clear exactly when the improbable date of 1975 was abandoned, but a letter dated 26 April 1973 discussing a BBC commission from Robert Ponsonby, controller of BBC Radio 3, makes it clear that the composer was still intending to write the opera within a couple of years of completing *Des canyons*:

> I am so pleased that you are hopeful that you could write to commission for the BBC a substantial work lasting between 60 and 90 minutes, either for orchestra alone, or for soloists and orchestra, or for chorus and orchestra. I appreciate that you have first to finish the new work for New York and that after that you have an opera for Paris! We are agreed, however, that the BBC commission would follow as soon as possible after that – in other words from 1976 onwards.[31]

Ponsonby had met the composer the previous day, for the Messiaens were in London for a brief concert tour culminating in a performance of *La Transfiguration* at St Paul's Cathedral. The trip had got off to a disastrous start when their taxi to the Gare du Nord, oblivious to the wild gesticulations and shouts from Messiaen and Loriod, drove away before they retrieved the suitcase with their concert outfits from the boot. It was not recovered until the driver returned to work after a three-day break.

Despite the agreement made in October 1972, it was not until November 1975 that Messiaen decided definitively to write *Saint François* and he only signed the contract in April 1976. Liebermann, whose term of office came to an end in 1980, ensured that it: 'stipulated very precisely the stages of writing'.[32] It is clear that Messiaen's thoughts on the scenario were already at an advanced stage and he had written much of the libretto. In fact, it would be more accurate to say that he constructed the libretto for, as he was the first to admit, much is derived more or less directly from other texts. Principal amongst these are the prayers written by Saint Francis, notably the Canticle of the Creatures,[33] together with early accounts of the Saint's life, such as the lives by Celano, St Bonaventure and the anonymous *Fioretti*, and there are also numerous quotations from Scripture and allusions to *The Imitation of Christ*. An early five-scene plan for the opera is outlined at the end of the 1971 diary:

1. La joie parfaite (Perfect joy)
2. La règle et les vertus (The rule and the virtues)
3. Le Prêche aux oiseaux (The sermon to the birds)
4. L'Ange au violon et les Stigmates (The Angel with the violin and the Stigmata)
5. Le Cantique et la mort (The Canticle and death)[34]

The elements of the final version missing from this prototype are 'Lauds', an 'everyday' scene of the brothers at prayer, the kissing of the leper, and 'L'Ange voyageur'. Only the second of these provisional scenes did not find its way into the final work. 'La joie parfaite' became 'La Croix', Messiaen not being so naïve as to realize that the original title could be misconstrued. The Stigmata scene was separated from the viol-wielding Angel, which became 'L'Ange musicien', and Saint

Francis's great paean of praise, the Canticle of the Creatures (also known as The Canticle of Brother Sun) was used as a unifying feature, the verses being split across three tableaux:

Act I   1. La Croix (The Cross)
           2. Les Laudes (Lauds)
           3. Le Baiser au Lépreux (The kissing of the leper)
Act II   4. L'Ange voyageur (The travelling angel)
           5. L'Ange musicien (The Angel musician)
           6. Le Prêche aux oiseaux (The sermon to the birds)
Act III   7. Les Stigmates (The Stigmata)
           8. La mort et la Nouvelle Vie (Death and new life)

The early lives of Saint Francis, on which the scenes are based, cannot be regarded as 'biographies' in the sense that we understand the word today. On the contrary, they were a record of the deeds of Saint Francis with the emphasis on the word *Saint*, and Messiaen follows their lead. Rather than biographical detail and an accurate chronology, we have instead eight stylized episodes, each characteristic of an aspect of the Saint's life, omitting the mundane and concentrating instead on the symbols of the spiritual development of Saint Francis and his followers. In this respect, each scene could be regarded as a fresco brought to life; the concern is spiritual rather than temporal. Events from the Saint's raucous early life, including the stormy relationship with his father, are omitted. As the composer later observed: 'Some people have told me, "There's no sin in your work." But I myself feel sin isn't interesting, dirt isn't interesting. I prefer flowers.'[35]

In September 1975, the Messiaens went to New Caledonia, a trip that the composer had been planning since April. A small French colony in the southern Pacific Ocean, it has symbolic importance in the opera as the point on the globe furthest from Assisi; *François* has a vision of the islands and its exotic birds during the sixth scene, 'Le Prêche aux oiseaux'. Moreover, the birds that Messiaen notated in New Caledonia permeate the score, usually as symbols of something 'other'. The Gerygone, in particular, is the theme-bird of the Angel, and its staccato song, combining chirpy innocence with crystalline beauty, is at the heart of several of the opera's most magical moments. Getting to New Caledonia was no small matter:

> Twenty-eight hours in the air! An exhausting flight [. . .] But I have a good remedy for fatigue. As soon as I hear birdsongs, I regain my strength and forget my cares. I can be dying, but if I hear a bird's song I'm cured! [. . .] Upon my arrival in New Caledonia it was the same. I listened to the birds and was wild with joy.[36]

Loriod, by contrast, was not so easily enthused:

> I never understood why he couldn't just go to Assisi. In the end I said to him, 'New Caledonia is a very long way away and it's going to be very expensive to get there; couldn't you make do with the birds of Europe?' But yes, yes, yes, he had to go. I found he was very stubborn about this, but I myself never understood why he needed the gerygone for his Angel.[37]

Nonetheless, New Caledonia made a big impression on them both:

> [. . .] there are magnificent green landscapes. They're extraordinary, with niaoulis, those famous exotic trees with white trunks, and flamboyants, which have vivid red leaves. But at the bottom of the island, which looks like an exclamation mark, there's the dot itself, which is a tiny island, called the Isle of Pines, or the Isle of Kuni, and there you have some extraordinary birds which are not to be found anywhere else, like the Gerygone warbler [. . .].[38]

This little bird heralds each arrival of the Angel in *Saint François* with its mesmerizing music.

Another essential field trip was to return in June 1976 first to Assisi, to notate birdsong and make notes on the scenery, and then Florence for Fra Angelico's paintings. Appropriately, it was during this excursion that the last refinements were made to the libretto. Now it was full steam ahead with the music, beginning with 'L'Ange voyageur' (No.4), the only scene not to feature François, and saving the largest scene,

22. Messiaen notating a blackcap at the Carceri, Assisi, 4 June 1976.

'Le Prêche aux oiseaux' (No. 6), until last. Messiaen showed every sign of being an old man in a hurry. He kept his diary completely clear during the summer of 1976 and, unusually, he continued composing back in Paris, completing the short score by the end of the following summer. On 6 October 1977, he recorded in his diary: 'Telephone Liebermann to show him the finished opera'.[39] Despite such astonishing speed at producing more than four hours of music, the composer, no doubt recalling the protracted gestation of *La Transfiguration*, was already pondering whether 1981 or even 1982 might be a more realistic deadline. When Messiaen unveiled *Saint François* to Liebermann, his concerns were overcome and the original plan of mounting the work in 1980 was re-confirmed.

23. Alan Civil and Messiaen during rehearsals for *Des canyons aux étoiles*, Utrecht 1977.

Shortly after this meeting, it was reported on the radio that Messiaen was writing an opera on Saint Francis of Assisi; the information could only have come from Liebermann. For a composer who was almost pathologically secretive about work in progress, this was a grave transgression. As was his usual practice, Messiaen had kept even

Loriod unaware of the subject-matter of his latest work. George Benjamin recalled that, on the day of the radio report, Messiaen 'came into the class in a really bad mood. He was really very upset.'[40] Unlike Debussy or Boulez, Messiaen rarely made even minor alterations to a work once it was performed. However, until that point of no return, the secrecy surrounding compositions was as strict as that of the confessional:

> [. . .] I don't like to talk about a piece before it's finished. Because when it is finished it doesn't always correspond to what I'd imagined at the beginning. And anyway, when you're composing you always hope you're writing a masterpiece. You have to. Otherwise you wouldn't compose at all. And then, once it's finished, it can be a great disappointment when you realise that you haven't written a masterpiece at all. You're still waiting for your Opus 1. That's why it's better not to talk about things before they exist. There's an old saying: Don't count your chickens before they're hatched.[41]

This caution covered even the rehearsal period for a work. For instance, each of the principals for Saint François was given tapes of Messiaen and Loriod playing and singing their scenes. Each set of tapes was recorded afresh as they did not have copying facilities and Messiaen did not wish anyone to hear the music unless it was absolutely necessary. Having an unwelcome spotlight shone upon the opera while still in embryonic form only added to the pressure to finish Saint François for the increasingly improbable date of 1980. By the time that he was celebrating his seventieth birthday a year later, expectation was high for early completion of this unexpected venture; the souvenir brochure for the birthday concerts even included an advertisement announcing 6 June 1980 as the date of the world première for the opera.[42]

In fact, in December 1978 Messiaen was recovering from the latest of several bouts of ill-health that had already delayed work on Saint François. On a trip to Vienna at the end of February 1976 he had contracted viral hepatitis. In the process of this diagnosis a gallstone was also discovered.[43] On 30 March of the following year, Messiaen fell heavily outside Guy Moquet Métro station. He was given stitches on his eyebrows, nose and lips at the Rothschild clinic, but a deep gash on his right ankle, caused by his broken glasses, was overlooked. Typically he still attended a rehearsal and concert of *Couleurs* that day. However, a week later he cut short a visit to his Aunt Madeleine in the Aube, and on 11 April Messiaen had an operation on his ankle. As a result of the delay, he suffered from leg ulcers for the remainder of his life.[44]

The first half of 1978 had been dominated by Messiaen's last two terms at the Conservatoire before compulsory retirement. As with the opera, there appears to have been a conscious summation of his teaching, with favoured topics, such as *Pelléas*, Greek poetic metre, *Siegfried*, *Götterdämmerung* and Claude Le Jeune's *Le Printemps*. Neither would it be the Messiaen Class without examining new avenues and recent trends. *Chronochromie* was analysed, as were works by Penderecki and Dutilleux. There was a demonstration of the tuba by Fernand Lelong, and a talk by Tristan Murail. For the final week, though, Messiaen returned to the other end of the historical spectrum with a brief course on plainchant. At the last class on 19 June, the students gave him a facsimile of the sketches for *Pelléas* as a farewell present. Astonishingly, neither the director, Raymond Gallois-Montbrun, nor any of the other senior members of the staff saw fit to mark the occasion.[45] After thirty-seven years of dedicated service, perhaps the greatest musical teacher of the twentieth century stepped out of the Conservatoire for the last time without even a handshake.

Retirement had not made finding time to work on *Saint François* any easier, for the remainder of 1978 was taken up with seventieth birthday celebrations. Work in Petichet on the orchestration of scene 2 had been interrupted for a short trip to Japan in July. On 2 October, the Messiaens had embarked upon a lengthy, and exhausting, tour of North America, returning to France on 18 November, where a month

24. Jessye Norman, Messiaen and Serge Baudo, February 1978.

of concerts began the following day. Once again, though, Messiaen fell ill, this time with prostate problems necessitating another operation. Typical of her devotion to the man and his music, Loriod slept in Messiaen's hospital room on a folding chair while also fulfilling her rehearsal and concert commitments for the birthday events.[46] Among the concerts that Messiaen missed was a performance on the evening of his birthday of *Des canyons*, conducted by Boulez and with Loriod as soloist:

> I had a radio, and as soon as the live broadcast concert began,
> I sent the nurse away and opened up the score in bed. The score
> had just been published by Leduc that very morning, and my wife
> had brought it triumphantly into my room! When the work was
> finished, I was furnished with more than just applause: Pierre Boulez
> addressed a very affectionate speech to me over the airwaves. It was
> very moving.[47]

Messiaen must have harboured hopes that, after two months' convalescence from his operation, with his seventieth birthday celebrations out of the way and having retired from the Conservatoire, he could make rapid progress on *Saint François* during 1979. However, in June he wrote to Liebermann making it plain that there was no hope of completing the work by 1980:

> I now find myself with all of the orchestration of the opera to do, which will be about 3000 pages for orchestra. Two scenes are already orchestrated, but six remain to be done, unfortunately the longest. There remain, therefore, about 2500 pages of orchestration for me to write. Each page represents close to three hours for finding the disposition and the combining of timbres, then three hours of drafting and three hours of copying. Therefore nine hours in all for average pages. The very difficult pages can require up to three days! It is necessary to add to all of these problems that my sight is diminishing progressively, which doesn't hasten my work ... I am, therefore overestimating my progress; and here is the truth: I will not finish my orchestration before January 1982.[48]

To his credit, Liebermann rejected a proposal by Bernard Lefort, his successor, for a performance of four scenes in 1980, and gave Messiaen an additional three years to complete the opera. For the next year steady progress was made on the orchestration. In parallel with his subject, Messiaen became progressively more cloistered, with work on *Saint François* taking precedence over virtually everything else. He did go to see several productions at the Opéra, but this tended to be to listen to potential singers for the principal roles. In April 1980, he recharged his batteries with another short trip to Assisi, and he certainly was not going to miss the visit to Paris of Pope John Paul II, standing for five hours among the crowd on 30 May. Even then, the opera was not far from his thoughts, with the combination of the bells of Notre Dame and the fanfare heralding the Pope's arrival inspiring the iridescent orchestration of the music after François's death in Scene 8.

Messiaen began work on this, the second longest scene, in Petichet at the beginning of July 1980. Now that he was retired from the Conservatoire, Messiaen was able to work all year round. However, his beloved Petichet could only be used as a compositional retreat for half of the year as it was snowbound during the winter months, while, even with improved roads and railways, it was too far from Paris to be practicable for short breaks. This left Messiaen with the unappetizing situation of working for the most part in the city, and with only the pigeons in the tiny municipal park opposite the apartment on rue Marcadet for inspiration. The constant noise made work there difficult: '[. . .] in spite of all the soundproofing I've used in my flat – double-glazing, boarding, fibreglass inside the walls – despite all that, you can still hear radios. I've actually written scores with a radio above me, one on the right, a radio on the left, and another underneath.'[49] The solution was to buy a second country house, La Sauline, but this time just a couple of hours' drive from Paris, in the Sologne region, the landscape that had inspired 'La Rousserolle effarvatte' from the *Catalogue d'oiseaux*. The property was bought in June 1981, and the Messiaens moved in on 26 October.[50] Unlike the house at Petichet, whose location was known to many friends and admirers, and had been publicly celebrated in *La Fauvette des jardins*, the existence of La Sauline was a closely guarded secret.

Work on Scene 8 dragged on through the winter and into the spring of 1981, so that the colossal undertaking of turning the short score of 'Le Prêche aux oiseaux' (Scene 6) into a fully realized orchestration could not be tackled until June 1981. Various health niggles, including concerns over an irregular heartbeat and painful aching in the ankle he had injured in 1977, further delayed progress and added to Messiaen's growing concern that he would not finish *Saint François*; a recurring refrain throughout the latter stages of its composition was that his only wish before death was to complete the opera.[51] By late 1981, Messiaen had fallen into a depression. Now that he had no teaching to do, he was barely going out at all. It did not help, as Messiaen later admitted, that the sixth scene was the one that he 'was most anxious about because I'm an ornithologist and wanted it to be absolutely my finest bird music'.[52] By December, he was periodically weeping, and paralysed by doubt and exhaustion. At the urging of his doctor, Messiaen began taking daily walks, making his way up the hill behind

Sacré Coeur to attend evening Mass. In the new year he also made the effort to attend concerts again, and he even began contemplating what he might compose after *Saint François*, his thoughts understandably turning away from anything involving an orchestra and towards his own instrument, the organ. Loriod had already been drafted in to prepare the vocal score of the opera after the radio report breaking Messiaen's compositional cover. Now he made the unprecedented step of agreeing to her making the fair copy of Scene 5 from his orchestral sketch so that he could concentrate upon Scene 6; once the first production of the opera was out of the way, he returned to Scene 5 to make his own fair copy.

In the orchestral works since *Réveil des oiseaux*, Messiaen had adopted a number of strategies for writing birdsong choruses in order to reconcile his desire for accuracy within individual songs while giving an overall sense of harmonious hubbub encountered in an early morning forest. Now, in the ornithological centrepiece of the opera, he found an elegant solution to the problem. All of the birds are notated precisely, but some, entering at a cue from the conductor, are liberated from the ensemble and allowed to fly free of the barlines. The result of this 'hors tempo' approach is a much greater fluidity; a genuine sense of controlled chaos. Messiaen interrupted work on 'Le Prêche aux oiseaux' to orchestrate scene 1, leaving until last the biggest challenge of the entire opera: the big bird concert that follows François's sermon. Aside from the creative effort involved, this task was physically exhausting involving standing for ten hours a day in front of the outsize manuscript paper. In October 1982 illness again threatened progress, Messiaen being hospitalized for five days with bronchitis. It was not until February 1983 that he completed the fair copy of scene 6, but it took until 22 August before the vocal score was approved by Messiaen and the opera was at long last, completely and utterly finished.

Saint François is a large work by any standards, even Messiaen's own. It consists of about four and a half hours of meticulously crafted music for the largest forces the composer ever requested. The manuscript score weighs about twenty-five pounds and contains approximately two thousand five hundred pages. It is scored for an orchestra of one hundred and nineteen and a choir of one hundred and fifty. The sheer magnitude of the orchestra, including many bulky instruments, would cause problems in even the most accommodating opera house pit. For instance, the opera contains five virtuosic parts for the *claviers* – glockenspiel, vibraphone, xylophone, xylorimba and marimba. The percussion section proper contains no less than three sets of tubular bells and a set of crotales as well as a vast array of instruments of indeterminate pitch including timbral subtleties such as the paper, wood and glass chimes which colour the principal theme of *Saint François*. Furthermore, with the exception of the percussion section, each member of the orchestra has an individual part which is specific to one instrument. Thus the three piccolo parts and the part for alto flute are entirely independent of the three flute parts. Similarly, each of the sixty-eight string players has a unique part. Inevitably, the scale of Messiaen's requirements caused tensions with the management at the Opéra. To Messiaen's frustration, Massimo Bogianckino, who had taken over as director of the Opéra after Bernard Lefort's brief steward-ship, pruned the size of the string section from sixty-eight to forty-eight, 'which is a bit inadequate'.[53] The chorus was also reduced, from the desired 150 to just 100 singers, 'but they sang well and the volume was sufficient'.[54] One point that was non-negotiable was the music itself. When he discovered on 6 July 1982 that Bogianckino was proposing to make cuts in the opera, the dismayed composer imme-diately refused permission. After so much time and effort, he was not about to allow *Saint François* to suffer from a fate similar to that which befell Berlioz's *Les Troyens*, which was cut and artificially split into two for its first production, remaining in this distorted form for the next century.

Messiaen gave *Saint François d'Assise* the subtitle 'Scènes Franciscaines', and the idea of Franciscan scenes intimates something of the apparently distinct nature of these eight musical frescoes. And yet, cohesive opera it is. Despite the slow-moving, internal nature of its drama, Saint François actually suffers more than most operas from being given in a concert performance. The fact that the visual drama moves only slowly does not reduce its necessity in appreciating the unfolding human drama of the work. For all that it lacks a real villain or crime or love interest, the progress of the spiritual journey in Saint François is centred on distinct characters and, for all that it conveys as much theology as La Transfiguration, Saint François is more than a staged oratorio. Rather than just presenting the 'truths' of the Catholic faith, Messiaen explores the relationship, albeit in exceptional and idealized form, between the human and the divine. The progress of this inter-action provides the dramatic thread of the opera. It is wrong-headed to entertain the notion that the scenes could be rearranged or omitted without detriment to the whole. Even the sermon to the birds, which is dramatically the most contrived scene, provides a necessary break between the interaction of François with a representative of the divine, in the form of the Angel, and his direct dialogue with God in the Stigmata scene. At the same time, it underlines the visionary qualities of François by this stage in the opera. Throughout, there is, as Messiaen claims in the preface to the score, a clear pattern of 'the growth of grace in the soul of Saint Francis'. In the first tableau, 'La Croix', François confidently opines upon the nature of perfect joy, placing it in the context of service and sacrifice, but it is not until the leper harangues him, essentially for being strong on talk and poor on action, that François confronts, and overcomes, the difficulties of the ideal. Later, he moves from being given a foretaste of the music of paradise, in the fifth scene, to becoming a second Paschal sacrifice through the receipt of the Stigmata in the seventh. Thus the promise of sacrifice and the acceptance of suffering in the service of God espoused in 'La Croix' reaches its culmination in 'Les Stigmates', which itself is only a prelude to the death of François and concluding resurrection chorale of the final tableau.

As the dramatic focal point of the opera, the quasi-Passion setting of 'Les Stigmates' reflects earlier examples in Messiaen's output where he portrays suffering, underpinning the bipartite structures found in, amongst others, the *Diptyque* and 'Combat de la mort et de la vie' from *Les Corps glorieux*. Indeed, the relationship of opposites between death and resurrection goes to the heart of understanding crucial aspects of Messiaen's compositional style. *Saint François* could be characterized as juxtaposing terrestrial and celestial elements, with occasional movement between the two. A crucial moment is the entry of the Angel in scene 5, 'L'Ange musicien', when the harsh yakking of the kestrel interrupts the song of the Angel's theme bird, the Gerygone. This piece of grit in the oyster magnifies the transcendent luminosity of the Gerygone's song, heard gently on the glockenspiel supported by a bed of a cappella humming voices. Hardly surprisingly, there is a general congruity between music in the higher register and the celestial, and music in the middle and lower registers and the terrestrial. The orchestral pounding when the Angel taps on the monastery door would seem to contradict this brazenly crude analysis. However, what is heard is the result of a celestial incursion into the terrestrial domain. The Angel only taps the door, but the noise to human ears is immense and it includes much lower registers than the other terrestrial music. Then there is Frère Léon's poetic reflection just after François dies:

Il est parti . . . comme un silence, comme un silence amical qu'on touche avec des mains très douces. Il est parti . . . comme une larme, comme une larme d'eau claire qui tombe lentement d'un pétale de fleur. Il est parti comme un papillon, un papillon doré qui s'envole de la croix pour dépasser les étoiles . . .

[He has left . . . like a silence, a friendly silence which is touched by very gentle hands. He is gone . . . like a tear, like a tear of clear water that drops slowly from a flower-petal. He has gone like a butterfly, a golden butterfly which flies from the Cross to go beyond the stars . . .]

On the dramatic level, this brief passage provides a moment of intimacy, of humanity, before returning the focus firmly to the sacred and divine. In musical terms, its tenderness provides the foil for the dazzling resurrection chorale that ends the opera. These may be simple observations, but many of the particularly memorable moments in the opera are ingeniously uncomplicated.

Messiaen oversaw almost every aspect of the opera. For instance, he spent day after day at the photocopying shop during February 1983 producing the 160 vocal scores, each consisting of separately bound volumes for each scene, needed for the chorus to begin rehearsals. Over the previous couple of years, he had already had numerous meetings going through the music of each scene with the conductor, Seiji Ozawa, his understudy, Kent Nagano, and the principal singers. Messiaen admitted that he would have liked to direct the opera, but, with his only experience of direction being the childhood productions of Shakespeare in his sweet-wrapper equivalent of The Globe Theatre, he recognized that he 'didn't possess the skills'[55]. Instead, Bogianckino brought in two compatriots, Sandro Sequi and Giuseppe Crisolini-Malatesta, as stage director and designer respectively; they had 'the great advantage of knowing the places where the opera unfolds, the landscape, the costumes, the paintings of Giotto, the Fra Angelico altarpiece'.[56] They had the tricky task of translating Messiaen's vision into the reality of an event at the Palais Garnier. The scenery and layout of the stage, with its deliberate emulation of mediaeval and early Renaissance art, reinforced the link with the frescoes that provided the inspiration for the costumes and much of the spirit of the opera.

Rehearsals began in September 1983. Robert Grenier, understudy to Philippe Courtis in the role of Frère Bernard,[57] later recalled the first time the 'astonished' singers encountered the vast orchestra: '[. . .] we were rehearsing what the French call an "Italienne", when the singers sit on stage and sing with the orchestra. After a moment's delay, I was summoned to sing my phrase. Unsure of the pitch, I called out in French, "Si bémol", whereupon a veritable shower of B flats of every imaginable sonority came at me from all directions.'[58] The composer was everywhere:

> I was present at every one of the preparatory stages before the first performance [. . .] rehearsals with singers, chorus, and orchestra;

staging rehearsals; the making of costumes and scenery. It was I who arranged for the purchase and transport of the three ondes Martenot, the installation of the brass players in the front boxes, the two-platform set-up for the woodwind and *claviers*, and the seating of the string and percussion players in the pit. I even ordered the laser beams for the projections – the cross, the moving flecks of colour.[59]

According to Grenier, Messiaen was generally calm, although there were alarums when he was told that the television crews needed ten complete vocal scores to follow the action during recording: 'His voice was quite high-pitched, and he departed from the room in some haste, as if to stomp out a fire'.[60]

With the first night barely a month away, Messiaen's health declined once more in October, traces of blood in his urine raising the spectre of cancer. Once again he feared that death was imminent, a concern shared by his own physician, Dr Bernachon, until the opera was finally performed, as he admitted to Loriod in a letter dated 20 April 1984: 'I must confide in you that I had a lot of anxiety for the health of your husband. My worries were only lifted when I saw him radiant on the steps of the Opéra.'[61] Messiaen himself was anxious about the demands the title role was placing on José van Dam. Grenier recalled the composer approaching the singer after one performance and 'inquiring if he was all right after six hours, nearly all of it onstage. Van Dam responded in the affirmative, but I still see the concern on Messiaen's face as well as the exhaustion evident in the body language of van Dam.'[62]

Saint François was the event of the year, causing a frisson of excitement way beyond Paris, with people coming from across the world to see the opera. The eleven performances from 28 November to 18 December played to packed houses, the list of those attending resembling an index for a musical *Who's Who*. As with earlier works, *Saint François* divided opinion. On the first night, the end of Act I was greeted with boos from some in the audience.[63] The detractors were in the minority, though, and, not for the first time, the greatest divergence of opinion was to be found between the tumultuous reception within the Palais Garnier, and the response of a number of critics. Some were enthusiastic, with Alan G. Artner concluding his review in the Christmas Day edition of the *Chicago Tribune* that 'despite its giantism, it goes unmatched by any other opera of our time in the authenticity of its feeling. It is a masterpiece.' Nonetheless, as Messiaen later observed: 'A few journalists wrote articles almost as malicious as those for my *Petites Liturgies*, although in more respectable turns of phrase [. . .] All things considered, I told myself that these attacks proved I had preserved a certain youthfulness.'[64] David Stevens, writing in the *International Herald Tribune* on 30 November, typified the sceptical response:

> There are moments of great beauty, certain scenes (the leper, the stigmata) had a convincing vigour and power, and the composer uses his immense orchestra with economy and consideration for the voices. But for those who cannot enter fully into Messiaen's sound world and time scale, it is hard to justify the Wagnerian length and slow-motion pace. [. . .]
>
> That the composer was given carte blanche and a prestigious platform for what is almost certainly his last major statement is to everyone's credit, but a reckless disregard of theatrical limitations and the stamina of operagoers will surely take its toll.

The palliative to such malevolent comments came courtesy of the television broadcast, which prompted 'innumerable letters from enthusiastic viewers, some even telling me that the work had brought tears to their eyes'.[65]

Saint François d'Assise had been composed and staged. Messiaen had surmounted this greatest compositional challenge, a work longer than *Turangalîla*, *La Transfiguration* and *Des canyons* put together. He had overcome the various health problems and the self-imposed burden of composing his very best music for what he increasingly saw as his swan-song. No doubt expecting death to be imminent, he announced just before the première: 'Twilight has arrived. I have finished. I will never compose anything else.'[66] But Messiaen did not die just after *Saint François*, and he now faced an unusual question: what comes next after you have composed your final work?

Notes

1. Samuel, *Music and Color*, p. 222.
2. ibid, p. 151.
3. PHNS, p. 284.
4. ibid, p. 285.
5. Samuel, *Music and Color*, p. 160.
6. PHNS, p. 286.
7. ibid, p. 287.
8. ibid, pp. 289–90.
9. Samuel, *Music and Color*, p. 161.
10. ibid.
11. Kent Nagano, private communication.
12. Samuel, *Music and Color*, p. 170.
13. PHNS, p. 234.
14. ibid, p. 284.
15. ibid, p. 287.
16. Some information from Messiaen's diaries on the genesis of the opera was communicated privately by Peter Hill.
17. Samuel, *Music and Color*, p. 207.
18. Private communication.
19. Massin, *Une poétique du merveilleux*, p. 95.
20. Founded in 1961, Les Percussions de Strasbourg was an ensemble of six young percussionists from Strasbourg orchestras. Over 170 compositions have been dedicated to the group.
21. For a thorough account of Messiaen's various ballet projects, see Nigel Simeone, 'Dancing *Turangalîla*: Messiaen and the Ballet' in Dingle and Simeone (eds), *Olivier Messiaen: Music, Art & Literature*, (Aldershot: Ashgate, forthcoming).
22. Patricia Malavard, *Visions de l'Amen* (Paris: Editions Albert Morancé, 1966), p. 2.
23. Rischin, *For the End of Time*, p. 94.

24. Almut Roßler, *Contributions to the Spiritual World of Olivier Messiaen with original texts by the composer* (Duisburg: Gilles und Francke Verlag, 1986), p. 132.
25. Samuel, *Music and Color*, p. 207.
26. Jaquet-Langlais, *Ombre et lumière*, p. 64.
27. Claude Samuel, *Conversations with Olivier Messiaen*, trans. Felix Aprahamian (London: Stainer and Bell, 1976), p. 82.
28. Samuel, *Permanences*, p. 250.
29. ibid.
30. Samuel, *Music and Color*, p. 209.
31. BBC WAC, 'R83/625/1. Music Registry Messiaen, Olivier, 1955–64'.
32. Rolf Liebermann, *En passant par Paris* (Paris: Gallimard/nrf, 1980), p. 410.
33. Also known as the *Canticle of Brother Sun*.
34. PHNS, pp. 304–5.
35. Samuel, *Music and Color*, p. 213.
36. ibid, p. 228.
37. Hill, 'Interview with Loriod', p. 297.
38. Messiaen, 'Entretien avec Claude Samuel' ECD75505.
39. PHNS, p. 318.
40. Private communication.
41. Messiaen, 'Entretien avec Claude Samuel' ECD75505.
42. *Hommage à Olivier Messiaen: novembre–décembre 1978* [brochure-program], Claude Samuel, artistic director.
43. PHNS, p. 310.
44. ibid, p. 316.
45. ibid, p. 319.
46. ibid, p. 321.
47. Samuel, *Music and Color*, pp. 205–6.
48. Rolf Liebermann, *En passant par Paris-Opéra*, p. 410.
49. Messiaen, 'Entretien avec Claude Samuel' ECD75505.
50. PHNS, p. 335.
51. Samuel, *Permanences*, p. 415.
52. Samuel, *Music and Color*, pp. 216–17.
53. ibid, pp. 221–2.
54. ibid, p. 219. N.B. The desired number is mistranslated in the English version as being 500.

55. Samuel, *Music and Color*, p. 247.
56. ibid.
57. Grenier sang in two performances.
58. Robert Grenier, 'Recollections on Singing Messiaen's *Saint François d'Assise*', *The Opera Quarterly* (vol. 18, no. 1, winter 2002), p. 61.
59. Samuel, *Music and Color*, p. 251.
60. Grenier, 'Recollections', p. 61.
61. PHNS, p. 340.
62. Grenier, *Recollections*, p. 62.
63. ibid.
64. Samuel, *Music and Color*, pp. 248–9.
65. ibid, p. 250.
66. *Libération*, 28 November 1983.

9 Tous les oiseaux des étoiles[1] 1984–92

> Afterwards, I felt empty, I imagined that I had said everything,
> I thought that I could stop composing.[2]

Having spent so long in the orbit of a musical object as colossal as *Saint François*, Messiaen understandably had trouble summoning the mental and physical strength to escape its gravitational pull. Loriod recalled that 'he became exhausted, and after the work was finished he became very depressed – he was unable to eat or walk or indeed do anything. And he told everyone that he'd finished composing.'[3] During the latter stages of the opera's lengthy gestation, excitement at seeing the work take shape was countered by numerous anxieties and setbacks. At the extremes, Messiaen had plumbed the depths of despair in December 1981, believing he would never complete *Saint François*, only to reach the height of jubilation with the first production, but there were numerous peaks and troughs in between. It is small wonder, then, that the evidence about his state of mind remains contradictory for several years afterwards, especially with regard to his creative aspirations.

Alan Rich reported in *Newsweek* on 12 December 1983 that '[. . .] before the opera opened, [Messiaen] said firmly that he had ended his career as a composer. A day after the première, he let it slip that he was ready to change his mind.' The tumble back into the abyss mentioned by Loriod occurred during January 1984, but by late in the month he was making notes about a new piece: 'For Boulez, *Vitrail* for Mary, Queen of Peace – two or three pianos, and small orchestra, lots of colours.'[4] Late in February, Messiaen was already making preparations for a new composition, but, rather than the work for Boulez, it was to be his largest cycle for his own instrument, the eighteen-movement *Livre du Saint Sacrement*. This two-hour *summa* for the organ can be regarded as a companion piece to the opera, just as the *Méditations* explore similar theological territory to *La Transfiguration*. Now, though, Messiaen faltered. His next works were miniatures, a sequence of minor satellites alongside the gas giants of *Saint François* and the *Livre du Saint Sacrement*. The composition of the first two of these thumbnail sketches, *Petites esquisses d'oiseaux* and *Un Vitrail et des oiseaux*, was as hesitant and lacking in confidence as work on the *Livre du Saint Sacrement* had been fluent. Messiaen was doubtful of their worth, and it seemed as if a career notable for the confident breadth of its vision might end in a dribble of inconsequential works. It was only in 1987 that Messiaen's self-belief began to return, allied to a new flexibility in his established harmonic style. This was achieved not by experimentation but by re-examining his most favoured compositional elements. In effect, Messiaen returned to first principles. In addition to three more miniatures, the reinvigorated composer now embarked upon his last great masterpiece, *Éclairs sur l'au-delà...*, a sequence of eleven meditations for large orchestra.

Like the *Méditations*, some of the music for the *Livre du Saint Sacrement* (Book of the Blessed Sacrament) originated in an improvisation:

> My post as church organist obliges me to improvise; my wife records me and I listen to these improvisations with a very critical ear. One Maundy Thursday evening, when the Church commemorates the institution by Christ of the Eucharist, I had three minutes to fill with music, and that was when I had a sudden inspiration. I played a piece which at first looks like nothing at all special: a very simple Bacchic rhythm (short – long – long), a commonplace first inversion chord . . . but I suddenly realized, on hearing it again, that this music was not like any other.

I believe that I was inspired by the moment, touched by this service which was very beautiful. I rewrote this piece, I called it 'L'Institution de l'Eucharistie' (The Institution of the Eucharist), and I began to write the Livre du Saint Sacrement [. . .] It was more than a year after Saint François.[5]

The impetus for the work came in 1984, commissioned jointly by the city of Detroit and the American Guild of Organists for the latter's biennial National Convention. However, just as seeds of the *Méditations* were formed several years before Messiaen officially began composing the work in 1969, the improvisation on which he based the 'Institution de l'Eucharistie' was in fact made on Maundy Thursday 1981 (16 April).[6] In fact, Messiaen had been thinking about writing another organ cycle for several years before this. Asked by Claude Samuel about his current projects at the time of his seventieth birthday celebrations in 1978, Messiaen replied: 'First, if my eyes permit it, to finish the orchestration of my *Saint François*. Then, perhaps, I shall write a large work for organ.'[7] In response to a request during March 1980 from the clergy of the Trinité for a recital, the composer noted in his diary that, by 1984 or 1985 'I shall be able to give the first performance of a work by me for organ'.[8] In fact, the new work was first performed not by Messiaen, but by one of his most devoted interpreters, the German organist Almut Rössler. Ideas fermented during the early 1980s; a time when, rather than composing, Messiaen was engaged with the orchestration and the logistics of *Saint François*. In 1981 he made plans for a *Prière au Saint Sacrement*, then, in 1982, his thoughts turned to studies ('Etudes on complementary colours, on grace notes, and on light and dark'), while also making notes on 'a series of pieces on the Blessed Sacrament', and a piece on the parting of the Red Sea.[9] In May 1983 he made his first visit to Israel, and the Messiaens returned in 1984 for a fortnight during Lent:

[. . .] for a Catholic like me, this trip was overwhelming, for I visited the sites where Moses, David and the great figures of the Old Testament lived; I saw the places Christ passed through. I was in Gethsemane, the garden whose three-thousand-year-old olive trees witnessed the agony of Christ. I saw the cenacle where Christ instituted the Eucharist and where, having risen from the dead, he twice appeared before the Apostles [. . .] visiting these sacred, almost divine, historic sites is an extraordinary experience. Added to this is the marvellous beauty of the landscape, its contrasts, the extreme aridity of the yellow-rock mountains, the extraordinary silence of the Judean desert, a silence hardly broken by the solitary song of a marvellous bird, the desert lark; and in the Valley of Jericho, the rich plant life with oranges, bananas, palm trees, and an abundance of springs where the water flows to profusion. You go from one landscape to the next with no transition.[10]

As with the canyons of Utah for *Des canyons*, the scenery and birdsong that Messiaen encountered in Israel and Palestine permeates the *Livre du Saint Sacrement*, notably with the desert portrait of the sixth movement 'La Manne et le pain de Vie' (Manna and the bread of Life) and the fifteenth movement's jubilant mélange of birds 'La Joie de la grâce'.

The superstructure of the cycle broadly mirrors the structure of the Mass. The first four movements are acts of adoration, analogous to the opening prayers. The next seven movements contain allusions to, and representations of, Scriptural narrative equivalent to the liturgy of the Word. The last seven movements are meditations on liturgical mysteries, corresponding to the consecration and subsequent participation in the Eucharist. This is redolent of the concert liturgy of *La Transfiguration*, and, like the oratorio, the emphasis seems to be on the awe and power of the mysteries being contemplated. Gillian Weir has commented on the 'stark strength and directness that is almost brutal' of the seventh movement, 'Les Ressuscités et la lumière de la Vie' (The Resurrected and the light of life).[11] The ninth movement, 'les ténèbres' (sic) (darkness), is even more uncompromising. The darkness in question is that of the Passion, and specifically the Crucifixion. As with the climax of 'Les Stigmates', which is also inspired by the Passion, the composer's contemplation of suffering provokes a ferocious outburst, with unrelentingly harsh chords during the opening section. The conclusion may be subdued, but no less unsettling, with a chilling, low rumbling representing the darkness which covered the land. The impact made by 'les ténèbres' is actually more desolate than that made by 'Les Stigmates'. Whereas the immense suffering depicted by the opera is immediately set into relief by the assuaging call of the chorus, 'les ténèbres' itself contains no hint of relief. A stark contrast of mood does come with the beginning of the next movement, 'La Résurrection du Christ', but Messiaen uses the power of the instrument to drive home an awe-inspiring message of jubilation with overwhelming force in a blaze of F sharp major; at no point is the hand of tenderness held out in response to the suffering. This has to wait until the simple humility of the Prayers before and after Communion, the fourteenth and sixteenth movements respectively. The concluding 'Offrande et Alléluia final' was the first piece to have been written when Messiaen began work on the cycle in February 1984. Originally called 'La Visitation et la joie de Jean Baptiste', this dazzling toccata had sat a little awkwardly before the 'Prière avant Communion' in Messiaen's original scheme,[12] until the composer realized that, with the change of name, it could become a more universal Magnificat.

Much of the *Livre du Saint Sacrement* was composed at La Sauline, Messiaen finally able to take advantage of being able to compose, as opposed to orchestrate, away from Paris during the winter months. Like the similarly proportioned *Vingt Regards*, it was composed at great speed, reflecting, perhaps, that the work had been at the back of his mind for more than half of the time that he was working on *Saint François*. The subject matter, the Blessed Sacrament, is closely related to the opera's charting of the Saint's ever closer communion with Christ, notably in the quasi-Passion setting of 'Les Stigmates'. It is as if, having created a magnificent *summa* for the public, secular world of the concert hall and opera house, Messiaen now wished to do the same for the more private, sacred realm of his organ music. The next step, though, was more difficult.

He still had the commission from Boulez to complete, but, despite making notes and even working on some harmonies, Messiaen struggled to get going with it. In fact, there was only one person capable of coaxing a piece from him at this time: Loriod. Anyone ignorant of his low confidence might have expected that Messiaen would now compose a monumental cycle for the piano fulfilling a similar function to the *Livre du Saint Sacrement*. Such a project could have been inspired by a religious topic and written on an even vaster scale than *Vingt Regards*, incorporating the compositional developments of the intervening forty years. Alternatively, he might have channelled his energy into producing a second *Catalogue d'oiseaux*, a project for which he had transcribed more than enough material. Birds would inevitably play their part, but in a far less grandiose manner. Loriod asked Messiaen why her favourite bird, the robin, had never been given a starring role in one of his piano works. His eventual response was to produce not one, but three portraits of robins. In addition, he interleaved this unassuming triptych with contributions from three further birds – a blackbird ('Le Merle noir'), a song thrush ('La Grive musicienne') and a skylark ('L'Alouette des champs') to produce a total of six *Petites esquisses d'oiseaux* (Little bird sketches). Rather than any grand plans, it is the unassuming proportions and deceptive exterior simplicity which characterizes these miniatures. He composed the *Petites esquisses* in secret during the summer of 1985 under cover of correcting proofs, so that it was a surprise and a delight for Loriod when one Sunday morning at La Sauline in late September he suddenly produced the new work,[13] less with a flourish than a wave of timidity: 'He was very doubtful about the *esquisses* and said "I am tired, I can no longer write. The pieces are not very good."'[14]

Given this low self-esteem, it is not surprising that Messiaen chose four particularly favoured birds all of which had appeared in *Saint François*. Taken in the context of his previous works, these vignettes contain a number of unusual features, not least of which is their length or, more accurately, their brevity. The entire collection takes barely a quarter of an hour to perform. The *Petites esquisses* are also atypical amongst the composer's birdsong works for piano owing to the complete absence of depictions of the birds' habitats. Each piece in

Catalogue d'oiseaux had been a portrait depicting a scene from nature, with all the sights, smells and sounds experienced as well as the songs of several birds. By contrast, each of the short movements of the *Petites esquisses* presents the song of a single bird placed on the pedestal of a few favoured chords. In this respect, the collection is closer in spirit, if not style, to his earliest birdsong compositions – notably *Le Merle noir*, *Réveil* and *Oiseaux exotiques* – rather than being an appurtenance to *Catalogue d'oiseaux* and *La Fauvette des jardins*. As Loriod sensed, the *Petites esquisses* represent the beginnings of a new economy of means in Messiaen's music, of which just one characteristic is a paucity of bass textures. At first, the pianist Peter Hill found that, physically, they were curiously tiring to practise until he repositioned his piano stool so that he was sitting an octave higher than usual.[15] As for Loriod, she certainly did not share her husband's reticence: 'I worked at them and I told him "they are marvellous, absolutely marvellous".'[16]

It is remarkable that Messiaen managed to compose anything at all during 1985 given the number of concerts, frequently abroad, that he agreed to attend in the wake of completing *Saint François* and the *Livre du Saint Sacrement*. Quite apart from trips to, among other places, Toronto, California, Italy and Metz during the Spring, it is the inroads into the normally sacrosanct summer months that catch the eye. Much of August was spent in Salzburg, and, during mid-September, the Messiaens were in Denmark. The Salzburg visit was made on account of the work that had caused Messiaen's creative impasse: *Saint François*. Four scenes (3, 6, 7 and 8) were semistaged, with Dietrich Fischer-Dieskau in the title role and Lothar Zagrosek conducting. Although the concert was on 22 August, the anxious composer arrived ten days earlier to attend the rehearsals: 'I'd been quite afraid of this partial performance, without the actual spectacle of a full staging, but it was so beautiful that I myself was quite carried away.'[17] The Autumn saw further trips, with a week in Bremen and then, in November 1985, the receipt of the prestigious Kyoto prize from Kazuo Inamori provided an excuse for the Messiaens to revisit their beloved Japan: 'There were four days of grand festivities, with mountains of flowers, dinners,

25. Messiaen and Loriod in Salzburg, August 1985.

gardens, and temples – and many speeches; I personally delivered two speeches, each an hour and a half long.'[18]

Busy it may have been, but 1985 was merely a warm-up for the virtually non-stop concerts of 1986, with the opera again featuring among the highlights. Four months after receiving the Kyoto prize, Messiaen was back in Japan on the first leg of a world tour that, in addition to Tokyo, would encompass London, Berlin, Boston and New York. Scenes 3, 7 and 8 of *Saint François* were presented in concert performances with varying personnel but Seiji Ozawa always at the helm. Typically, Messiaen popped back to Paris the day after the London performance on 26 March to play for the Holy Saturday and Easter Sunday services at the Trinité, before going on to Berlin. Each of these performances of bleeding chunks from the opera was a tremendous success, but even better was to come. The entirety of September was spent at the Bonn Festival, which that year was dedicated jointly to Beethoven and Messiaen. Just about all of Messiaen's output, including *La Transfiguration*, was performed, the culmination being a complete concert performance, repeated in Utrecht and Madrid, of *Saint François* under Kent Nagano.

The other major event of 1986 was the first performance of the *Livre du Saint Sacrement*, given by Almut Rössler on 1 July in Detroit in a 'private' performance in front of 2,000 members of the American Guild of Organists. Despite the dry acoustic, oppressive summer heat and a persistent noise from a ciphered pipe on the large five-manual organ,[19] Messiaen enthused a couple of weeks later to Claude Samuel that it was 'a very great success'.[20] Having survived this baptism of fire, Rössler repeated the work in Detroit, Ann Arbor (Michigan), and during the Bonn Festival in September before finally being able to perform it at her own organ in the Johanneskirche in Düsseldorf as the centrepiece of another festival of Messiaen's music.

Aside from these major events, Messiaen traversed Europe and the Atlantic repeatedly during the course of the year. The trips to the United States and Bonn, at the beginning and end of the summer respectively, meant that Messiaen had not much more than a month scheduled in Petichet. However, even this was cut short, and once again *Saint François* was the cause. Since the first production, Messiaen had been trying to interest record companies in releasing a recording. In August, Eric Alberti, a member of the Opéra orchestra, informed Messiaen that he intended to set up a company, Cybelia, that would produce a recording. Crucially, he had secured an agreement from the musicians that they would only be paid if the discs made a profit. Messiaen rushed back to Paris to oversee the editing process.[21]

After such frenetic activity, 1987 was a relatively quiet year for concerts; a kind of collective drawing-in of breath before Messiaen's eightieth birthday year. With a little more stability in his schedule, he now began to find his feet again as a composer. In effect, upon completing the *Petites esquisses* in September 1985, Messiaen took a sabbatical from composing which lasted until the time of their première on 26 January 1987. The only problem was that this was not a planned break. He was finding it impossible to make headway with the commission for Boulez. With numerous distractions, quite apart from the almost continual concerts, there was plenty of scope for prevarication by a composer short of confidence. Nor was there any false humility about Messiaen's attitude to the *Petites esquisses*. Their first performance saw them placed rather awkwardly within an Ensemble Intercontemporain concert: the result of an attempt, shortly after he presented them to Loriod, to withdraw from the commission for the ensemble and proffer the piano pieces as recompense. Boulez was not about to let his former *maître* give up so easily:

> Brigitte Marger has told me that in a moment of discouragement – at least I hope it's only a moment – you've given up writing a work for the Ensemble. I am truly sorry. We would of course be ready and willing to ask Yvonne to play the new piano pieces which you have written for her. But I would like all the same for you to reconsider your decision. The Ensemble and I very much wish to give a first performance, and in addition to the première to play it in various tours abroad.
>
> Once you have decided, let me know what you are able to do. But I've no doubt myself that you'll find a way of overcoming this obstacle and write for us the work which you have promised and to which we will devote ourselves.[22]

Both the score of the work he finally produced, *Un Vitrail et des oiseaux* (A Stained-glass window and birds), and Messiaen's note for the first performances state that it was composed in 1986. In fact, the only thing written that year was a short 'Chant donné in the style of Mozart' for the Conservatoire harmony examination, but, like improvisations, such pastiches did not count as true composition to Messiaen. He had had another go at the Boulez commission in January 1986, but noted dispiritedly in his diary that these were 'laboured attempts'.[23] Once he eventually found a way forward early in 1987, progress was rapid, the score being finished by 27 March.[24]

As we have seen, the idea of stained glass (Vitrail) had been in Messiaen's mind since the first mention of the piece in January 1984, initially envisaging a Marian work. He mused further about the subject matter at the time of his abortive attempts in January 1986: 'Vitrail en fleur ... amaryllis ... Carpathian campanula'.[25] Like the Petites esquisses, it was, ultimately, a few of Messiaen's favourite things, already tried and tested, that held the answer, rather than any grand scheme or new departure. Un Vitrail opens, like his first birdsong work for orchestra, Réveil des oiseaux, with a solo nightingale, and the other birds are all regular characters in his music, such as the garden warbler and the blackcap. The chorale, the Vitrail of the title, is an adaptation of a melody that had appeared in Turangalîla, Cinq Rechants and Cantéyodjayâ. Anyone unaware that it was written in 1987 could be forgiven for mistaking Un Vitrail as being a preparatory sketch for Saint François, with the same trinity of xylophones at the opening, hors tempo ('outside time') passages recalling the birdsong choruses from 'Le Prêche aux oiseaux', periodic interjections from the blackcap on woodwinds, and the piano taking the role of protagonist. Then again, Un Vitrail certainly does not resemble the opera in terms of scale, being, at a little under nine minutes, Messiaen's shortest orchestral work.

Having broken the creative block caused by one Boulez commission, Messiaen felt confident enough to accept another, this time to write a work for the 1989 Festival d'automne in Paris. Quite apart from the Boulez connection, the parallels between Un Vitrail and La Ville d'en-haut, are so striking that there is justification for suggesting that La Ville is little more than the re-composition of

Un Vitrail. Phrased more sympathetically, *La Ville* displays greater self-assurance in exploring the same musical and theological territory as that charted in Un Vitrail. Messiaen's confidence is audibly returning. Admittedly, this is due, in part, to the substantially bigger ensemble used in *La Ville*, although, like Un Vitrail, it omits strings. Messiaen's use of a full brass section in *La Ville* evokes the monumentalism which had dominated his soundworld since the mid-1960s. In particular, the opening call to arms is the one significant trait that distinguishes it from Un Vitrail in terms of musical style, *La Ville* being a distinctly monumental miniature – a monumentalette, perhaps. The other feature that differentiates the two works is their titles. In the context of Messiaen's works, *Un Vitrail et des oiseaux* is a purely functional title. A religious subtext is implicit – stained glass is primarily experienced in churches, after all – especially with Messiaen's mention of the 'aspect invisible' in his note for the work. However, for once, there is no Biblical inscription. There is no such reticence with *La Ville d'en-haut*, a work unequivocally about the celestial city.

By the time that he began writing *La Ville* in August 1987, Messiaen had accepted the commission from Zubin Mehta that would result in *Éclairs sur l'au-delà. . . .* Then Music Director of the New York Philharmonic, Mehta wanted a work for the orchestra's 150th anniversary season in 1992–3. Messiaen's response, in a letter dated 2 August, was positive, albeit tempered by a series of caveats:

> I was very touched that you thought of me for a commission. I accept with pleasure to write: a work for large orchestra [. . .] I shall soon be 79, and I already have two other commissions for large orchestra to fulfil, to say nothing of my ceaseless travelling for concerts abroad. I feel very well and I hope that I shall still be in good health for 1992–93. Anyway, I shall try to write a work worthy of you and the orchestra, but it is impossible to tell you so far in advance what the duration and instrumentation will be. We shall, therefore, have to decide the material details of the commission a little later. In any case, you can count on me, it's yes!

In marked contrast to La Transfiguration and Saint François, Messiaen's US commissions all seemed to flow easily, and this new work was to be no exception.

Messiaen had found it difficult to compose amidst the incessant concerts of 1986, even if they ultimately rejuvenated him. His letter to Mehta suggests that he was anxious about encountering similar problems during 1988, his eightieth birthday year. Just about the entire musical world wished to mark this milestone by celebrating the many achievements of his long career. During the course of the year, he heard the entirety of his œuvre several times over; the festivals held from May to June in Australia and during December in London were particularly thorough. However, having broken the creative deadlock encountered with Un Vitrail, it seems that, time-consuming and tiring though they were, the travels (and travails) of 1988 galvanized Messiaen. To start with, he got as much done as possible during the relative calm of the summer and autumn of 1987, but he also managed to note ideas and compose between the numerous commitments of the anniversary year. A draft score of La Ville was complete by September 1987 and, spurred on by a meeting with Mehta, Messiaen was at La Sauline by the end of October with thoughts clearly forming about the nature of the piece for New York:

> Take books on astronomy, on painting. The same music can change in substance by being high or low, fortissimo or pianissimo, very fast or very slow. Pack the cassettes of New Zealand birds.[26] Devise harmonies, rhythms, melodies for the Prélude à l'Apocalypse.[27]

As with earlier large-scale works, Messiaen's early thoughts were more modest than the eventual work. Given the caveats in his letter to Mehta, it is possible that the original scope of Messiaen's ambitions was for a work of similar dimensions to La Ville. By the beginning of 1988, he was thinking in terms of a seven-movement work, rather than the eleven movements of what became Éclairs sur l'au-delà.... The 'Prélude' from October 1987 was now a brass chorale, 'Apparition du Christ glorieux', balanced by a final slow movement for strings, provisionally called 'Song of the Lamb', and this early plan also provided for two birdsong movements.[28]

The six-week trip to Australia in May and June 1988 had a decisive impact upon *Éclairs*. As usual, especially when visiting a country for the first time, Messiaen had ensured that there was time in the schedule for some trips to collect birdsong. In particular, he wanted to seek out the lyrebird. His first encounter with this remarkable creature was on a visit to Sherbrook Forest early in June. In the preface to the score of *Éclairs*, Loriod recalls that:

> The composer was in this sunlit forest, with giant eucalyptus, like cathedral columns, in the vibrant light, when all of a sudden he saw the bird several metres from him majestically raise its plumes to form a lyre more than twice his height. This ritual touched him and prompted him to think of the betrothed of the Apocalypse 'adorned for her husband'.

Messiaen was so struck by the song of this 'master mimic' that, uniquely in his orchestral music, an entire movement of *Éclairs*, 'L'Oiseau-lyre et la Ville-fiancée', is dedicated to its song. This exuberant, high-speed flight around the orchestra by the superb lyrebird is based upon a transcription made at Tidbinbilla, near Canberra, about a week and a half after the composer's first sighting of the bird:

> Its song is by turns whistling, fluting, screeching, radiant, brassy, disjointed, where the sounds of water mix with imitations of other birds, with a prodigious virtuosity, range of attacks and nuances. Three lyrebirds singing together give the impression of an orchestra filling an entire forest with bright and joyous colours.[29]

As well as this jubilant outburst, the score of *Éclairs* is filled with numerous other Australian birds; souvenirs of a happy and fruitful trip.

The official French celebration of Messiaen's eightieth birthday was a concert given by the Ensemble Intercontemporain conducted by Pierre Boulez at the Théâtre des Champs-Élysées on 26 November at which *Un Vitrail et des oiseaux* received its première. However, Messiaen was in London on the actual date of his birthday where a semi-staged production of Saint François marked the peroration of a two-week festival. Stretching back to the Préludes and incorporating the UK premières of the Petites esquisses and Un Vitrail, together with performances of La Transfiguration and Des canyons, and also music by former students, this was an especially complete survey of Messiaen's output with which to conclude this anniversary year.

Messiaen made good progress on Éclairs throughout 1989. By July he was ready to begin orchestrating, and in April 1990 he had completed the draft score and was ready to begin making the fair copy.[30] As if this was not enough, he had, in the meantime, also composed and orchestrated another work. At the end of 1988, Marek Janowski had asked Messiaen to write a work 'for small orchestra in the spirit of Mozart'. Despite being immersed in Éclairs, the idea of writing a piece for the bicentenary of Mozart's death (5 December 1991) captured Messiaen's imagination, and within a week he had decided upon a title: Un Sourire (A Smile).[31] This charming little piece intersperses a slow, tender melody for strings (without double-basses), coloured by woodwind solos, with chirpy birdsong episodes for woodwind and xylophones. It is not surprising that Messiaen was particularly enthused by this tribute. His lifelong love of Mozart's music is clear from the inclusion in Traité of his analyses of the Mozart piano concerti. The only other composers accorded such prominence are Debussy, Le Jeune's Printemps and Stravinsky's The Rite of Spring. Moreover, it is Mozart who makes repeated surprise appearances regarding the 'etymology' of Messiaen's most characteristic chords in 'Tome VII' of the Traité. At the British première of Un Sourire in 1992, Kent Nagano related how, the afternoon before the work's first performance in Paris the previous December, Messiaen had told him:

> It's a very special piece because I've always written works and I've been really scared what people would think about [them] after they've heard the piece. I've always wondered if they would really be able to accept the

pieces. This is a piece that I just wrote for myself. It's a piece where I really wanted to do something particularly beautiful, something particularly personal, and I felt so determined to make it a piece for myself that I called it *Sourire*.[32]

In retrospect, it can be seen that *Un Sourire*, with its simplicity of expression and strings floating free of the mooring provided by double-basses, was the first intimation of the soundworld of *Éclairs*.

La Ville d'en-haut received its first performances, by the BBC Symphony Orchestra under Boulez, in November 1989. After the première at the Salle Pleyel on 17 November, Messiaen followed the orchestra to Milan, London and the Huddersfield Festival, where there was a reunion with John Cage. Aside from being pleased with the performances of the bite-sized chunk of monumentalism of *La Ville*, Messiaen was struck by another piece receiving its first outings, Boulez's substantial re-working of *Le Visage Nuptial*. Given that he was still in the midst of orchestrating *Éclairs*, the manifest similarity of spirit between the cascading points of light of 'La Constellation du Sagittaire', and the rhythmic interaction of eight spacially separated crotales in 'Gravité. L'Emmuré' from Boulez's masterpiece is surely no coincidence.

1990 was a relatively quiet year for the now elderly composer. On 10 May, Alain, his 'petit frère', died. Visibly shaken, Messiaen typically found consolation by immersing himself in his work.[33] Alain had been suffering from Parkinson's Disease, with things coming to a head in the spring of 1988, when it became clear that he could no longer look after himself. The Messiaens' tour to Australia, which left such a profound mark upon *Éclairs*, was nearly cancelled. Initially Alain came to stay at the rue Marcadet, but this was an ill-fated solution for he was long used to living on his own; caring for him was not easy. Finally, shortly before departing for Sydney, a place was found in a nursing home.[34]

Messiaen spent more than a year making the fair copy of *Éclairs*, underlining both the numerous other calls on his time, and the

26. Messiaen at a performance of *Turangalîla*, Israel, summer 1990.

extreme care that he took over this definitive document of a work. Anyone who witnessed the meticulous way that he signed his name on a concert programme would be amazed that he would have enough time to write out a line of plainchant, never mind a large-scale orchestral score. Loriod recently recalled that Messiaen 'was very very slow in his work, but he always worked well and exceptionally thoroughly. But while he was doing that, I could have done two things – though possibly badly.'[35] *Éclairs* was completed on 27 July 1991,[36] although, while he was in hospital the following April, he went through the score, singing the themes to Loriod so that she could add metronome markings.[37]

At the time that he was composing *Éclairs*, the perceptions of Messiaen were dominated by *La Transfiguration*, *Des canyons* and *Saint François*, what Paul Griffiths has characterized as 'Trois Grandes liturgies', to which *Et exspecto* can be regarded as a forerunner: a kind of *Das Rheingold*. When it emerged that he was composing a large work for the New York Philharmonic Orchestra, expectations were raised of another colossal monument in a similar manner. Such speculation was hardly undermined by the revelation that, with 128 instrumentalists, the orchestra for *Éclairs* would be the largest ever used by Messiaen. In fact, when *Éclairs* was finally performed, the most striking characteristic was its restraint, reminding us that Messiaen's music is instantly recognizable but never predictable. In contrast to the monumentalism of the previous twenty-five years, *Éclairs* is often disarming in its charm and intimacy. Whereas *Des canyons* is an enormous aural protrait created using barely forty players, *Éclairs* frequently sounds like chamber music which just happens to require an orchestra of 128 to perform it. The music is essentially put together from the same materials, but it is as if Messiaen has reversed the polarity. The most successful purveyor of musical overstatement since Wagner became in his final years a master of delectable understatement.

Éclairs also exhibits a freshness and vitality which, with the possible exception of *Un Sourire*, had been a little in short supply in the music written since *Saint François*. Nevertheless, *Éclairs* shares some characteristics with the series of miniatures composed after the opera. In particular, it shares the reluctance to venture below the tenor register which has been noted in *Petites esquisses*, which characterizes *Un Vitrail* and *La Ville*, and is a defining feature of the bass-free string writing in *Un Sourire*. Most striking, perhaps, is that Messiaen somehow manages to blend the effervescence of these 'lightning flashes'[38] with a prevailing sense of serenity.

Like several earlier works, Éclairs draws inspiration from the vivid imagery of Revelation. Lasting just over an hour, it is built upon three beautiful slow movements. The majestic opening chorale for winds, 'Apparition du Christ glorieux', sedately unfolds at a pace designed to ease the listener into the broad timescale of Messiaen's depictions of the eternal, and away from the hustle and bustle of modern living. This is balanced in the fifth and eleventh movements by two great adagios for strings, 'Demeurer dans l'Amour' (Abide in Love) and 'Le Christ, lumière du Paradis' (Christ, light of Paradise) which find Messiaen unashamedly wearing his heart on his sleeve. Within this broad framework, Messiaen presents us with the music of stars and nebulae, dazzling kaleidoscopes of colour, entire aviaries of birdsong, and the trumpets of the Apocalypse. Even in his eighties, he was still prepared to be musically ruthless; the enchanting world of 'Demeurer dans l'Amour . . .' abruptly disappears with the three resounding thwacks of the bass drum that herald 'Les Sept Anges aux sept trompettes' (The Seven Angels with seven trumpets). The following 'Et Dieu essuiera toute larmes de leurs yeux. . .' (And God wiped away every tear from their eyes), is as tender as the Angels were forthright. Rather than overwhelm us with the glory of the Almighty, Messiaen here presents God as the assuager, comforting humanity, in a movement as delicate as the gossamer thread of string trills with which it begins.

Except for the three slow movements, birds, not surprisingly, permeate Éclairs. The movement dedicated to the lyrebird is balanced by the ninth, 'Plusieurs oiseaux des arbres de Vie', which is constructed exclusively from the songs of twenty-five rather exotic birds played in free tempo on ten flutes and eight clarinets, thus providing the sole outing for many of Messiaen's large woodwind contingent. The bass instruments, on the other hand, are kept back until their dramatic entry at the beginning of the eighth movement, 'Les Étoiles et la gloire', returning for its resounding concluding chorale, and the leap into the abyss that opens and closes the penultimate 'Le Chemin de l'Invisible'. Despite such dramatic moments, the abiding impression of *Éclairs* is of an understated charm.

Messiaen did not live to hear *Éclairs*. A slow, but inexorable decline in his health had begun at least as early as 1988. He started to suffer from momentary blackouts, the first occurring on 1 June in his lodgings during the trip to Sherbrook Forest. Another blackout a month later left him lying in scalding water in the bath at La Sauline, but tests at Vierzon hospital were inconclusive. Further blackouts followed during the summer, culminating in a particularly bad fall that saw Messiaen whisked back to Paris in an ambulance.[39] However, unlike 1978, he was able to attend the various birthday concerts towards the end of the year. This fragility of health continued throughout the last few years of Messiaen's life. For instance, Yvonne Loriod withdrew from a performance of *Turangalîla* with the LSO under Kent Nagano on 15 June 1989 on account of Messiaen having another fall. He was experiencing pain and mobility problems, and by the time that he went to Israel for a fortnight in the summer of 1990, Messiaen needed to use a wheelchair at the airport.[40]

Despite this, Messiaen still played the organ for the Christmas services in 1991. As usual, Midnight Mass was preceded by a carol service, during which he played several improvisations whose vitality and invention belied the ailing composer's physical condition. Undeterred by his poor health, Messiaen was full of plans for 1992, with the highlights promising to be Peter Sellars's brand-new staging of *Saint François*, the first since the original production, at the Salzburg Festival in August, followed by the première of *Éclairs* in November. He was in and out of hospital in the early months of 1992. In mid-February it was discovered that the increasingly excruciating pains he had been suffering, previously attributed solely to arthritis, were caused by cancer, although Messiaen remained unaware of the diagnosis.[41] On 22 April he had an operation to insert two pins in the top of his back to support collapsed vertebrae. Two days later, he saw Pascal and Josette for the last time, and, on Sunday 26 April, Messiaen received communion in his hospital bed. Early the next evening he began to cough up blood:

> Nurses rushed to help, while Loriod ran to find Messiaen's doctors: they attempted resuscitation but were unable to save him. Loriod remembered having lost track of the time. Outside darkness had fallen, and she noticed that the watch on Messiaen's bedside table had stopped at 8.30 pm.[42]

Messiaen died on the evening of Monday 27 April 1992.

It is a sign of his stature that news of Messiaen's death was carried on the front pages of many newspapers, and not only in France. However, none of the many obituaries surpassed the words spoken by Pierre Boulez on Messiaen's birthday back in 1978 for succinct insight: 'Beneath the very real complexities of his intellectual world he has remained simple and capable of wonder – and that alone is enough to win our hearts.'[43] Messiaen's life and work were commemorated publicly on 14 May with a Mass and concert at the Trinité. However, his funeral was held not in Paris, but in his beloved Petichet. The first performances of *Éclairs* inevitably acted as memorial concerts for the world at large. At both the world and the UK premières, the audience observed a long, respectful silence after the final chord of 'Le Christ, lumière du Paradis', before breaking into enthusiastic applause. Inevitably, *Éclairs* was initially viewed as Messiaen's *Nunc Dimittis*, a musical last will and testament, tying up the loose ends to the long career of the *Maître*. As it turned out, the conclusion to Messiaen's career was not quite so neat. He had been wrong in presuming that *Saint François* would be his last work and that death would follow soon after; although he had many talents, Messiaen could not count prophecy among his gifts. Having struggled to compose for several years in the wake of the opera, it seems that, as he entered his eighties, Messiaen was composing very freely. After his death, Loriod ventured into the inner sanctum of Messiaen's composing studio and discovered an extensive draft on his desk for, of all things, a quadruple concerto.

Written for five musicians whom Messiaen admired greatly, the flautist Catherine Cantin, oboist Heinz Holliger, Rostropovich, the conductor Myung-Whun Chung and, of course, Loriod, Messiaen had begun writing the *Concert à 4* in July 1991, as soon as *Éclairs* was complete. The original impetus had come from Holliger, who had played the *Vocalise* (a study for voice Messiaen had written in 1935) to the composer in 1984, demonstrating how circular breathing enables the oboe to sustain an extended melodic line.[44] Messiaen incorporated the *Vocalise* into the *Concert*, transforming it into an exquisite slow movement, contrasting with the relatively abrasive conclusion to the first movement. Despite the characteristically large orchestra, the work is rather Classical in spirit, though not in content. Whilst pastiche would be out of the question, a debt to Mozart, Scarlatti and Rameau is acknowledged. By the beginning of October 1991, Messiaen was ready to photocopy the drafts of four movements for the *Concert*, but the work was left incomplete at his death. He intended to compose at least one further movement, a fugue with four subjects,[45] and, on past practice, several more might have been added before the work was regarded as complete. Loriod completed the work in consultation with Holliger and Messiaen's former student, George Benjamin. The first performance, at a packed Opéra Bastille on 26 September 1994, was an emotionally charged occasion.

So long his constant companion in life, Loriod has continued to dedicate herself tirelessly to Messiaen's cause since his death. Aside from completing the *Concert*, she undertook the Herculean task of preparing the *Traité de Rythme, de Couleur et d'Ornithologie* for publication according to Messiaen's plan, as well as the scores of his final works and various rediscovered pieces from much earlier in his career. In one of the short films accompanying his 2005 DVD of the *Vingt Regards*, Roger Muraro relates that he and Loriod had visited Messiaen's grave ten days earlier; 'Madame Loriod told me: "I loved him, and I love him still"'.[46]

****

27. Messiaen's grave in the churchyard of Saint-Théoffrey, Petichet.

At the southern end of Petichet, just above the route Napoléon, is the tiny church of Saint-Théoffrey. The 'bald mountain' made famous by Messiaen's nature portraits looms in the background; Lake Petichet at its foot. In front of the church, hidden from the road, is a modest walled graveyard. As with so many village cemeteries the name of a single family, in this case Troussier, is a frequently encountered leitmotif. Towards the centre is the grave of a musician; Marcel Carraud, a local accordionist. The next grave to the left is Messiaen's. From the front, the white headstone is clearly a bird, from the back the wings are transformed into soaring Pentecostal flames. The earthly setting is Messiaen's beloved landscape, but the inscription, a bar of music from *Harawi*, raises the sights heavenwards: 'Tous les oiseaux des étoiles'.

Notes

1. 'All the birds of the stars': a phrase from 'Amour oiseau d'étoile', the tenth song of *Harawi*.
2. Jean-Christophe Marti, 'Entretien avec Olivier Messiaen', *Saint François d'Assise: Libretto, Analyse, Kommentare, Dokumentation* (Salzburger Festspiele, 1992), p. 17.
3. Hill, 'Interview with Loriod', p. 301.
4. PHNS, p. 350.
5. Marti, 'Entretien', p. 17.
6. PHNS, p. 343.
7. Massin, *Une poétique du merveilleux*, p. 75.
8. PHNS, p. 331.
9. ibid, p. 343.
10. Samuel, *Music and Color*, p. 106.
11. Gillian Weir, 'Organ Music II', in Peter Hill (ed.), *The Messiaen Companion* (London: Faber and Faber, 1995), p. 382.
12. PHNS, p. 348.
13. ibid, p. 353.
14. Hill, 'Interview with Loriod', p. 301.
15. Private communication.
16. Hill, 'Interview with Loriod', p. 301.
17. Samuel, *Music and Color*, p. 253.
18. ibid.
19. Weir, 'Organ Music II', p. 380.
20. Samuel, *Music and Color*, p. 258.
21. PHNS, p. 356.
22. ibid, p. 353.
23. ibid, p. 354.
24. ibid, p. 357.
25. ibid, p. 354.
26. Some of these had been supplied to Messiaen by Nicholas Armfelt, a long-standing enthusiast and supporter of his music.
27. PHNS, p. 360.

28. ibid, p. 362.

29. Yvonne Loriod-Messiaen, preface to the score.

30. Peter Hill, private communication.

31. PHNS, p. 370.

32. Platform speech by Kent Nagano during the Hallé Orchestra concert on 20 September 1992 at the Free Trade Hall, Manchester.

33. PHNS, p. 373.

34. ibid, p. 366.

35. 'Yvonne Loriod interviewed by Irene Tüngler' in booklet for Warner Classics' 'Messiaen Edition' (2564 62162-2), p. 138.

36. PHNS, p. 376.

37. Hill, 'Interview with Loriod', p. 302.

38. «Éclairs» is one of those words which stands in resolute defiance of adequate translation. A literal translation would be 'lightning flashes' with all the suggestions of rapidity, brilliance and immediacy that entails. However, in the context of Messiaen's title, it also suggests the enlightenment of 'illuminations'.

39. PHNS, p. 370.

40. ibid, p. 374.

41. ibid, p. 380.

42. ibid, pp. 382–3.

43. Boulez, *Orientations*, p. 420.

44. PHNS, p. 374.

45. Yvonne Loriod-Messiaen, programme note for first performance.

46. Accord DVD 476 719 0.

SELECT BIBLIOGRAPHY

**Messiaen's major writings (in chronological order; in French
unless stated otherwise)**

'Ariane et Barbe-Bleue de Paul Dukas' in La Revue musicale, no. 166 (June
   1936), 79–86.

'Le Rythme chez Igor Strawinsky' in La Revue musicale no. 191 (June,
   1939) 91–2.

Vingt Leçons d'Harmonie (Paris: Alphonse Leduc, 1940).

Technique de mon langage musical, 2 volumes (Paris: Alphonse Leduc,
   1944; trans. John Satterfield, 1956). Single volume edition (Paris:
   Alphonse Leduc, 1999 (French); 2001 (English)).

Conférence de Bruxelles, prononcée à l'Exposition Internationale de Bruxelles en
   1958 (Paris: Alphonse Leduc, 1960).

'Olivier Messiaen', in Marc Honegger (ed.), Dictionnaire de musique, vol.
   2 (Paris: Bordas, 1970), 713.

Conférence de Notre Dame (Paris: Alphonse Leduc, 1978).

Les 22 concertos pour piano de Mozart (Paris: Séguier-Archimbaud, 1987).

Conférence de Kyoto (Paris: Alphonse Leduc, 1988).

Entretien avec Claude Samuel, rec. Paris, October 1988, Erato disc
   ECD75505.

Messiaen, Olivier, Traité de rythme, de couleur, et d'ornithologie, 7 Tomes
   (Paris: Alphonse Leduc, 1994–2002). N.B. Tome V in 2 vols.

Olivier Messiaen and Yvonne Loriod-Messiaen, Ravel: Analyses des
   Œuvres pour Piano de Maurice Ravel (Paris: Durand, 2003).

Books and longer articles by other authors

† denotes books in French

Aguila, Jésus, *Le Domaine Musical* (Paris: Fayard, 1992).†

Boivin, Jean, *La Classe de Messiaen* (Paris: Christian Bourgois, 1995).†

Boivin, Jean, 'Messiaen's Teaching at the Paris Conservatoire: A Humanist Legacy', in Siglind Bruhn (ed.) *Messiaen's Language of Mystical Love* (New York: Garland, 1998).

Boulez, Pierre, *Orientations – Collected Writings*, trans. Martin Cooper (London: Faber and Faber, 1986).

Boulez, Pierre, *Stocktakings from an apprenticeship*, trans. Stephen Walsh (Oxford: Clarendon, 1991).

Brothier, J. J., *La Jeune France: Yves Baudrier, André Jolivet, Daniel-Lesur, Olivier Messiaen* ([Paris] Les Amis de la Jeune France, [1954]).†

Bruhn, Siglind (ed.), *Messiaen's Language of Mystical Love* (New York: Garland, 1998).

Buckland, Sidney (ed. and trans.), *Francis Poulenc, Echo and Source, Selected Correspondence 1915–1963* (London: Victor Gollancz, 1991).

Chimènes, Myriam (ed.), *Francis Poulenc: Correspondance 1919–1963* (Paris: Fayard, 1994).†

Collaer, Paul, *Correspondance avec des amis musiciens*, ed. Robert Wangermée (Sprimont, 1996).†

Dingle, Christopher, 'Charm and Simplicity: Messiaen's Final Works', *Tempo*, no.192 (April 1995), pp. 2–7.

Dingle, Christopher, 'Frescoes and Legends: the sources and background of *Saint François d'Assise*' in Dingle and Simeone (eds), *Olivier Messiaen: Music, Art and Literature* (Ashgate, forthcoming).

Dingle, Christopher, 'La statue reste sur son piédestal: Messiaen's *La Transfiguration* and Vatican II' *Tempo*, no.211 (April 2000), 8–11.

Dingle, Christopher, *Messiaen's Final Works: an examination of style and technique* (Ashgate, forthcoming).

Dingle, Christopher and Simeone, Nigel (eds), *Olivier Messiaen: Music, Art and Literature* (Ashgate, forthcoming).

Dupré, Marcel, *Marcel Dupré raconte...* (Paris: Éditions Bornemann, 1972).†

Goehr, Alexander, *Finding the Key* (London: Faber and Faber, 1998).

Goehr, Alexander, unpublished interview, Cambridge, 4 July, 1996.

Goléa, Antoine, *Rencontres avec Olivier Messiaen* (Paris: Julliard, 1960).†

Grenier, Robert, 'Recollections on Singing Messiaen's *Saint François d'Assise*', *The Opera Quarterly* (vol. 18, no.1, winter 2002), 58–65.

Griffiths, Paul, *Olivier Messiaen and the Music of Time* (London: Faber and Faber, 1985).

Gut, Serge, *Le Groupe Jeune France* (Paris: H. Champion, 1977).†

Halbreich, Harry, *Olivier Messiaen* (Paris: Fayard, 1980).†

Hill, Peter, 'Interview with Yvonne Loriod', in Hill (ed.), *The Messiaen Companion* (London: Faber and Faber, 1995).

Hill, Peter (ed.), *The Messiaen Companion* (London: Faber and Faber, 1995).

Hill, Peter and Simeone, Nigel, *Messiaen* (New Haven and London: Yale University Press, 2005). [PHNS]

Hommage à Olivier Messiaen: novembre–décembre 1978 [brochure-program], Claude Samuel, artistic director.†

Jacquet-Langlais, Marie-Louise, *Ombre et Lumière – Jean Langlais 1907–1991* (Paris: Edition Combre, 1995).†

Johnson, Robert Sherlaw, *Messiaen*, 2nd edition (1st published 1975), (London: Dent, 1989).

Jolivet, Hilda, *Avec André Jolivet* (Paris: Flammarion, 1978).†

Kurtz, Michael, *Stockhausen – a biography*, trans. Richard Toop (Faber & Faber: London, 1994).

Lauerwald, Hannelore, *In fremdem Land. Kriegsgefangene in Deutschland am Beispiel des Stalag VIIIA Görlitz* (Görlitz: Viadukt Verlag, 1997).

Liebermann, Rolf, *En passant par Paris-Opéras* (Paris: Gallimard/nrf, 1980).†

Mari, Pierette, *Olivier Messiaen: l'homme et son œuvre* (Paris: Éditions Seghers, 1965).†

Marti, Jean-Christophe, 'Entretien avec Olivier Messiaen', *Saint François d'Assise: Libretto, Analyse, Kommentare, Dokumentation* (Salzburger

Festspiele, 1992), pp. 8–18; repr. in disc notes for Deutsche Grammophon recording of *Saint François d'Assise*, 445 176–2.

Massin, Brigitte, *Olivier Messiaen: une poétique du merveilleux* (Aix-en-Provence: Éditions Alinéa, 1989).†

Massip, Catherine (ed.) *Portraits d'Olivier Messiaen* (Paris, 1996).†

Matossian, Nouritza, *Iannis Xenakis* (Paris: Fayard-SACEM, 1981).†

Messiaen, Pierre, *Images* (Paris: Desclée de Brouwer, 1944).†

Nattiez, Jean-Jacques (ed.), *The Boulez-Cage Correspondence*, trans. Robert Samuels (Cambridge: CUP, 1993).

Nichols, Roger, *Messiaen*, 2nd edition, (1st published 1975) (Oxford: Oxford University Press, 1986).

Nichols, Roger, *The Harlequin Years: Music in Paris 1917–1929* (London: Thames & Hudson, 2002).

Olivier Messiaen, homme de foi: Regard sur son œuvre d'orgue (Paris: Trinité Media Communications, 1995).†

Périer, Alain, *Messiaen* (Paris: Seuil, 1979).†

PHNS – see Hill, Peter and Simeone, Nigel.

Pople, Anthony, *Messiaen: Quatuor pour la fin du Temps* (Cambridge: Cambridge University Press, 1998).

Rischin, Rebecca, *For the End of Time – The Story of the Messiaen Quartet* (Ithaca, New York: Cornell University Press, 2003).

Rößler, Almut, *Contributions to the Spiritual World of Olivier Messiaen with original texts by the composer* (Duisburg: Gilles und Francke Verlag, 1986).

Rostand, Claude, *Olivier Messiaen* (Paris: Ventadour, 1957).†

Samuel, Claude, *Entretiens avec Olivier Messiaen* (Paris: Pierre Belfond, 1967).†

Samuel, Claude, *Conversations with Olivier Messiaen* trans. Felix Aprahamian (London: Stainer and Bell, 1976).

Samuel, Claude, *Olivier Messiaen: Musique et couleur – nouveaux entretiens avec Claude Samuel* (Paris: Pierre Belfond, 1986).†

Samuel, Claude, *Olivier Messiaen: Music and Color – Conversations with Claude Samuel*, trans. E. Thomas Glasow (Portland, Oregon: Amadeus 1994).

Samuel, Claude, *Permanences d'Olivier Messiaen: Dialogues et Commentaires* (Actes Sud, 1999).†

Samuel, Claude, *Olivier Messiaen (1908–1992): Les couleurs du temps. Trente ans d'entretiens avec Claude Samuel* (Paris: Radio France, 2000).†

Sauvage, Cécile, *Oeuvres complètes* (Paris: La Table Ronde, 2002).†

Schlee, Thomas Daniel and Kämper Dietrich, *Olivier Messiaen: La cité céleste, das himmlische Jerusalem: über Leben und Werk des französischen Komponisten* (Cologne: Wienand, 1998).

Seifert, Charles E., 'Messiaen's *Vingt Regards sur l'Enfant-Jésus*: A Historical and Pedagogical Study', PhD thesis, University of Illinois (1989), pp. 4–5.

Simeone, Nigel, *Bien Cher Félix. . .: Letters from Olivier Messiaen and Yvonne Loriod to Felix Aprahamian* (Cambridge: Mirage Press, 1998).

Simeone, Nigel, 'Dancing *Turangalîla*: Messiaen and the Ballet' in Dingle and Simeone (eds), *Olivier Messiaen: Music, Art & Literature* (Aldershot: Ashgate, forthcoming).

Simeone, Nigel, 'Group Identities: La Spirale and La Jeune France', *Musical Times* (Vol. 143, Autumn 2002) 10–36.

Simeone, Nigel, 'Messiaen and the Concerts de la Pléiade: "A kind of clandestine revenge against the Occupation"', *Music and Letters* (November, 2000), 551–84.

Simeone, Nigel, 'Offrandes oubliées: Messiaen the 1930s' *Musical Times* (Vol. 141, Winter 2000), 33–41.

Simeone, Nigel, 'Offrandes oubliées 2: Messiaen, Boulanger and José Bruyr', *Musical Times* (Vol. 142, Spring 2001), 17–22.

Simeone, Nigel, *Olivier Messiaen: A Bibliographical Catalogue* (Tutzing: Verlegt bei Hans Schneider, 1998).

Simeone, Nigel, 'Olivier Messiaen: *Vingt Regards sur l'Enfant-Jésus*', booklet essay for Hyperion disc CDA67351/2.

Simeone, Nigel, 'The Science of enchantment: Music at the 1937 Paris Exposition', *Musical Times* (Vol. 143, Spring 2002), 9–18.

Simeone, Nigel, 'Towards "un success absolument formidable": the birth of Messiaen's *La Transfiguration*', *Musical Times* (Vol. 145, Summer 2004), 5–24.

Stockhausen, Karlheinz, *Stockhausen on Music, compiled Robin Maconie* (London: Marion Boyars, 1991).

Toesca, Maurice, *Cinq ans de Patience (1939–45)* (Paris: Emile-Paul, 1975).†

Toesca, Maurice, *La Nativité* (Paris: M. Sautier, 1952).†

Tual, Denise, *Le Temps Dévoré* (Paris: Fayard, 1980).†

INDEX